The Victoria and Albert Museum
The Making of the Collection

Anna Somers Cocks

Designed by Philip Clucas MSIAD

Produced by Ted Smart and David Gibbon

Featuring the photography
of Clive Friend FIIP

Windward

Acknowledgements

First of all, I must say how grateful I am to my colleagues in the Metalwork department who have put up with me while I have been writing this book, and I am especially indebted to the Deputy Keeper, Mrs Shirley Bury, who generously made available a great mass of her notes on the early history of the museum. Much of the information is, of course, unpublished and derived from the museum files and registers. Mr Anthony Burton also helped a great deal by allowing me to ransack his excellent lecture on the history of the library, by choosing from among the thousands of possibilities the most telling illustrations, and kindly correcting various errors which I had made. Robert Skelton, Keeper of the Indian Section, gave me a great deal of his time, and a firm guiding hand in unfamiliar artistic territory. John Ayers and Joe Earle in the Far Eastern department gave me comparable advice, and Lionel Lambourne offered me his extremely useful essay on 'The Growth of the National Collection of British Watercolours in the V & A' before publication. Irene Whalley was endlessly helpful with the intricacies of the library. The Keepers who read the chapters relevant to their department very kindly did all they could to prevent mistakes of nuance and fact; any which remain are mine alone. Photography would have been a great deal more arduous than it was had it not been for the unstinting help of Len Joyce, Charlotte Sillavan, Linda Parry, Zara Fleming, Dick Bartlett, Anne Manningham-Buller, Tony North, Eric Turner and Julian Litten.

Lastly, my thanks go to John Hardy in Furniture and Woodwork who helped me a great deal with that department and, because he happens to be my husband, also had to put up with me at home, writing this book.

A.S.C.

First published 1980 by Windward
An imprint owned by W. H. Smith & Son,
registered no. 237811 England,
trading as W.H.S. Distributors, St. John's House, East Street, Leicester, LE1 6NE, England.
Text copyright © Anna Somers Cocks 1980
Photographs copyright © Colour Library International Ltd and The Victoria and Albert Museum 1980

Colour Separations by Fercrom, Barcelona.

Photoset by The Printed Word Ltd, 19 Briset Street, London EC1M 5NR

ISBN 0-7112-0042-4

Printed and bound by Jisa Rieusset, Barcelona, Spain.

Contents

Front Cover: Pendant of the Royal Order of Victoria and Albert, First Class. Onyx cameo surrounded by diamonds and pastes, mounted by an imperial crown of diamonds, rubies and emeralds. The Order was instituted by Queen Victoria, 10th February 1862, and comprised the Sovereign and forty-five ladies. The Order, First Class, was conferred only on Royal Personages. Museum number (m 180-1976).

For my mother
without whose excellent advice I would never
have come to work in this museum

Preface

It is obvious to any visitor to the Victoria and Albert Museum
that it is full of marvellous treasures in every material, of all
ages and countries. But it is also peppered with the surprising,
the odd and the touching. It is not only a vast repository
delineating the history of style, but of the modes and
manners, habits and customs, eccentricities and extravagances
of over a thousand years of human creativity. These objects
must not only be seen as dead artefacts but in human terms as
evidence of time past. The story of how this huge assembly of
objects of every size and proportion, from a shoe buckle to a
life-size cast of Trajan's column, came to rest in South
Kensington has never been told before. And it is this that the
present book sets out to remedy, to describe how this
happened and to illustrate in all its infinite variety both the
glories and lesser stars in the firmament of what is
affectionately known throughout the world as the V & A.

Dr Roy Strong
Director of the Victoria and Albert Museum

*1. A huge silver and gilt wine flagon, 24½ ins. high,
made by C. T. and G. Fox for Lambert and Rawlings,
and purchased from the Great Exhibition (2743-1851).*

1
A Short History

The Victoria and Albert Museum is the greatest decorative art museum in the world. Nowhere else can the history of Renaissance bronzes, of Edwardian ladies' underwear, of great tapestries, and of porcelain, furniture, silks, silver and jewellery (to list only a few of the objects it contains) be studied better under one roof. It is also the oldest museum of its kind, fostering offspring in Vienna, Budapest, Nüremberg, Zagreb, Berlin, Basle, Paris and the great cities of America. This book is about how it came to exist and how its collections have evolved up to the present day.

The museum was born out of the spirit of free trade and radicalism which flourished after the passing of the Reform Bill of 1832. This had brought a completely new class of person into power, the men of the new industrial Britain who had a confident belief in progress and in the importance of technical and mechanical innovations, but who also felt that the dislocation of the traditional crafts by mechanisation was leading to a decline in standards of execution and design. As early as 1835 the House of Commons was so worried about the effects of declining standards that it set up a Select Committee of Arts and Manufactures to enquire into the problem. The crucial sentence in the Report which emerged is: 'To us, a peculiarly manufacturing nation, the connection between art and manufactures is most important — and for this merely economical reason (were there no higher motive), it equally imports us to encourage art in its loftier attributes . . .'

This utilitarian attitude towards art remained a recurrent theme through the history of the museum, swelling louder, one suspects, when it suited museum officials trying to winkle money out of the government. In this case, the Committee recommended setting up state-supported schools of design for the upper artisan classes in the various cities of England. This, it was hoped, would lead to an improvement in standards so that the dreaded French with their superior designs would no longer steal our markets.

Thus the first London School of Design, the progenitor of the Victoria and Albert Museum, was founded in 1837. It was situated in Somerset House, with a small collection of books, later to evolve into the museum library, and of plaster casts, the foundation of the museum collections. A small budget was made available for specimens of manufacture, both old and new, to be bought for the purpose of edifying the students, and from the mid-1840s, when the first provincial Schools of Design had been founded, these were being trundled around Britain in two railway carriages.

Two men were crucial to the next stage of the museum's development: one was Henry Cole (1808-82); and the other was Prince Albert of Saxe-Coburg, who married Queen Victoria in February 1840.

Henry Cole was an example of every attribute for which the Victorians are now generally admired: wide-ranging in his interests, self-reliant, improving, self-righteous and slightly humourless. In his lifetime he was to become involved in dozens of schemes, from the Penny Post to standardising the gauge for railways, and from early contraception to industrial design. He was also, incidentally, to become the museum's first director.

In the 1840s, convinced that the best way to improve industrial design was to involve fine artists, that is sculptors and painters, in their creation, Henry Cole set up a scheme whereby he would act as an entrepreneur, commissioning designs from artists such as Richard Redgrave, R.A., and getting them executed by well-known manufacturers. The business was launched under the title of Felix Summerly's Art Manufactures, and although it had little financial success and its effects on design, whether good or bad, are difficult to judge, it was a very strong pointer in the direction the museum was to take after Cole became director; and of course a number of Felix Summerly pieces found their way into its collections during the 1850s and 1860s (plates 2 and 3).

A major step forward in the realisation of Cole's ambitions was his appointment by Prince Albert to the board organising the Great Exhibition of 1851, at which the variety and ingenuity of British design, manufacture and industry were to be displayed in the great 'Crystal Palace' built by Joseph Paxton in Hyde Park. Cole quickly established himself as one of the most influential members of the board; and when the Exhibition was over — a triumphant success — he was appointed to a selection committee charged with the task of purchasing objects from it which would form the foundation collection of a new museum of manufactures (plates 1 and 4). A fund of £5,000 was voted by the government for the purpose, and in 1852 Queen Victoria gave the museum its first permanent home in Marlborough House.

4. Another piece bought from the Great Exhibition, a steel 'thalwar' (sword) mounted in enamelled gold, from Rajputana in India. It dates from the mid-19th century (110-1852).

2

3

The other members of the selection committee were the architect and designer Owen Jones, the painter Richard Redgrave, and A.W.N. Pugin, the designer of the interior details of Barry's Houses of Parliament. When the museum was set up, as the 'Department of Practical Art' under Board of Trade control, Henry Cole was appointed its head, at the quite generous salary of £1,000 per annum. Richard Redgrave became Art Superintendent — in effect, head of the Art Schools — at £300 per annum; and John Charles Robinson (1824-1913) became Curator of the Museum, at the same salary.

The collecting policy of the new museum at first retained strong links with the regional Schools of Design, and numerous modern pieces were acquired from firms like Minton and Sèvres, together with plaster casts, electrotypes and modern drawings for important works of art. J. C. Robinson and Cole, however, made a promising start with the antiquarian side of the collections (which nowadays is the museum's *raison d'être*). They were lucky in that two of the great early collections of decorative art objects, one made by the English M.P. Ralph Bernal, and the other by the Toulouse lawyer Jules Soulages, both came up for sale in the 1850s. The way in which the Soulages Collection was bought shows how flexible and unbureaucratic such dealings were in those days, but also how unreliable financial support from the government could be.

Soulages had been a pioneer collector in the 1830s and 1840s of objects of decorative art, such as maiolica, iron-work, armour, goldsmiths' work, and so on, instead of the 'high art' which had always been admired. Cole saw these objects when he visited Paris as Commissioner for the British Section of the Paris Exhibition of 1855, and decided that the British nation needed them; but on his return he met only with the support of Prince Albert, who gave him £1,000 towards the total cost of £11,000. John Webb, the London dealer friend of the museum, negotiated the purchase with M. Soulages, who accepted £3,000 down and Cole's own promissory note for the balance, to be paid within three years.

The collection was shipped over to London and put on show in the museum at Marlborough House in October 1856. Palmerston, then Chancellor of the Exchequer, refused to provide any money, but Cole was undeterred. He was a pioneer of public relations, which he called creating a 'climate of opinion', and he calculated that if he could give the collection enough publicity the Treasury would eventually have to give way. He therefore agreed to sell it *en bloc* to the Man-

2.   This papier-mâché tray inlaid with mother-of-pearl and ivory was designed for the Summerly company by Richard Redgrave, R.A., in 1847 (132-1865).

3.   Another Richard Redgrave design for Summerly: a painted glass water carafe, 10¼ ins. high (4503-1901).

4

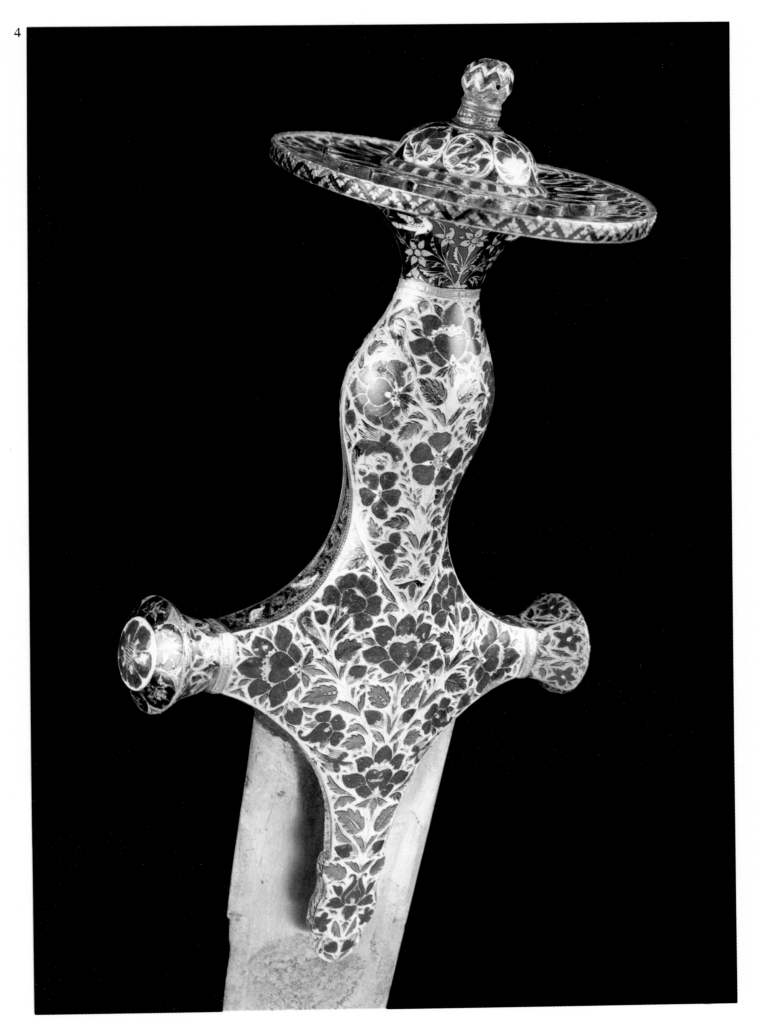

chester Art Treasures Exhibition of 1857, in the hope that he would be able to buy it back afterwards as funds became available. Soulages was asked whether he would accept the whole amount due to him plus interest in exchange for Cole's promissory note, but he

5 and 6.   *The refreshment room designed by Sykes and Gamble, and opened in 1868. It has recently been restored after decades of neglect and even threatened 'modernisation'. The decorated ceiling is itself the product of a technical innovation introduced to the School of Design: it is of enamelled iron, a technique revived at the Sèvres factory in 1843, and shown at the 1851 exhibition, where Cole was so impressed that he encouraged its use throughout the building.*

7. *The William Morris restaurant.*

7

answered, rather charmingly, that he preferred to hold the promissory note of an Englishman to any other security. Eventually, however, he was persuaded to accept payment.

Meanwhile two further applications by Cole to the Treasury were refused, and he was forced to devise a completely new means of securing the collection: he would hire it from the Manchester Committee and make purchases from it annually as his purchase grant came in. And so, despite some official murmurings, the collection was eventually bought at the rate of £2,000 per annum.

Then, on 20 June 1857, the museum reopened in its new buildings, still surrounded by fields, at South Kensington. A Royal Commission (which, inci-

dentally, still exists today) had been set up in 1851 to administer the profits of the Great Exhibition, and at Prince Albert's suggestion the present site of the museum was bought and the beginnings of what was intended to be a vast educational and museum complex were set up. Building was in fits and starts, under the architectural direction of Captain F. Fowke of the Royal Engineers, from 1856 to 1865. Cole had always admired the Sappers, as the Royal Engineers were called, because they appealed to his eminently practical and progressive nature; in later life he gave an address on the desirability of their employment in all branches of civil life during peace-time, and he certainly made use of them in the museum. They built it, maintained it, acted as its fire brigade and to some extent guarded it, although this was really the job of the helmeted London bobby, who warded it until its reorganisation at the beginning of this century. Cole's own son became a Royal Engineer and made use of his regimental facilities to make the vast plaster cast of the façade of the Sānchī temple in Central India; and the museum's good relations with the regiment must have been a factor in persuading Major Murdoch-Smith, who was putting up the telegraph across Persia in the 1870s, to volunteer to buy Persian art for its collections.

Fowke's architectural style can still be seen in the north wing of the quadrangle; he favoured the Italian Renaissance, with dark red brick and ornate terracotta mouldings. The interiors were elaborately decorated by Godfrey Sykes, Reuben Townroe and James Gamble (plates 5 and 6). These were all pupils of the sculptor Alfred Stevens, who had himself worked at the School of Design in London for eighteen months in the 1840s, and then left for Sheffield where he was to be the idol of the students at the local School of Design.

Cole also commissioned the firm of Morris, Marshall, Faulkner and Co, William Morris's company, to execute the West Dining Room (plate 7), next to the Refreshment Room. This was completed in 1866 to the designs of William Morris, assisted by Philip Webb. The stained glass windows and painted panels

8

beneath represent the seasons of the year, and were designed by Sir Edward Burne-Jones. There is obviously no intention to integrate the two very different interiors, but rather to show what was considered good of its kind.

The two gigantic, vaulted Architectural Courts were put up under Fowke's successor, also a Royal Engineer, in 1868-73. The West Court, with its rich polychromy, has recently (1978-9) been restored to its original magnificence after decades of a depressing uniform grey, which the anti-Victorians regarded as more

tasteful (plate 8). The East Court, still unrestored, was a simple inversion of the red-green colour scheme, with the green predominating instead. Sadly, it seems likely that the opportunity to revive this second great Victorian interior is going to be passed over in favour of a modern colour scheme.

The last phase in the early building campaign of the museum was in 1884 when the Art Library was built. Not surprisingly, the museum throughout these years presented a very heterogeneous appearance. It still lacked a proper frontage, and much of it was built in the cast iron sections beloved of the Sappers which attracted the nick-name 'the Brompton boilers'. It was also uncomfortable and inconvenient: the museum files include a furiously scrawled minute from the irascible Robinson after a windy day in March 1864: 'Would it not be possible to put a chimney pot or some other scientific contrivance on the top of the flue in my room — I am again smoked out, and the place is not tenable in windy weather — under any circumstances the room is most comfortless.' Nonetheless, the South Kensington Museum, as it was now known, was enormously popular with the public who flocked to see its combined artistic and scientific displays. These included the Sheepshanks collection of paintings and drawings, the collection of modern sculpture contributed by members of the Sculptors' Institute, the collection of ornamental art accumulated with government funds since the earlier days of the School of Design, the collection of architectural casts and drawings, and the Circulating Art Library. Then there was a mass of architectural models and materials relating to building, from the 1851 and 1855 Paris exhibitions, educational models and diagrams and patented inventions on loan from the Patent Office. Finally there was a section called 'Animal Products', presented to the public by the Commissioners of the 1851 exhibition.

Cole ran this with a very small staff. In the first place he held two of the most important posts himself: he was both Secretary of the Department of Science and Art (as the Department of Practical Art was now renamed), and General Superintendent (that is, Director) of the museum. He was empire-building as fast as possible at this time, and preferred to have good administrators around him rather than encouraging scholars to join the museum. Philip Cunliffe-Owen (1828-95) was the Deputy General Superintendent of the museum and in charge of everyday administration. Richard Redgrave was Inspector General for Art in the Department of Science and Art until 1875, which meant that he was responsible for the art school network, but he was also an Art Referee which involved his advising on purchases. Then there were three Keepers in charge of the Art collections, the Art Library and Educational Collections respectively; four,

9

10

8. *A watercolour painted around 1875 of the western architectural court (the Cast Court), looking north, and showing some of the plaster casts in place. The artist is unknown (D564-1905).*

9. *Etching of the Prince Consort gallery (c. 1876) at the South Kensington Museum, showing the decorative cast iron structure. The rich curtaining and the London policeman are features which have since disappeared, although the objects in the cases, and the cases themselves, can still be seen today.*

10. *Memorial to Sir Henry Cole on the Ceramic staircase, recording the twenty years (1853-1873) which he devoted to the creation of the museum.*

11. The electrotype store, where reproductions of many of the finest pieces of plate from all over Europe are kept. The originals of the leopard and of the large flagon in the left foreground are in the Kremlin, Moscow.

later twelve, Assistant-Keepers, and then the clerks. Realising that catalogues had to be written, Cole employed outside experts to do so, with John Hungerford Pollen, the minor aesthetic artist, as general editor. One of the first, C. D. Fortnum's *Catalogue of the Maiolica Collections,* was published in 1873.

Robinson continued to be a very important figure in the early history of the museum, making bold and distinguished purchases in nearly all fields of the decorative arts, until he quarrelled with Cole for the last time in 1867 and his employment ended, partly at least because he was suspected of buying objects for his own collection and reselling them at a profit to the museum. In the following decades, however, no single man was to equal his purchasing skill, and he went on to be Keeper of the Queen's Pictures and to receive a knighthood.

In the meanwhile Cole was organising exhibitions, such as the Art Treasures Exhibition to coincide with the 1862 London International Exhibition, where large quantities of works of art in private hands were put on show to the public. He also drafted the Convention of 1867, signed by the Prince of Wales and fourteen of the European princes, including the Czarevitch, the Crown Prince of Prussia and the Prince Royal of Italy, in which all the countries involved agreed to exchange reproductions of their works of art. This now seems a mere historical curiosity, since interest today lies so much in the unique qualities — the genius of the artist, not to say the potential financial value — embodied in the 'genuine' article; but in those days, when few people travelled and much art was shut away in royal palaces and private collections, plaster casts and electrotypes seemed a marvellous way of spreading the knowledge of art – hence the magnificent galleries in the South Kensington museum devoted to plaster casts of Trajan's Column, the Pisano pulpit, Michelangelo's David (a present from the Grand Duke of Tuscany) and hundreds of other examples of architecture and ornament. Electrotypes were the other form of reproduction mentioned in the Convention and they need a word of explanation: they are made by a method invented by Elkington's, who also invented electroplating. A mould is made of the object to be reproduced, it is attached to the negative pole of a battery, and then immersed in a plating bath in which metal is dissolved. When the battery is actuated the metal in the electrolyte is released and deposited gradually on the mould, ultimately creating a perfect reproduction of the original object. The museum possesses electrotype reproductions in silvered and gilt copper of many of the most famous pieces of goldsmith's work in the world, including part of the Kremlin treasury. Plate 11 shows two of these pieces from Russia in the left-hand foreground of the Ali Baba's cave where all these reproductions are kept. Until very recently it was thought dishonest to display them to the public, who expected 'real' works of art, so

they emerged only for the occasional museum party; but the climate of opinion on this matter is gradually changing. It is also changing about the worth of the plaster-cast collections. These are no longer regarded as white-elephants, but as important teaching aids, and in some cases much more than that — the only surviving record of something which has either completely disappeared, or which has deteriorated since the cast was made in the nineteenth century. For example, at Shobden in Herefordshire, the twelfth-century carved doorway was removed from the church and placed on the hillside as a Gothic folly by the late eighteenth-century owner. A hundred-and-twenty years ago these delicate grotesque carvings were still clearly visible, and one single cast was made of them for the museum; this was destroyed in the 1930s as being of no interest, and the original is now so weathered that nothing can be seen any more of the original design. Such a tragedy will not happen again.

Having got the museum well on its way, Cole retired in 1873. He was unable to cut himself off completely from the museum, however, and to the irritation of the officials he left behind him he settled as close as he possibly could to the building, in the large house opposite on the corner of Thurloe Square. In 1875 he was knighted, and he spent the remaining years of his life, until his death in 1882, in characteristically entrepreneurial form trying to further a scheme to turn sewage waste into concrete and mortar. He was succeeded by Philip Cunliffe-Owen who was director until 1893. Under him the museum's growth slowed down considerably, and unlike Cole he was never both Director and Head of the Science and Art Department, with serious consequences eventually for the balance of power between the museum and the bureaucracy. European purchases made during his two decades were also less distinguished because of the system of relying on Art Referees to ratify acquisitions. The Referees were mostly distinguished artists in their own right — they included Mathew Digby Wyatt, the architect, William Morris, the designer, and Arthur Gilbert, the sculptor — but many seemed to lack the acquisitive urge and the critical faculty which had made Robinson such a brilliant collector.

Cunliffe-Owen did, however, take a great interest in the museum's first outstation, the museum at Bethnal Green in the East End of London which had been opened in 1872 and was housed in part of the 'Brompton boilers', moved by the sappers from South Kensington as the new buildings went up. He also had a gift for making use of men who were geographically in the right place to help the museum; for example, it was he who gave Major Murdoch-Smith such a free hand in collecting for the museum while he was in Persia; it was his idea to get the Japanese exhibiting at the Philadelphia Centenary Exhibition in 1876 to choose Japanese works of art on the museum's behalf, and he also employed Dr Bushell, physician for many years to the British community in Peking, to buy

12. *A picture from* The Illustrated London News *showing the foundation stone of Aston Webb's façade being laid by Queen Victoria on 17th May 1899. This was the last major ceremony which she was to perform in her life, and it was then that she directed that the building was henceforth to be called the Victoria and Albert Museum.*

12 ceramics, since Bushell could reasonably be assumed to know more on that subject than anyone in Europe.

It was also under his directorship, in 1880, that the important decision was taken to remove all modern works of art from South Kensington to Bethnal Green. This decision confirmed South Kensington as a museum for antiquarian collections, despite the fact that the move was not completed for many decades. The circulating side of the collections was also expanded in the 1880s to include provincial museums and galleries, but it was precisely this aspect of museum policy which was the first to come under attack. The museum was simultaneously accused of putting priceless works of art at risk, and of sending out pointless conglomerations of objects with inadequate labelling. This was in 1891, the beginning of the decade during which the museum reached its all-time low.

Cunliffe-Owen had allowed power to drift into the hands of the Secretary of the Department of Science and Art, Major-General Donnelly of the Royal Engineers, who seems to have had a malign influence on the museum. He interfered with appointments, vetoed purchases, and prevented any changes. There were even whispers of nepotism. The natural desire on the part of the Keepers to be allowed to specialise in parts of the collections was thwarted by their arbitrary reappointment, say, from Accounts to the Indian Museum, or to the Circulating Section. The librarian, W.H.J. Weale, was the strongest internal critic and he had an ally in M. H. Spielman, editor of *The Magazine of Art,* who published detailed criticisms of the museum's policy. The general public was also beginning to be impatient with the cramming together of cases, the prominence given to gutta-percha boots, stone-breaking equipment, pen holders and models for Her Majesty's Theatre, while fine old tiles had to be peered at in the gloom of a back corridor. Labelling was also very poor, and one hostile Member of Parliament complained of a fatuous example which read: '94 Objects, chiefly of oak. English, Flemish, etc. 15th and 16th centuries.'

Then there were more serious criticisms: that fakes had been bought, that the building was in danger of burning down, that funds had been misapplied and that there had been waste and extravagance. Finally, criticism came from abroad as well. A famous French art historian, Charles Yriarte, Inspector General of Fine Arts in his own country, wrote a letter to *The Times* which received a great deal of publicity. The tone is more of sorrow than of anger as it begins: 'Today, for all of us foreigners South Kensington is a Mecca. England there possesses the entire art of Europe and the East, their spiritual manifestations under all forms, and Europe has been swept into the stream in imitation of England.' But it goes on to say:

'The splendour of the start (excessive as it seems to me) contrasts with the inertia of the last fifteen years; the inconceivable treasures are becoming so much heaped up as to be a veritable obstacle to study.'

After Cunliffe-Owen's retirement in 1893 there was a brief and unhappy period under Professor J. H. Middleton, a good art historian who became utterly enfeebled by morphia addiction, and who was found dead one morning in 1896 from an overdose. Sir Caspar Purdon Clarke was then appointed director, and immediately embarked upon reforms. He began with the reorganisation of the museum into departments by material. Then in 1897 a select parliamentary committee of enquiry was set up, charged with investigating all the charges that had been levelled at the museum over the preceding ten years.

The enquiry sat for nearly twelve months, and much of the evidence given sheds light on the administrative chaos that had prevailed since Cole's retirement. Some of this was merely comic: it emerged in answer to a question about security, that in 1870 two pistols, a sword, and two sets of false teeth had disappeared from the Meyrick Collection. But other disclosures were more alarming: for example the fire hydrants in the museum, it transpired, were of a different gauge from the stand-pipes of the Metropolitan Fire Brigade, and were thus entirely useless. Any major fire would almost certainly have burned the place to the ground. Another typical absurdity was the discovery that the director of the Art Museum was only allowed on his own authority to buy objects up to £20 in value, despite the fact that the annual purchase grant was £10,000; for a more valuable item he had to summon the Art Referees, which was both expensive and time-wasting.

The formal report, 935 pages long, appeared on 29 July 1898. It recommended that the long-standing involvement of the Royal Engineers with the museum be ended and that the Sciences should once and for all be severed from the Arts, and moved west of Exhibition Road to the new Science Museum; that expertise should be encouraged in the curators by allowing them to settle in one post, and there should be a special entrance exam to sift candidates; that the labels in the museum were to be revised and cheap catalogues written for the use of the general public; that the director was to have sole responsibility for the museum; and that paid Art Referees (several of whom M. H. Spielman comments in his note-book were wealthy and aristocratic amateurs) should be abolished and an Advisory Board set up instead. Finally, the Fire Brigade and not the Sappers were to protect the building, and 'objects of vicious taste' at the Bethnal Green Museum were to be destroyed. One wonders what precisely these can have been. Gradually, all these recommendations were implemented.

Thus, bureaucratically and morally revived, the museum approached the twentieth century. In 1899 the

13

13. *The façade of the museum with its imperial crown dome, designed by Aston Webb and completed in 1908.*

new building which everyone now knows was begun, and completed by 1908. Queen Victoria laid the foundation stone (plate 12) and graciously consented to rename the museum 'The Victoria and Albert Museum', trusting that 'it will remain for ages a Monument of discerning Liberality and a Source of Refinement and Progress'. The architect was Aston Webb who, against seven other entrants, had won the competition which had taken place in 1890. Alfred Waterhouse, the president of the Royal Institute of British Architects, was the professional assessor, and Webb was chosen on the grounds of the excellence of his plan and elevations and his 'artistic treatment of detail'. Webb, nonetheless, has been cursed by practically every museum curator since for his failure to connect his vast façade in any logical way with the older buildings at the back, so that one must forever be going up and down little flights of stairs; and the moving of heavy works of art, let alone a wheel chair, around the museum is tedious and frustrating. Unaccountably, he also forgot to plan any office space for the curatorial staff, who now live in partitioned corners of the vast galleries, as often as not looking onto a dreary vista of drain pipes and soot-blackened brick. On the other hand, he provided a suitably imposing façade (plate 13), which the building had always lacked, and which is really fine when seen by floodlight.

14

15

16

The bureaucrats finally departed from South Kensington to Whitehall, as the Department of Science and Art was wound up and the museum put under the Board of Education. This, in turn, was being changed by the great reforming civil servant Sir Robert Morant. It was he who was ultimately responsible for the museum's arrangement on craft lines – Metalwork, Textiles, Woodwork, etc. – rather than on chronological or cultural lines. His committee for the rearrangement of the museum included three industrialists, and decided emphatically in favour of first principles: the museum was there first and foremost to stimulate the craftsman and manufacturer, and only secondarily to spread the knowledge of art. This meant that the vast new galleries were filled with objects of one material – entirely maiolica, or entirely silver, instead of the new fashionable arrangements of objects of different kinds from the same period and culture which Bode had pioneered at the Kaiser Friedrich Museum, Berlin. The criticism started immediately. It was a form of artistic oversimplification, said the *Burlington Magazine*; designers should be able to compare different materials but of similar artistic background; it was boring and off-putting to the students, said *La Chronique des Arts;* and, as a German editor pointed out, it was irrelevant to the modern designer as no one felt any longer that the slavish copying of the ornament of the past was the way to set about producing good design. Nonetheless, the scheme went ahead and remained more or less unchanged until after the Second World War. The museum settled down to a period of consolidation. The departments were now structured like those at the

14.   Mr David Northrop of Metalwork Conservation, examining a replica silver figure made by him to replace one vandalised from the Wellington centre-piece at Apsley House, London.
15.   Mr Ennio Panetta of Furniture Conservation, replacing missing 'intarsia' in an Italian chest of about 1500.
16.   Mrs Marian Kite of Textile and Tapestry Conservation, putting back some of the dark areas in the design of a Dutch table carpet dated 1549.

17. The ceramic fountain which
was the centre-piece in the Royal
Doulton exhibition, sponsored by
Royal Doulton in 1979.

British Museum, each with a Keeper and two or three Assistants, plus junior staff. The names of the staff begin to be familiar: for example, Bernard Rackham, the great ceramics specialist, joined in 1899; Eric (later Sir Eric) Maclagan, the respected Renaissance scholar, in 1906; Leigh (later Sir Leigh) Ashton, the post-war director, in 1923; and Charles Oman, famous for his writings on English silver, and father-in-law of the present director, in 1925. By all accounts it was a peaceful life. Exhibitions were infrequent, displays static, and the number of visitors small and select (well under 750,000 in 1938, compared to 1,594,137 in 1978). The curatorial staff spent much more of its time discussing the finer points of, say, Queen Anne silver, with a discerning collector, than answering letters from the public at large, giving opinions, arranging exhibitions, or advising the Department of the Environment, all of which and much more takes up a great deal of its time now.

Before war broke out in 1939, the museum was closed and the finest pieces evacuated to Montacute House and deep storage in London. Less valuable material was put in strengthened parts of the basement, and a huge brick shed was built in the back drive to hold the Raphael cartoons. Further evacuation of the rest of the collections took place in 1941 to the caves at Bradford-on-Avon, but a skeleton staff remained, and special exhibitions were put on until 1944 when London was under attack again from the V2 bombs. The library also remained open. In the meanwhile a school for child evacuees from Gibraltar was established in certain galleries from 1941 to 1944, and one of the courts was used as a canteen for the Royal Air Force.

By 1948 the collections were all back and the new Director, Sir Leigh Ashton, decided at last to bring in the kind of display adopted years before by every large museum on the continent: that is, a chronological arrangement of works of art of every material. Thus the Continental Primary Galleries were created on the ground and lower ground floors, and the English Primary Galleries on the first and second floors in Aston Webb's part of the building, up the marble stairs on the left as the visitor enters the museum. These display selected works of art which are shown with more space around them than in the study collections, and the visitor can move from the artistic culture of the Early Middle Ages to Gothic, to Italian, then to German Renaissance, and so on.

Around the turn of the decade the museum acquired its three great houses, seventeenth-century Ham, eighteenth-century Osterley, and the Duke of Wellington's early nineteenth-century town residence, Apsley House. This was eventually to launch the museum into its present involvement with the country houses of England, and with the history of interior decoration in general.

The 1950s were years of consolidation, but from the 1960s onwards the museum began to woo its public as

17

never before. The education department, which arranges lectures and guided tours on every subject for children and adults, was set up and then greatly expanded. The workshops, which since the nineteenth century had repaired museum objects rather as the estate carpenter would have looked after the running repairs on a country house, were reorganised to form a conservation department with a greatly increased, and more qualified, staff (plates 14-16). This has become heavily involved in helping and advising outside bodies — a well known recent case has been the museum's work in the restoration of stonework in Venice — and the textiles section has been particularly influential, with workshops springing up all over the country in imitation of its methods.

The exhibition programme has been expanded, until, in the last few years it has been usual to hold five or six exhibitions every year (plate 17). As the ultimate gesture towards the demands of the media and the public, a large Public Relations department has developed.

Recently, under Dr Strong, a proportion of the annual purchase grant has been devoted to twentieth-century acquisitions, and even the occasional commissioning of a work of art (plate 44). A temporary twentieth-century study collection has been arranged but a great reworking of the English Primary Galleries is planned, turning them back to front, correcting the old imbalance towards the art of the eighteenth century and culminating in a twentieth-century primary gallery near the front entrance. In this emphasis on the importance of contemporary design it is indeed a return to the first principles on which the museum was set up.

18. The Eltenberg Reliquary, copper gilt, enamelled, and with walrus
ivory figures and plaques, dating from about 1180. This was bought
from the Soltykoff collection in 1861. Height 1ft. 9½ins. (7650-1861).

2
Metalwork

If every print, button, scrap of lace and fragment of wall-paper is taken into account, the Victoria and Albert Museum probably owns at least a million objects divided between the nine curatorial departments. To keep order in this artistic time machine a quartermaster's discipline is required. Every single object has a number and the date of its acquisition painted on it, and this corresponds with an entry in the large, leather-bound ledgers which are kept in each department. The very first entry for Metalwork, for example, reads: 'Hinges, pair of. Tinned iron. With plates of pierced floriated scrolls. German. 17th century. 6¾ inches by 5 inches. Bought, 6s 8d. 891,892-1844.'

The style, with its echoes of 'Boots, soldiers for the use of', suggests that a quartermaster's method was indeed used initially to catalogue works of art, and the entry is so brief that it cries out for the gaps in the information to be filled in. To take, first of all, the date of acquisition, 1844: this seems at first surprising, since the museum was not founded until after the Great Exhibition in 1851, but the answer is that this unassuming pair of objects (plate 20) dates back to the pre-history of the museum, when the London School of Design in Somerset House was allowed a small sum of money to buy plaster casts, books and didactic objects for the edification of the students — in this case obviously for students of blacksmithing.

During the 1840s provincial schools of design were set up in nearly all the great manufacturing cities of England. Making use of the new railroads, the study collections of the London School were circulated around the country, bringing among other things that pair of hinges to the sight of an audience which had probably never looked at works of art before. What precise message the hinges were supposed to convey we can only guess at, but the careful fretting and craftsmanship of the smith who made them may have been what attracted the attention of the unknown buyer who paid 6s 8d for them. The next twenty items or so in the registers are either relatively humble objects of this sort, or contemporary pieces by the envied and admired French manufacturers. With the year 1851, however, the picture changes almost at once.

Among the pieces singled out for purchase from the Great Exhibition to form the foundation collection of the Museum of Manufactures, in 1851, was the wine flagon shown in plate 1. Augustus Welby Northmore Pugin, it will be remembered, was one of the selection committee formed for this purpose, and Pugin brought all his zeal as a Roman Catholic convert to bear on his aesthetics. He believed firmly that the Gothic style was the only one appropriate, indeed, morally permissible, for a Christian country, and he utterly despised all classicism as being pagan. He was clearly something of a trial to his less doctrinaire colleagues, who would sometimes wait until he was absent to sneak in the purchase of some neoclassical piece. This wine flagon would, however, have appealed to him because it echoes in a distant way the lobed forms and tight embossed Gothic foliage of late fifteenth-century German goldsmith's work, but it is a supreme example of the non-functional, and indeed non-commercial, piece which the nineteenth-century exhibitions were to encourage. It stands two feet high, has a capacity of twelve quarts, and took a craftsman twelve weeks, working entirely by hand, to make it for the firm of Lambert and Rawlings of Coventry Street. Its impractical nature did not strike the experts as undermining whatever design virtues they considered it to have, and it was some fifty years before the tide of fashion made it an object of ridicule to be banished to the stores, and another fifty before admiration of the Victorians caused it to be removed from store and put on display once again.

To the purchases from the Great Exhibition were added the collections of the London School of Design, and so the hinges, the flagon, and many other objects beside, were put on show in Marlborough House, by gracious permission of Queen Victoria who took a passionate interest in all Prince Albert's projects. In 1852 the Museum of Manufactures was renamed the Museum of Ornamental Art, and almost immediately the profits of the Great Exhibition began to be used to erect a suitable building for it at South Kensington. In accordance with the Prince Consort's wishes, Science was added to its brief, and in 1857, when the museum moved to its new galleries it was in its last incarnation but one, as the South Kensington Museum.

Under Sir Henry Cole's directorship the museum of course acquired pieces from his manufactory which had attempted to put some of the early orthodox principles of design into practice. In 1865, for example, it bought for £1 11s 6d the bread knife with its ivory

19

20

handle carved as a maize cob, and the blade engraved with children sowing and reaping. The designer in this case was the sculptor John Bell, who registered the design in 1848.

After 1852, however, the museum quickly turned to collecting old works of art in preference to new, partly because they were supposed to inspire artists and craftsmen by their superior technique and design qualities, but also because the antiquarian urge, and the desire to possess a complete 'series' of any given category of works of art, took over. Cole no longer made use of the same team which had advised on the purchases from the Great Exhibition, but he had an expert counsellor with the curious title of 'art referee'. This was J. C. Robinson, an irascible, opinionated, handsome, brilliant polymath. More power was vested in this individual expert than would now be imaginable, and he was constantly called upon by 'My Lords of the Science and Art Department', the board which controlled the finances of the museum, to travel abroad, view sales, advise upon purchases and recommend which objects should be reproduced, whether by coloured drawings, plaster casts or electrotypes. On his advice, for example, the museum in 1854 bought the rosy agate standing cup with silver-gilt mounts (plate 21) for the large sum of £80. It was a good purchase despite the fact that no one realised its lid was missing. It is one of a small number of surviving late Gothic drinking vessels made perhaps in Freiburg-in-Breisgau, where the mountain streams flow powerfully enough to drive the great wheels which grind semi-precious stones like agate, rock-crystal and serpentine. The mounts, which may have been made elsewhere (such as Nüremberg, then a great centre for goldsmithing), conceal within their contorted foliage tiny cast figures of dogs hunting stags, and a piece as exotic as this would have been made for presentation, perhaps by the burgers of a city to a visiting prince. If it was used at all it was for ceremonial drinking of people's health.

The registers show that at the same period the museum was also buying quite large quantities of German silver and other metalwork from the sixteenth and seventeenth centuries. The selectors' taste seems to have run to the heavily decorated, the most expensive pieces being those embossed with figurative scenes. Robinson's eye was, except in a few and consistent cases, a good one, but by modern standards of art historianship and simple observation he could be oddly blind, failing to notice modern additions or glaring regilding, such as that on the otherwise very distinguished clock by the Augsburg maker, Jeremias Metzger (plate 19). The delicate etched arabesque

---

19.   *A copper-gilt clock with enamelled silver dial, made in Augsburg by Jeremias Metzger, 1564 (4273-1857).*
20.   *The first object acquired by the Metalwork department, one of a pair of hinges (891, 892-1844).*

21

22

ornament on the foot and the clock face, and the quaint straddling figure of Atlas on the pierced base, combined with the unusual form known as a 'mirror-clock', must have been what appealed to him, but the date 1564 in the inscription was misread as 1504, and the name of the maker totally ignored, so that it was a hundred years before a German scholar realised that this was a key work by Metzger, enabling a large number of other works to be attributed to his workshop.

The trouble with Robinson was that he replaced Pugin's violent prejudices by ones of his own: namely, that good goldsmithing died out in 1700, and that 'merely useable plate' (one of his favourite phrases) could not be regarded as decorative art. He believed that only objects 'of unusual importance and finely decorative intention' should be bought. These views, combined with his refusal to pay any attention to the researches that were then being made into the significance of English hallmarks, meant that he positively delayed the forming of the English silver collections which are now such an important part of the museum.

In January 1864 Robinson was reprimanded for not even bothering to report fully on something which he regarded as beneath his interest, a college tankard. If anyone dared to recommend a purchase while he was on one of his frequent trips to the continent, he blasted their Lordships with withering rudeness. In 1865, for example, he returned from France to find that a number of pieces, including the sugar box (plate 22) decorated with chinoiserie engraving had been bought at Christie's on the advice of an enterprising and knowledgeable dealer, William Chaffers. He exploded: 'the best of these specimens even, under any circumstances, would have been scarcely worthy of a place in the Museum, whilst all of them have been bought at a very extravagant rate . . . I except to a certain extent one piece which from its quaint and characteristic but by no means commendable style, it might be right to acquire . . . The rest of the specimens are of very common type, and one or two are positively bad in style and of rude workmanship . . . This sale was, I believe brought to the notice of the secretary (Cole) by Mr Chaffers. Mr Chaffers' habitual indiscretion is such as to make him unsuitable to be associated with the expenditure of public money. Mr Chaffers' acquired knowledge is only enough to give him a dangerous amount of self-confidence.' It need hardly be said that the chinoiserie box, hall-marked London 1683-4, and the four other pieces still occupy honourable places in the museum.

Sometimes, of course, he was right, and during his absence truly unworthy pieces had been bought by more gullible officials than himself, for it is clear from his reports that there was a constant stream of third rate and fake art objects being sent from dealers in England and on the Continent. While he was on his great reconnoitering trip in Spain, for example, a supposedly early eighteenth-century silver tankard, a silver dish embossed with Androcles and the lion, a silver tureen dated 1698, and a sixteenth-century knife, fork and spoon were bought. Robinson immediately and rightly declared them all to be modern fabrications of a fraudulent kind. The extraordinary thing about the last items is that they came from a manufacturer in Vienna called Ratzersdorfer who was well-known for making Renaissance revival pieces so the unfortunate person responsible for that particular purchase should have smelled a rat. Encouraged by his success Ratzersdorfer sent two enamelled gilt vases and candlesticks a few months later, but met with a curt reply from Robinson.

Some of his reports give an insight to the places where forgery was being done: for example shortly after the previous incident he turned down some plate offered by Payne of Bath, including a re-embossed eighteenth-century tankard, and remarks that for some time Bath had been notorious for forgery and objects of silver plate. On another occasion he scornfully rejects a mounted nautilus sent over by a Herr Dux of Hannover,

22.   *A silver sugar-box made in London in 1683-4. The maker is unidentified (53-1865).*

saying: 'The precious pokal is expressly described by Mr Dux as an ancient work. This piece is, however, entirely modern, it belongs to a clan of spurious fabrications . . . of which any number of equally precious examples may be found in the third rate curiosity shops at Oxford Street, Holborn and the City.' He ends censoriously: 'I have no doubt that Herr Dux is perfectly aware of the real character of these objects and I recommend that they be returned to him with a sharp rebuke for having attempted so impudent an imposture.' Thus, if one is not indebted to Robinson for any especially important pieces of English silver, one should at least be grateful to him for what he kept out. Furthermore, he set his sights high. He tried, for example, to buy Lord Radnor's extraordinary chiselled iron throne — the one for which Goering was later to offer a million pounds — but the price of £10,000 was

too steep for the Board. If he had had his way, the museum and not the Pierpoint Morgan Institute in America would own the famous twelfth-century enamelled ciborium exhibited by the Rev. G. W. Brackenridge at the 1862 Art Treasures Exhibition. Through his determined bullying of the faint-hearted Board the museum bought lavishly from one crucially important sale in particular. In 1861 the millionaire Russian Prince Peter Soltikoff, who had bought *en bloc* 4,000 principally medieval objects from Débruge Dumenil after the 1848 revolution, put them up for sale at the Salle Drouot, the Paris auction house. In the first of those years the museum bought six objects from him, of which by far the most important were the Gloucester candlestick, made for the Abbey of St Peter in Gloucester in the early twelfth century — a unique survival from that period of English art; and the Eltenberg reliquary (plate 18). This piece, in an almost perfect state of preservation and dating from the 1180s, has every quality which was bound to make it appeal to the antiquarian nineteenth-century collector. The

enamelling is intact and brightly coloured, the patterns of decorations bold, rich and diverse; the form is ecclesiastical yet exotic, with its echoes of Byzantium in its Greek cross ground-plan and lobed dome; and the scriptural quotations on the prophets' scrolls incorporate a complicated theological programme which is only now being explained. It is an almost perfect example of the combined skills of the theologian, goldsmith and ivory carver, and the museum did not hesitate to pay the then enormous sum of £2,142 for it (but, incredibly, this was only £142 more than the museum was to pay in 1868 for a parade shield made by Messrs Elkington to illustrate Milton's 'Paradise Lost'), despite the fact that nothing was known about its origins. This was rectified, however, by the engagement of Canon Bock, an antiquarian priest in Aachen, who was also much involved with the purchasing of textiles for the museum, to set out on its trail and track it to the church or monastery whence it came. He discovered that, ever since it was made, probably in the Cologne area, it had been in the same convent for aristocratic canonesses at Hochelten. It had escaped the furies of the Napoleonic Wars owing to the presence of mind of the last canoness, a Princess Salm-Reifferscheidt, who, after the suppression of the chapter house (part of the general suppression of ecclesiastical institutions which took place in the Napoleonic period, releasing thousands of works-of-art on the market), kept it hidden up the chimney of her house. When peace returned she handed it over to a Canon Poel of Emmerich who died in 1842. His relations sold it to a small dealer in antiquities, Jacob Cohen of Anhalt, who, as the story goes, called one day on Prince Florentin von Salm-Salm, and offered him one of the walrus ivory figures for sale. One figure after another was sold to him and eventually the whole reliquary appeared, blackened by smoke and smelling of tobacco. Later, Prince Florentin's son, Prince Felix, persuaded him to sell the piece to a dealer in Cologne, and it is at this stage, one suspects, that modern fakes were substituted for the Journey of the Magi, the Virgin and Child with St Joseph, and some of the prophets. These must be hidden in a private collection somewhere, and the department lives in hope of buying them back for the reliquary some day. In any case, Prince Soltikoff bought the reliquary from the Cologne dealer and by this chain of events the museum came to own one of the most important medieval works of art in the world.

In 1862 Robinson bought another twenty objects from Soltikoff, among which were others that had until as recently as 1836 also spent their existence in their place of origin: the Basel treasury silver. These objects are now scattered all over the world because

23.   *A German standing cross of enamelled silver gilt set with pearls, and silver parcel gilt, dating from the 14th and 15th centuries. Height: 1ft. 7½ins. (4939-1862).*

24. *A pair of guns made in Paris about*
1750-60, probably for Louis XV,
whose portrait is chiselled on the locks.
Length: 19½ins. (2243 & a-1855).

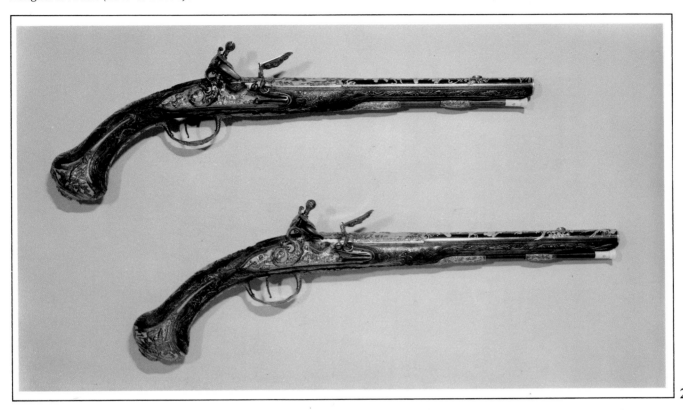

24

the canton of Basel decided to quarrel with the city of Basel, and in the ensuing debacle the Treasury of the Cathedral was auctioned piece by piece. Plate 23 shows what is certainly the museum's most distinguished work of art from this source. It is a reliquary altar cross, the enamelled cross being about a century older than the stand and the figures of the Virgin and St John, which date from around 1475. The whole is of silver, finely gilt in parts, and the two statuettes are embossed rather than cast. We know that the fifteenth-century parts of the cross were made with money from the sale of indulgences and commissioned by the Cathedral chapter and the master of works, Heinrich Gugelin. The goldsmith responsible was probably the Augsburg goldsmith, Hans Rutenzwig, who came to Basel and settled there around 1460.

Robinson did not neglect firearms if he considered them decorative enough, and he bought a pair of guns which form the cornerstone of the collection. The museum paid £104 for a pair of flintlock holster pistols (plate 24) at the 1855 sale of the decorative art collection of the Member of Parliament, Ralph Bernal, who had collected avidly in the 1830s and 1840s when medieval arms and armour appealed more than these relics of the more recent past. The walnut stocks are profusely inlaid with gold wire scrollwork, while the steel mounts are chiselled by hand in unusually high relief with characters and scenes from classical mythology. As works of exceptionally fine craftsmanship by the gunsmiths Jean Baptiste La Roche and his son, they would be desirable enough;

but what makes them really special is that they were almost certainly made for Louis XV of France (1715-74) because the gold escutcheon plates bear the royal arms, and his portrait is chiselled on the lock.

After the resignation of Robinson in 1867 the metalwork collections suffered from an undistinguished if well-established art referee, the architect Sir Mathew Digby Wyatt. He was completely unsuited for the task of building up the collections in the most important areas of English and continental silver. His main preoccupation seems to have been to save the museum money, and since he also felt it was beneath his dignity to discover how the hallmarking system, now thoroughly worked out by scholars, operated, he made a number of serious blunders, buying pieces which had been re-embossed in the early nineteenth-century, or which were composite, one part dating from the 1750s and the other from the 1780s. Fortunately he died in 1877, and although his place was never officially filled an excellent enthusiast, Wilfred Cripps, who was the leading expert in the country, took over as informal adviser. He helped to negotiate some of the most important purchases for the whole collection, such as the Mostyn plate, a superb hoard of Elizabethan silver found in a plate chest at the bankers of the Mostyn family after having been forgotten for many years.

With the death of a great collector, John Jones, in 1882 practically every area in the museum was enriched with eighteenth-century works of art of great distinction. This was a fortunate windfall, for at the period when the museum was founded, academic

25

26

27. A brass candlestick
inlaid with silver and
black composition. West
Iran, about 1220-40.
Height: 7⅝ ins. (775-1892).

opinion tended to be prejudiced against much of the art of the eighteenth-century; it was still too close to be regarded dispassionately, and the rococo in particular was regarded as intrinsically inferior. Public taste, however, had not shared this prejudice, and from the 1830s onwards there had been a distinct vogue for it, especially for anything which might have been associated with the doomed court of Louis XVI and Marie Antoinette. Jones had made a fortune out of the supply of uniforms to the British army; the Crimean war had been his particular enrichment. Afterwards he lived a simple life with one man-servant in his house in Piccadilly, but spent his money lavishly on the French decorative arts of the late seventeenth and eighteenth centuries.

The gold snuff-box (plate 25) epitomises his taste, for not only is it technically very splendid but the miniatures on the lid and base depict Marie Antoinette and the royal family of the day. With her are three of her children, and a bust of the king. The sides are set with lapis-lazuli, while the gold is decorated with enamel. It was made by the Paris goldsmith Pierre-François Drais around 1780. The other box (plate 26) Jones almost certainly bought under the impression that it was French. It is, however, definitely English, for it was precisely this sort of exquisitely fine embossing of gold in which English box- and watch-case makers specialised around the middle of the eighteenth century. Here the gold work has been set in tortoiseshell which is also piqué with fine points of gold. Jones's collection of gold boxes came to the museum just in time to make up for the disappointment when in 1880 a large group of 190 boxes, the Charles Goding collection, which had been on loan to the museum for four years, was snatched away and sold (making, incidentally, a record sum for such items, £40,000). The price of these small and exquisite bibelots soared thereafter, with individual specimens regularly fetching over £1,000, and they became beyond the reach of the purchase fund.

Throughout the second half of the nineteenth century the museum was also buying regularly in the areas of non-European art, although it must be remembered that the Far Eastern and Indian Sections did not yet exist, and even today there is no single department to deal with Middle Eastern culture. The Great Exhibition, as with so much in the museum's history, lay behind this. It had revealed to Cole and his associates that the craft traditions they admired were still flourishing in eastern countries not yet endowed with the advantages and disadvantages of the new technology. Indeed, with its initial budget of £5,000 the

27

purchasing committee bought more items from India, Tunisia, Turkey, China and Japan, at a total cost of £1,501 9s 6d, than it did from western sources. Of these, the Middle Eastern and North African metalwork still remains in this department. 246 items from the Jules Richard collection in Teheran, for example, were bought on the museum's behalf by Major Murdoch-Smith in 1875, and shipped back by the Royal Engineers. The foundation collection too continued to grow under the general influence of artistic interest in the east — one need only think of the large group of painters, later called the Orientalists, beginning with Delacroix, and including David Roberts, Edward Lear, Thomas Seddon and others, who lived and painted for longer or shorter periods in the east. The museum also bought directly from dealers in Constantinople, and from the British Consul there, St Maurice. This inheritance has proved particularly valuable in the last few years since the great boom in all matters to do with Iran and Arabia, and it is now recognised that the museum has the most distinguished collection of such metalwork outside the Middle East. An especially fine example is the candlestick (plate 27). It is of brass, inlaid with silver and black composition; it comes from Western Iran and dates from 1220-40. Remarkably the silver inlay is almost completely intact, while most objects decorated in this manner have suffered a great deal of damage. The small figures represent revellers at a feast and huntsmen, and the name of an owner, perhaps the first, is engraved on the base. It was acquired in 1892 for £25 from a dealer called Jedag Eskanazi in Constantinople. In the register it is described, as indeed are numerous other pieces from widely scattered parts of the Middle East, merely as 'Saracenic', a quaintly old-fashioned as well as inaccurate term.

As the art referees became more and more involved with the purchase of old works of art, the museum's founding policy of encouraging good design among contemporary craftsmen almost fell into abeyance. The Arts and Crafts movement, which in many ways shared a common ancestry of ideas with the museum, seemed particularly neglected. From time to time, however, there was an exception to this rule, and in 1900 fifteen guineas were spent on buying a tall vase on an octagonal marble stand by the partnership of Omar Ramsden and Alwyn Carr (plate 28). This has been given its form by hand-hammering, and has been left with the un-planished and uneven finish beloved of the movement, which not only wanted things to be made by hand, but to look as though they had been. It is a sign, however, of how little regard the South Kensington museum had for contemporary work that this piece was immediately consigned to the part of the museum which circulated its works of art around the country, the Circulation department having maintained much of the early didactic fervour with which the museum was begun.

1901 was the year of the great 'New Art' controversy (see page 88), caused by the acquisition of numerous Art Nouveau pieces from the Paris Universal Exhibition of 1900. £72 13s 5d was spent there on metalwork objects, but when the whole new collection was shown in the Tapestry court the art referees, led by Walter Crane, complained bitterly at the false aesthetic principles embodied in these pieces. Angry letters were sent to *The Times*, and Purdon Clarke, the director, was browbeaten until the bulk of the collection was banished to the outstation at Bethnal Green in 1909. A recurring failure of nerve in the museum when faced with contemporary art can be traced back to this episode.

The turn of the century was also a turning point for the whole structure of the museum, and in 1910 the new departments were created, each with a Keeper and Assistant Keepers. W. W. Watts was appointed Keeper of Metalwork, and his department included all gold-smiths' work, jewellery, arms and armour, ironwork, brasswork, pewter and Middle Eastern and Far Eastern metalwork, until the foundation of a separate department for the last. All metal-cased clocks also belong to the department, while wooden and boulle-cased clocks went to Furniture and Woodwork. There are obviously some illogical boundaries: for example, bronze vessels of a utilitarian nature such as mortars, inkstands and bells belong to Metalwork, but if they were made by a great Renaissance sculptor like Andrea Riccio they become 'Fine Art' and are claimed by the Architecture and Sculpture department. Similarly, cameos and intaglios normally belong to Architecture and Sculpture, but if they have elaborate settings they become jewellery, and are treated as Metalwork.

W. W. Watts had entered the museum in a

28. Ramsden and Carr's silver vase on a marble stand, made in London, 1900. Height: 11¾ ins. (1346 & a-1900).

28

relatively lowly position, in a clerical grade. Under the pre-reform regime, he had managed to get himself transferred to the curatorial side and showed a gift for administration, so that he ran a number of different sections at different times. Although by no means a scholar, he produced perfectly competent catalogues of the chalices and the pastoral staves in the collections. Together with his deputy and friend, Hugh Parker Mitchell, he reorganised them completely in a way which remained unchanged until the Second World War. They showed a joint talent for making good purchases and getting objects and money out of people. This was fortunate because at the turn of the century the English silver collections still had serious gaps: the Middle Ages were represented by a single mazer, the Tudors by eight salts and mounted Rhenish stoneware jugs, but only one important cup. For the early Stuart period there was a marvellous standing cup of 1611, the Dyneley casket of mounted alabaster, four wine-cups and little else. Charles II and William III were scantily but adequately covered, but there was no Queen Anne silver worth mentioning. This had had little appeal, as Robinson made clear, for a generation of ornamentalists, and when Joseph Bond gave to the museum his large collection of English eighteenth-century silver in 1875 it included a

29

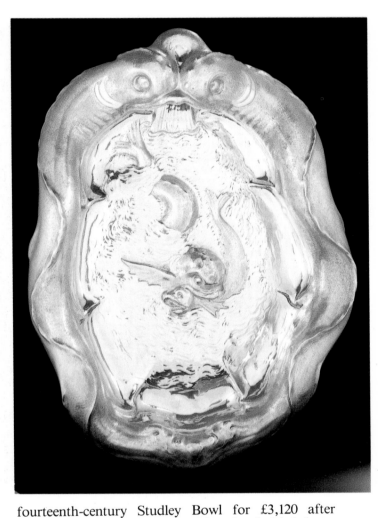

29. A silver teapot made in London, 1718-19, by Jonathan Lambe and Thomas Tearle, and given to the museum by Mrs W. Simpson through the National Art Collections Fund in 1914. Height: 6¾ ins. (M1066-1914).
30. A silver dish made in England by the Dutch silversmith Christian van Vianen in 1635. 19ins. by 14¹/₅ins. (M1-1918).

30

great deal of Rococo and much fine Adam silver (the 1880s onwards had been years of the Adam revival), but nothing which showed the clear lines and pure quality of early eighteenth-century English silver.

A fine example of this style is the silver teapot (plate 29) which came to the museum in 1914. Enthusiasm for English decorative art of all sorts had gathered momentum by the turn of the century, particularly for the achievements of the English silversmiths of the early eighteenth century. Yet funds at this time were low, and the available money was usually spent on any really exceptional piece, from any period, which might come up in the sale rooms — such as a rare silver-gilt standing dish with the London mark for 1564-65, acquired in 1912. Watts therefore decided to publicise the museum's need for good basic examples of Queen Anne silver, in the hope that the public's generosity would fill the gaps. The number of individual gifts of English silver rose dramatically (between 1855 and 1901 there had been only three), and Watts' policy was triumphantly vindicated.

The policy of buying outstanding pieces continued. They were exceptional either for their early date, their rarity, their historical associations, or their quality; and Watts deserves the credit for building the reputation of the English silver collections. It was he who bought the fourteenth-century Studley Bowl for £3,120 after launching a public appeal, and he who decided that a piece by Paul de Lamerie was vital and so bought the Newdigate Centrepiece, 1743-4, for just under £3,000 with the assistance of the Goldsmiths' Company and the National Art Collections Fund. Meanwhile, a very rare piece of continental silver had arrived: in 1918 Sir John Ramsden Bt gave the fish dish (plate 30) by Christian van Vianen, the nephew in the uncle-father-nephew team which constituted the most inventive and brilliant family of Dutch silversmiths in the seventeenth century. It is inscribed 1635 and therefore dates from Christian's English period when he was working for Charles I, making the altarpiece for St George's Chapel, Windsor. Embossed out of a single sheet of silver it is an extraordinarily inventive piece, so far out of the mainstream of contemporary design that many people hesitate when asked to date it, thinking briefly of the wilder flights of Rococo and Art Nouveau.

H. P. Mitchell, an able and enterprising man, eventually succeeded Watts in 1925. Earlier in his career his enterprise had led him into trouble with the authorities. Noting that nothing was being done to publicise the exhibits, he wrote the museum's first popular guide, *The Red Line Guide,* giving a brief account of the most important pieces, and a diagram

31. The Burghley Nef, a nautilus shell
mounted in silver gilt. It was made in
Paris in 1542; Height: 14ins. (M60-1959).

31

Today, many areas of the silver collections are almost complete and money can be spent on refining them, and on saving outstanding work from being exported. Something like the Burghley nef (plate 31) is obviously so rare, beautiful and important that the museum cannot possibly let it slip by. It is a nautilus shell mounted in silver parcel-gilt, an elaborate salt, and so far as is known only one similar piece of the same period has survived, and that has already been captured by the Germanisches Nationalmuseum, Nüremberg. It is not only a superb and rare piece of Parisian goldsmithing from the year 1542 but it encapsulates both the world of late chivalry, with the tiny figures of the lovers Tristram and Iseult playing chess below the main mast, and the world of courtly pomp and ceremony, where a large and imposing salt was the presiding lord's mark of rank. Its importance was recognised by the then Head of the Silver department at Christie's Auction Rooms, Mr Arthur Grimwade; he was at the Marquess of Exeter's house, Burghley, when he saw this piece, which the plate book recorded as 'one small boat' among a list of silver coming from Cowdray — another stately home. On 17 July 1959 it was Lot 118 in a sale at Christie's; the department paid £8,500 for it, and regarded this as a bargain, although it was a record price for continental silver at the time.

Certain objects also become compulsively attractive because the Keeper involved knows some special fact about them; he may, for example, have that flash of recognition which puts together two visual images, the design with the finished object, and which is the real test of a connoisseur's skill and visual memory. This happened recently with a set of candlesticks which came up for sale at Sotheby's on 2 June 1977. A drawing for a candlestick shaped as Daphne (plate 179) had been bought in 1968 by the Prints and Drawings department, signed by George Michael Moser, R.A. (1706-83), the Swiss chaser and enameller, and a founder-member of the Royal Academy. The drawing was published by two colleagues, who remarked on its fine quality and speculated about whether the design had ever been carried out. Nine years later another colleague was thumbing through a Sotheby's silver catalogue and saw illustrated the set of four of them, two Apollos and two Daphnes (plate 32), dated to around 1740-45, but unattributed, as they were unmarked. It was immediately clear that they were based on the design by Moser and they were bought for £14,850 at the auction.

It is well-known that museum curators tend to become slightly obsessive about the areas in which they specialise, but few can have been as single-minded as the man who succeeded Mitchell as Keeper, Albert Koop. He had a degree in Classics from Cambridge, but became completely addicted to Japanese art after joining the Department. During his Keepership hundreds of Japanese sword mounts were acquired, but every other aspect of the collection was ignored and he actually discouraged visitors and potential benefactors

marked with a red line to show the reader how to get there. Instead of being commended he was almost sacked for breaking the rule which forbids civil servants from making a personal profit out of knowledge acquired in museum time. Mitchell nonetheless made an important contribution to the department during his period as Keeper, and his purchases included the Sterne cup, a New Year's gift from Charles II to Archbishop Sterne, which J. C. Robinson had rejected in 1864.

Thus between them Watts and Mitchell had made the collection the kind of prestigious one which attracts donations and bequests.

Their policy not to buy eighteenth-century silver was still a viable one, for most fine examples still belonged to the descendants of the original owners, and the public-spirited gentry could often be prevailed upon to donate a few spares.

32.   G. M. Moser's Apollo and Daphne
candlesticks, dated around 1740-45.
Height: 14½ ins. Compare plate 179
(m 329 & a-1977)

33. *The Canning Jewel, gold, enamelled*
and set with a baroque pearl and gemstones.
It was made in Europe about 1560, but
its exact provenance remains unknown
(M2697-1931).

in other fields. His only wise decision regarding the rest of the collection was to allow the silver to be cleaned, because Mitchell had been terrified of wearing away the decoration, so that the collections all had a rich blue patina like the silver in the Kremlin. Fortunately, unlike the private collector, the museum operates, if not in the sight of eternity, at least against a panorama of centuries, so the collections balance out over a hundred years or so, short fall in one area being compensated for by later acquisitions.

A striking and still slightly contentious illustration of this is the forming of the collections of nineteenth-century art. As we have seen, after its initial brave beginnings as a patron of industry, the museum gradually gave up acquiring contemporary works of art, or if it did it sent them into the obscurity of the Circulation department. It is a commonplace that every generation dislikes the taste of the generation immediately preceding it, and in the case of the anti-Victorians, who have held sway since well before the First World War, the dislike is still remarkably entrenched. Imagine then the incredulity and mockery shown by the main departments whose collections ended abruptly around 1830, when the Circulation department announced in 1952 that they intended to celebrate the centenary of the opening of the Museum of Ornamental Art in Marlborough House with an exhibition of Edwardian and Victorian decorative art. Its Keeper, Peter Floud, intended this exhibition to include the best and most influential work arranged under the names of the designers, in order to quell both the academic indifference and the dilettante enthusiasm which had infected the subject hitherto.

His research assistants hoped the manufacturing houses might be able to help with information, but found that although Victoria had been dead only half a century the records from that period were nearly all destroyed; but they were in time to catch the children and pupils of members of the Arts and Crafts Movement, such as Charles Robert Ashbee (1863-1942), Ernest Gimson (1864-1919) and Phoebe Traquair (1852-1936), and to quiz them on their memories.

This exhibition, like the 1853 Gore House Exhibition of French eighteenth-century art, or the 1896 Bethnal Green Exhibition of English eighteenth-century art, was vital to the reappraisal of the period in question. Resistance continued to be fierce — indeed the recently retired Keeper of Architecture and Sculpture, John Beckwith, a distinguished early medievalist, prided himself on the fact that he had been almost successful in preventing a single nineteenth-century work defiling his department — but the Circulation department continued consciously to collect in those areas where it knew the other departments would eventually feel a need. One of the research assistants involved in that 1952 exhibition, Mrs Shirley Bury, eventually became Deputy Keeper of Metalwork, and has been responsible for bringing the silver collections up to date, with pieces including the most recherché unica from designers to high quality commercial productions of the nineteenth and twentieth centuries. She has also done the same for the jewellery collections, which are the widest-ranging of any museum in the world. J. C. Robinson had begun to collect for them with pieces bought on his Spanish tour in 1864 and they were gradually added to, with a particularly strong emphasis on Renaissance jewels.

One which has become so famous that it is almost a visual cliché is the Canning Jewel (plate 33). Traditionally it is supposed to have been a present from a Medici prince to one of the Mughal Emperors, but like many convenient and romantic traditions this turns out to be untrue as no Medici prince ever sent an embassy to the Mughal Court. Although of Western workmanship (whether Italian, Flemish or South German is uncertain) it was definitely in India long enough for the Indian carved ruby to be set into its belly, and the Indian ruby and pearl pendant to be hung from it. It was bought in Delhi after the Mutiny by Earl Canning, Governor-General and Viceroy of India, and then passed from the first Marquess Clanricarde to Viscount Lascelles. As Earl of Harewood he sold it at Sotheby's on 16 July 1931 when it was bought by Mrs Edward Harkness, wife of the American philanthropist, for £10,000 and presented to the museum.

Without a doubt the greatest benefactress to the collection was Dame Joan Evans (1893-1977), the only woman so far to hold the office of President of the Society of Antiquaries (1954-64). The much younger half-sister of Sir Arthur Evans, the excavator of Knossos, Dame Joan grew up in a scholarly atmosphere, and her first book, *English Jewellery,* was commissioned before she even went to Oxford as an undergraduate. She became well-known as a writer on medieval art and jewellery, and at the time when Mitchell was Keeper of the department she contemplated becoming an Assistant-Keeper in the museum. Her family was well-off, deriving its money from John Dickinson & Co, with its paper mills; and so she was able to put together a remarkable collection of predominantly fifteenth-, sixteenth-, seventeenth- and eighteenth-century jewels. She began lending them to the museum in 1926, until by 1975 her collection in the museum reached some two hundred and fifty items. Then the government threatened to introduce a wealth tax and her friends warned her that she might have to pay tax on her collection even though it had been on loan to the museum for so many years. Her characteristically generous reaction was, instead of selling it, to present it *en bloc* to the museum. With great modesty, and aware of how problematical these things can be for curators, she stipulated that anything 'not of museum standard' should be sold, and that the collection should be rationally incorporated with the existing pieces. Her charming letter of gift included the sentence: 'My Jewels come to your Department with love and gratitude; it has been kind to me for 65 years.' Plate 41 is of one of these jewels.

34

34 and 35.   Pugin's brooch, headband and necklace, which he designed for Helen Lumsden but eventually gave to Jane Mill when she became his wife. They are of gold, enamelled and set with gems (720-1902, M10, 21-1962).

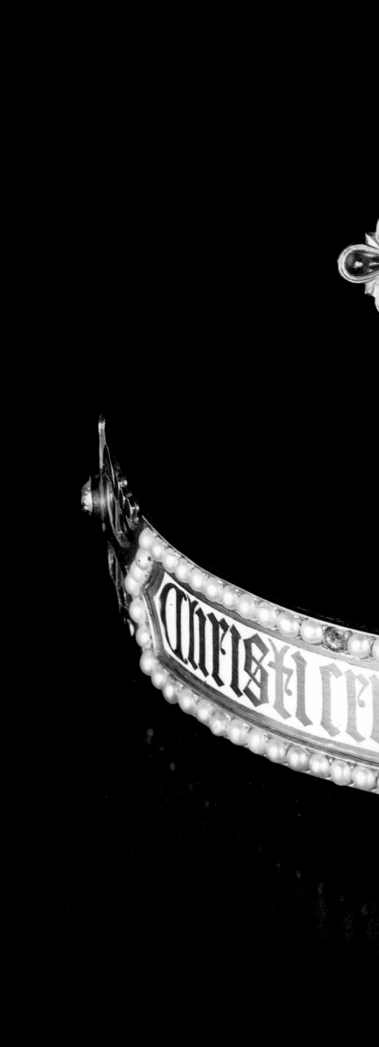

Until 1951, when Lady Cory bequeathed the department, to use her rather Edwardian phrase, 'her diamond ornaments, jewellery and trinkets' (even then more than £30,000 worth of fine early and high Victorian jewellery) there was nothing from the nineteenth century in the jewellery gallery. This has now been exhaustively remedied, and a purchase of particular significance to the history of the museum was the head-band, brooch and necklace designed by Pugin who, of course, had been intimately involved in the 1851 Exhibition (see plates 34 and 35).

These pieces are decorated with champlevé enamel in imitation of twelfth and thirteenth century work, and set with cabochon stones, also in the medieval manner. Stylistically, of course, they draw heavily on medieval sources, and they were displayed in the Medieval Court in the Crystal Palace which Pugin had designed and

36

36. A gold box, enamelled and set with diamonds, made by the St Petersburg firm of Fabergé (M1-1974).

arranged, and where, it is said, they were especially commented on by Queen Victoria. But their interest does not rest there: not only are they fine examples of Pugin's style in the 1840s, and of execution by John Hardman & Co of Birmingham, but they are mementoes of a particularly difficult time in Pugin's life when he was sorely tried for his Roman Catholicism. Pugin had intended them to be for his third wife, Helen Lumsden, with whom he was very much in love. He spent much time designing her medieval wedding dress, this jewellery and altering his house in Ramsgate, but at the last moment her family discovered to their horror that she had become a Catholic, and brought such pressure to bear on her that she called the marriage off

in March 1848. Fortunately Pugin met Miss Jane Mill that summer, proposed to her, and thus, among other blessings, had a new bride to whom to give the jewellery made for Helen. It is obvious that there could be no better resting place for it than the Victoria and Albert Museum.

Despite the fact that the museum held a record-breaking successful exhibition in 1977 of the Czarist court goldsmith, Carl Fabergé's work, it has very little from those prolific but prestigious workshops. Indeed,

37. An Art Nouveau head ornament and brooch made of tortoiseshell, horn, opaque glass and semi-precious stones, made around 1902 by René Lalique (M116 & a-1966).
38. A brooch of diamonds, platinum and stained chalcedony, made about 1913 by Cartier's of New York. Length: 2ins. (M212-1976).

37

38

if it were not for a public-spirited ex-ambassador to Moscow, Sir William Seeds, K.C.M.G., it would own nothing that was characteristic of that luxurious neo-eighteenth-century style. Plate 36 shows the box which came to the department on Sir William's death in 1974; in May the previous year he had written a delightful letter ending: 'its (the box's) fate depends on the grim race, during the next one or two years, between the Angel of Death and the Demon of Inflation.' It seems morbid, but one cannot help being pleased that the right side won.

The jewellery collections have been carried forward into the Art Nouveau period (plate 37) and recently attempts have been made to fill the Art Deco gap. This

39

40

is expensive as that was a period when much fine jewellery, especially by Cartier, was pavé-set with diamonds, so one is paying not only for good design but for considerable intrinsic worth. An appeal to the public was launched in 1976 which produced a certain amount of interesting costume jewellery, and a few spectacularly generous gifts like plate 38, given by Lady Reigate to get the appeal off to a good start. It was bought by her father from Cartier of New York as a Christmas present in 1913.

1956 brought a gigantic bequest from a slightly eccentric American, Dr W. D. Hildburgh, who for years had had the endearing habit of giving the museum presents at Christmas and on his own birthday. There is a dashing photograph of him as a young man pirouetting on iceskates in the Alps at the beginning of the century, but this is the only demonstration of frivolity this amateur scholar and antiquary ever gave. He had become involved with the department through the Keeper, H. P. Mitchell, who caught him on the rebound after he had given some ironwork to a minor New York museum only to find when he called two years later that his gift had been sold. Mitchell widened his horizons from being merely a collector of folk-lore and peasant art to becoming a discriminating collector of foreign goldsmiths' work. Plates 39 and 40 show two of his pieces, the former being part of his particularly large number of Spanish purchases which prompted Charles Oman to produce a catalogue of the by now very strong collection of Hispanic silver in the department. He bought immense quantities of objects for every department, filling in wherever he saw a glaring gap and, with great skill, buying pieces which were still underestimated and so quite cheap — seventeenth- and eighteenth-century German boxwood carvings were one example of this. Although a rich man when young, by the end of his life Hildburgh had probably spent most of his money on the museum, and his life was eccentrically austere. The retired Keeper of the department, Basil Robinson, visited him one day at his house in Kensington to find him cooking lunch by placing an open tin of sardines between two enamelled plates and heating them on a gas ring.

The arms and armour collection is relatively small when compared to the great armouries in Vienna and Madrid, but for an acquired rather than inherited collection it is distinguished. Nearly everything is in very good condition, and predictably was bought for its decorative qualities rather than to be typologically representative. There is only one rusted sallet here, but a large number of a really outstanding group of rapiers

39.   A Spanish reliquary bust of silver, parcel gilt, made in Saragossa in the early 16th century. Height: 14½ins. (M46-1956).
40.   A late 17th-century French table-top of silver, engraved with Venus presenting a shield to Aeneas. The boulle-work border is a 19th-century addition. 4ft. by 2ft. 8ins. (M53-1949).

and guns with a sprinkling of royal pieces (see plate 24), and some fine examples of embossed steel. Plate 43 shows a breast plate and a pair of gauntlets, both probably by the famous Milanese armourer, Luigi Piccinino, and both with a distinguished pedigree. The breast plate is from the suit of armour B1-B3 in the Royal Armoury Madrid, which is said to have been given by Charles Emanuel, Duke of Savoy to the Infante Philip, later King Philip III. The gauntlets, on the other hand, formed part of an armour which belonged to his successor, Philip IV; they came up at the sale of the famous early nineteenth-century collector, Ralph Bernal, in 1855, and fetched £53 11s. Both breast-plate and gauntlets were finally given to the department in 1921 by David Currie, together with a large quantity of armour, swords, steel caskets, keys and decorative knives and forks.

The arms and armour collections continue to be added to as exceptionally fine pieces turn up, and a recent acquisition has been a jewelled English small sword (plate 42) of about 1760, bought for £30,000 from the Earl of Gainsborough.

Having a Deputy Keeper with a training in Circulation, the Metalwork department has been a great deal less prejudiced than some where contemporary art is concerned. When the present director, Dr Roy Strong, decreed that as museum policy twentieth-century art was to be bought, and indeed set aside a proportion of the annual purchase grant in order to do this, it was not much of a revolution for Metalwork. It has meant, however, that the department can be a great deal more lavish with its purchases, and recently it actually commissioned a piece. Gerald Benney, a famous goldsmith and Visiting Professor at the School of Silversmithing and Jewellery at the Royal College of Art, was asked to make a jug. Technically it is a tour-de-force, with the silver body covered by a very large area of black enamel which had to be completely smooth. The chemists of Johnson Matthey were consulted and they produced a black lead enamel with a low melting temperature of 760° Fahrenheit. Despite this, it was only third time lucky: on the first attempt at firing the enamel cracked; the second attempt succeeded, but then the jug was dropped and the enamel broken; the third attempt was successful and is shown in plate 44. Thus, appropriately, the latest piece to be illustrated is completely in accord with the museum's earliest founding aim of encouraging good design, and of providing exemplars to inspire contemporary craftsmen.

43

44

43.   An Italian breastplate made around 1570 by Lucio Piccinino of embossed steel, damascened with gold and silver. The gauntlets, russeted, embossed and damascened with gold, are also Italian and of the same date (M144, 143 & a-1921).

44.   The jug commissioned by the museum from Gerald Benney in 1978. It is silver, with a gilt interior and the exterior enamelled, and with a carved ivory handle. Height: 7ins. (M166-1978).

45. *The Portland Vase, made by Wedgwood around 1790. It is of unglazed black stoneware with applied white decoration. Height: 10¾ins. (854-1882).*

3
Ceramics and Glass

Ceramics, in the Victoria and Albert Museum, is pronounced *à la Grecque, K*eramics, just as cinema used to be pronounced Kinēma. This Victorian pronunciation sounds affected, but like the hat brush in the Metalwork department for cleaning the Keeper's top hat, it gets passed down from generation to generation. It was spelled out in large letters in the new Keramic galleries opened in 1868 with the most lavish decorations of any part of the museum — great pillars covered with colour-glazed reliefs by Messrs Minton in what they misnamed 'majolica', incorporating the names of the great centres of production around the frieze, and appropriate old artistic chestnuts on the wall such as Bernard Palissy, the sixteenth-century French potter, throwing his last sticks of household furniture on the kiln in a desperate effort to solve the technical problems of firing. These marvellous decorations, alas, were encased in plain plaster just before the Second World War when the appreciation of Victorian art was at its nadir, and the ceramics collection had been moved up to the top floor, which it still occupies in its entirety, as early as 1909. These are silent, warm, bright galleries with a good view over the roof tops of South Kensington and housing thousands of objects. Practically every single aspect of the history of pottery and porcelain (glass is on the floor beneath) can be studied here, and this is the point to be stressed. Occasionally visitors who have found their way up to this eyrie complain about the display. 'Surely,' they say, 'you could modernise it — put 99 per cent of it away and make a feature of the best pieces — you know — some good dramatic lighting and modern cases, not those old mahogany ones with piano legs.' The answer, of course, is that some of the very best pieces are already shown in this way in the Primary Galleries, which are so much less exhausting to reach as they are mostly on the ground floor, but this is the study collection for specialists, for scholars, dealers and collectors, who like to be able to see the complete range of any category in existence; also for the ordinary member of the public who brings in his great aunt's tea-pot and who can then go and look at other pieces from the same manufactory. How much better than keeping reserve collections behind locked doors, which can only be seen by appointment, and which make even specialists bashful about troubling the curators.

What then was the early nucleus of this vast collection, which is perhaps the best in the world in its range and variety? The first twenty-four objects in the registers reflect the early School of Design's desire to provide admirable exemplars: they are all contemporary French pieces. The very first one, sadly got rid of in 1938, gives an idea of what the instructors admired. It was a large semi-opaque glass vase, enamelled and gilt, with a wreath of naturalistic glass flowers and ormolu mounts, made by La Roche and Co, and bought for the by no means small sum of £34, compared with the 10s paid for the extraordinarily rare and now highly prized Medici oil and vinegar flask in 1859 (plate 46). The first antiquarian purchases, in 1845, were of eighteenth-century Sienese earthenware, crisply painted and enamelled with bright colours after sixteenth-century prints. These must have appealed partly because of their accomplished technique and partly because of their association with fine art. Much contemporary work was bought after the Great Exhibition of 1851, but the beginnings of an English historical collection were made at the same time, when for £30 a proportion of the English wares assembled by the potter Enoch Wood (1759-1840) was bought. Part of his collection was considered distinguished enough to be accepted in an exchange for Meissen products by the Elector of Saxony in 1832, and the museum's share included a dish with the inscription which made a direct historical link with the Staffordshire industry: 'This dish was modelled by Aaron Wood about the year 1759 or 1760 and was deposited in his building by his youngest son Enoch Wood 1836 who at this date was Chief Constable of Burslem and Treasurer of the Market.'

J.C. Robinson's taste, however, was for maiolica, and this dominated his purchasing during the 1850s and 1860s. He also admired the products of the French Renaissance: Limoges painted enamels, Henri II ware, with its romantic echoes of the King's mistress, Diane de Poitiers, and Palissy ware with its cast snakes and lizards.

Maiolica, of course, had been admired in a modest way in England since the eighteenth century. Then it was called Raphaelle-ware, because the great painter himself was believed to have been responsible for some of the painted plates early in his career. Josiah Wedgwood, Horace Walpole and the Earl of Bess-

46

46. *Italian oil and vinegar flask, Medici porcelain, late 16th-century. Height 6ins. (5759-1859).*

borough all owned some, but the price was still quite low when the museum started collecting. Almost immediately, partly because of the museum's interest, prices began to rise steeply, a dish painted with the Labours of Hercules selling for £2 5s in 1817, and a comparable dish in 1858 for £205. Maiolica was certainly Robinson's second love, after Renaissance sculpture. He regarded it quite simply, as 'one of the most important categories of industrial or decorative art which the world has ever seen', and every bit as excellent in degree as the great works of painting and sculpture of the same period. He always intended to write a catalogue of the museum's collection in this field, and had the satisfaction of discovering Piccolpasso's treatise on pottery making (1565) (plate 191) in Casteldurante, one of the great centres of maiolica-making (this is now in the library). He never got around to doing the catalogue before he quarrelled with the museum authorities, but his influence in the subject survived for over a hundred years. He was responsible for buying 125 from among the 374 pieces of maiolica in the Bernal sale of 1856. This was an

interesting event because it was one of the first sales by the early generation of bargain hunters, at which connoisseurs and the institutions bid seriously and to unprecedented heights.

It is worth pausing over Ralph Bernal (1783-1854) because every department benefited from his sale at Christie's which lasted thirty-two days, comprised 4,294 lots, and made £63,000. He had trained as a lawyer, and entered Parliament in 1818 where he sat until 1852. He was modestly successful and became Chairman of the Committee in 1830. Compared to the amount which he spent on electioneering, £66,000 over his entire career, the £20,000 which he spent on works of decorative art seems modest; but of course he was buying in the 1830s and 1840s when practically everything was cheap. For example, from the first of the great country house sales, at Stowe, in 1848, he bought one maiolica plate from Cafaggiolo for £5, but Robinson had to bid £120 for it at his sale. Robinson went on to bid even higher, £131, for a Gubbio dish painted with the Three Graces, but this stuck in the throat of the Board who refused to ratify the purchase. At first it looked as though the museum had missed a bargain, because two years later it was sold in Paris for £480, and then returned to Christie's auction rooms in 1884 where it went for £819. But it all turned out for the best, illustrating the advantage of being a perennial institution: the buyer at Christie's was none other than George Salting, the museum's great benefactor; which shows that if you fail to get something in one century, you can sometimes pick it up in the next.

The next collection from which Robinson bought heavily was the Soulages, which had been shown *en bloc* at Marlborough House in 1856 with a catalogue by Robinson, and was being acquired piecemeal by the museum over the following few years. It is a pity that of the two pieces of maiolica illustrated by the early photographs, one should have turned out to be a fake, a rare instance where Robinson was taken in. It is a dish with a portrait of Perugino in the centre. This has subsequently turned out to be a later insertion into a genuine rim, the join being concealed by refiring.

Apart from Robinson, C. D. E. Fortnum (1820-99) also bought for the museum, particularly after Robinson had left. He was a well-to-do connection of the Fortnums of Fortnum and Mason's store in Piccadilly, and under Robinson's influence he had become a discriminating collector of decorative art, and of maiolica in particular.

On a number of occasions between 1859 and 1871 he was empowered by Henry Cole to buy for the museum and adamantly refused to accept a commission on the grounds that he was a gentleman and not a dealer. Eventually he was engaged by Hungerford Pollen, editor of the museum's catalogues, to compile the first on the ceramics collections, *Maiolica, Hispano-Moresque, Persian, Damascus and Rhodian Wares* (1873). Later, in 1884, he emerges once more in the history of the museum.

48

49

The enthusiasm for the products of the French Renaissance had much to do with a romantic fervour, comparable to the later one for Marie Antoinette, encouraged by that historical romantic Alexandre Lenoir, who created the Musée des Monuments Français in Paris at the height of the Revolution and then in the Napoleonic period. Salvaging what he could from the French royal past, he constructed a kind of monument to Diane de Poitiers with her figure from the fountain at the castle of Anet, and around her some vast Limoges enamel plaques by Pierre Courteys, supposedly from the façade of the Château de Madrid begun by François 1. Historical novels did the rest and by the 1850s the Rothschilds were vying with the museum for relics of this past. In 1864, for example, the museum paid £300 for a salt (plate 47) in Henri-II ware, with the interlaced crescents of Diane de Poitiers, which had previously been in Prince Soltykoff's great collection. Quantities of painted enamels were also

48.   *A Limoges enamel triptych made by Pierre Reymond in the 16th century (4401-1857).*
49.   *A maiolica plate from the service made around 1519 for Isabella d'Este (2229-1910).*

bought over those two decades and are shown in handsome nineteenth-century ebonised cases. The museum bought from practically every major sale of the 1850s, 1860s, 1870s and 1880s. Plate 48 shows a characteristic piece, a triptych with the crucifixion in grisaille by Pierre Reynard for which £350 was paid in 1857. But it was Palissy ware, that sixteenth-century French pottery usually covered with frogs, lizards or large cabbage-like leaves, that made collectors really enthusiastic in the last quarter of the century. Fortunately the museum had already acquired a number of good pieces before the prices rocketed, but the Board still paid £1,102 10s for a large oval wine cistern at the Andrew Fountaine sale of

1884 when J. C. Robinson, by this time Keeper of the Queen's Pictures, reappeared in old entrepreneurial form to organise a buying syndicate for the museum; the stimulus of a sale full of objects exactly to his taste must have been too much for him.

This was uncharacteristically lavish expenditure during the last two decades of the century, and luckily George Salting was collecting on the museum's behalf throughout the period. When he died in 1909 he left it no less than one whole case full of Palissy ware, three of Limoges enamels, ten of Italian maiolica, and of course much else besides. One especially important maiolica dish singled out in *The Times* of 25 December 1909 is a Casteldurante plate, with Phaedra and Hippolytus painted on it (plate 49), a part of the service made for Isabella d'Este, wife of Gianfrancesco Gonzaga (1484-1519), Marquess of Mantua. Other pieces from this service are in the British Museum, the Museum für Kunst und Gewerbe, Hamburg, the Museo Civico,

Bologna, and the Fitzwilliam Museum, Cambridge. This had also descended from the Bernal to the Fountaine sale.

But in those same early decades when the museum was helping make record prices in some categories, it was also buying some unrecognised rarities for almost nothing. In 1859 it bought the oil and vinegar flask in Medici porcelain mentioned earlier, together with another piece of the same material, for £2. This was extraordinary considering that there are only about fifty pieces in the whole world of this experimental porcelain, the fruit of the sixteenth-century Grand Dukes' of Florence efforts to imitate the ware being imported so expensively from the east. The craftsmen hit on a formula for making it, but the experiment was abandoned a few years later. A much simpler recipe was then discovered at the court of Augustus the Strong of Saxony (1694-1733) by Tschirnhausen, the nobleman with chemical interests, and Böttger, the alchemist. The Victoria and Albert Museum now boasts of eight of the surviving Medici pieces.

If the 1850s and 1860s were the heroic years of fifteenth- and sixteenth-century acquisitions for Ceramics, then the 1870s were remarkable for the Islamic collections built up by Robert (later Sir Robert) Murdoch-Smith, an officer in the Royal Engineers (always Henry Cole's favourite regiment). He was a Scot who in 1864 was sent out to Persia to supervise work on the telegraph line which the British were building across the country, linking Europe and India. Murdoch-Smith seems to have been a tactful diplomatist and good soldier, and he was quickly made Director of the Persian Telegraph Department. But he was more than just a soldier: earlier in his career he had taken part in the excavations at Halicarnassus and on his own initiative had carried out archaeological work at Cyrene in North Africa. Then, after some years of

purely military activities, he obviously felt a need to make himself useful in some more cultural sphere and in 1873 wrote to Sir Philip Cunliffe-Owen, the director of the museum, offering his services as a roving agent in Persia. After interviewing him Cunliffe-Owen obviously decided that he could be trusted implicitly, and over the next twelve years Murdoch-Smith submitted sixty-eight reports. For example, in his first he says: 'I have the honour to report that I have already purchased a considerable collection of old Persian fayence, a suit of damascened steel consisting of helmet, armpiece, and shield, and a number of carved metal vessels of different kinds, and a few other articles of artistic interest.' With the resources of the army to help him the logistics of the matter were not too arduous, and objects were taken to Bushira by caravan and then shipped to London. Unlike Robinson in Spain, Murdoch-Smith also seemed to receive his money fairly regularly, especially after the telegraph, which he had built, was in operation. His greatest coup was the acquisition of the Richard collection in 1875. Jules Richard was a Frenchman who worked at the Persian court as tutor to the royal children, went 'native', became a Moslem, married a Persian and lived in Teheran. Over thirty years he had collected works of art of every sort and Murdoch-Smith negotiated with him to buy the whole lot. All sixty-two cases of it were finally purchased for £1,778 7s 3d and by April 1876 the collection was on show to the public in the Persian galleries where the exhibits aroused considerable excitement. The exhibition was accompanied by an introductory *Handbook of Persian Art* written by Murdoch-Smith himself.

Murdoch-Smith continued to buy for the museum until 1883, especially through Richard — for example, in that year he bought from him about a hundred pieces of old Persian earthenware and twenty pieces of

50. 'The Luck of Edenhall' with
its 14th-century 'cuir bouilli' case.
The beaker is of enamelled glass,
made in Syria in the 13th century, and
stands 6¼ ins. high (C1 a & b-1959).

51

52

glass for about £145. These all went to making a very disinguished showing of Islamic ceramics in the department. After the Second World War the Keeper, Arthur Lane, wrote the two books which laid the foundations of the study of Islamic ceramics *Early Islamic Pottery* (1947) and *Later Islamic Pottery* (1957). In 1979 Ceramics acquired its first professional Islamicist with a thorough knowledge of the language, to carry on research on the collection which includes Syrian glazed pottery, early lustre tiles, Isnik ware from Turkey (what Fortnum catalogued as 'Rhodian' and 'Damascene'), and a fine collection, principally of remarkably intact lustre-ware, excavated in Gurgan, N.E. Persia, recently given to the museum by Clement Ades. The most romantic piece of enamelled glass from the Middle East is certainly 'The Luck of Edenhall' bought in 1958 for the then huge sum of £5,000, jusifiable not only on grounds of the intrinsic qualities of this thirteenth-century Aleppo beaker in perfect condition, but the history associated with it (plate 50). It had obviously come to Europe soon after it was made, probably in the baggage of a crusader, because the case, with the sacred monogram on top, must be fourteenth-century and no later. From the eighteenth century the cup has had a legend associated with it to do with the Musgrave family who owned it. This tells that it had been left behind by fairies drinking at St Cuthbert's well near Eden Hall; on being interrupted they fled, but one screamed out, 'If this cup should break or fall, farewell the Luck of Edenhall'. The family needless to say drank from it with great care and only when someone was holding a napkin beneath to catch it. It never was dropped. One may doubt whether the cup still has this supernatural power vested in it, since museums are very unnuminous places, sanitising all objects equally of their darker and their more spriritual associations.

Another, and more intrinsically precious piece from the Islamic collection is an Egyptian pottery lustre bowl (plate 51) bought in 1952. This not only shows a Coptic, therefore Christian, priest, which makes its subject matter a cultural rarity, but is signed by the maker, a certain Sa'ad.

Plate 52 shows a vase which could hardly be in more piquant contrast with the former piece. It is the Tippoo vase painted with Jupiter and Callisto after François Boucher. It is of Sèvres porcelain, painted against the ground known as *bleu de roi*. It came to the department together with a large number of other Sèvres pieces from John Jones, the military tailor who had made a fortune and spent a quarter of a million

51. An Egyptian white earthenware plate painted in gold lustre on a white glaze, dating from the first half of the 12th century. Diameter: 8⅜ ins. (649-1952).

52. The Tippoo vase, which was once the property of Tippoo Sultan (see plate 125). It is of Sèvres porcelain, about 1788, and is 18½ ins. high (747-1882).

collecting French court art of the eighteenth century. This bequest in 1882 was even more welcome than was Salting's in 1910, because, while the museum had already managed to put together a very respectable showing of sixteenth-century ceramics on its own, Sèvres was always almost beyond its price range. The first sign of the heights which this opulent art form — particularly the specimens with the sumptuous ground colours, dark blue, apple green, turquoise, pink and yellow — would reach was with the Prince Regent, who collected it regardless of price early in the century. Demand dropped somewhat after his death, but from the 1850s, the early collecting days for the museum, it rocketed again, with Lord Hertford, Lord Dudley and the Rothschilds all competing against each other. Significantly, the museum did not buy a single piece from the Bernal sale where there were 254 lots; this was partly because of the prices — Lord Hertford paid £1,942 10s for a pair of *rose Pompadour* urns on plinths — but also partly, one suspects, because Robinson did not care for the stuff. So, up to 1882, when the Jones Bequest arrived, the museum had bought very few pieces of eighteenth-century Sèvres, among which there were two plates from the Empress Catherine service at £15 each, a picture plaque by Dodin at £250, and a biscuit vase in blue and white in the Wedgwood style for £232. After 1882 the picture changed completely, for Jones had bought lavishly, despite the fact that he entered the market in the 1850s. He owned a number of the *garnitures* which were highly prized because they decorated a mantelpiece so elegantly, and some parts of *garnitures*, two with distinguished historical as well as artistic backgrounds. The Tippoo vase, for example, was commissioned by Louis XVI as a present for Tippoo Sahib, Sultan of Masulipatam (whose roaring tiger is shown in plate 125), and an important ally of the French in India against the English. Jones had bought it in 1870 at the H.L. Wigram sale for £1,078 10s. This was typical of the kind of price he was prepared to pay, for ten years later he bid up to £1,240 for a vase painted with a harbour scene, and also with a *bleu de roi* ground, which was adapted by Gustav III of Sweden for presentation to Empress Catherine II of Russia. The collection also includes a ewer and basin, *jardinières,* pot-pourri vases, bulb-vases, parts of tea services, and some fine examples of the more lavish sorts of English porcelain, notably Chelsea gold anchor, and some Meissen and oriental porcelain with ormolu mounts. He must have spent some tens of thousands on his small but distinguished collection, when Lady Charlotte Schreiber the other great ceramics donor of the nineteenth century spent a tenth of the amount on a much larger collection, but her approach was more sporting — literally — for she called her buying expeditions on the continent her 'chasses,' and she regarded £10 as a lot to spend on an item. She was an admirable woman, vastly intelligent, energetic, diverse, devout and passionate. We know a great deal about her because of a diary which she kept from the age of ten until, sixty-nine years later, she wrote: 'And here I close a journal which I have kept for very many years. I can no longer see to write, or to read what I have written . . . I feel confident the end cannot be far off, and now adieu to all.'

She was born in 1812, the daughter of Albemarle, 9th Earl of Lindsay. She scandalised contemporary society by making a love match with the great Welsh industrialist Josiah John Guest, to whom she bore ten children. She supported him in all his work, learned Welsh, made a translation of the Welsh epic the 'Mabinogion', on which Tennyson was to base the 'Idylls of the King,' and after Guest died she ran the steel mill very efficiently. Soon afterwards she fell in love with and married her son's charming tutor, Charles Schreiber, and then, ten years later, she was afflicted by china mania. For the next fifteen years, until his death in 1884, they toured the continent together in search of good pieces, particularly ones which were bargains. Here is a sample entry in her diary for one of these trips.

'Aug 17th. In the train before 6. At Amsterdam about 11. Set off immediately 'en chasse'. First to Van Houtens in the same street — Very little in our way. Our purchases of him consisted only of a small purple enamel pot and Cover (10/-). A Chelsea pug (tail replaced) 10/- Derby biscuit group (arm replaced) 10/- Good Chelsea Derby figure of a youth sacrificing a goat (head replaced) 10/-. After Van Houtens we had a grand chasse at Ganz's, and a rather successful one, though not to be compared to that of two years ago when we pulled down from his rafters one or two fine Bristol jugs (I may here remark that we have not seen a scrap of English hard paste since we have been abroad). At Ganz's we have found 2 excellent Chelsea *jardinières*, painted with flowers, which he sold us as old Dresden for £1 15s. A tall Freemason's mug, Worcester black transfer printed, 10/-. Blue and white Worcester tea-pot, raised ground 2/6. Milk jug ditto 1/10. Small Worcester vase with acrobat 5/-. Our next best haul was at Speyers, Breestraat: from him we made several purchases, some of them likely to prove good. Two groups of Chelsea-Derby figures, man and girl in bocage of leaves, good condition, only two fingers wanting 'Proposal' and 'Acceptance'? £15. Five small statuettes of which two already imperfect (and one of which two had the misfortune to drop and break still more) £1. 15. One small Menneçy figure (marked) and a white Capo ditto (unmarked) 15/-. An oriental group of a man and girl dancing, and complete copy and imitation of a Dresden one £1. Enamel box top 3/-, enamel box with swan 7/-. Ditto with bird 5/-. Pair of white salt cellars with Bouquets 25/-.'

And that is by no means all that she did on that day! Then, on 23 May 1876, her journal reads: 'Went on to Rotterdam, where we obtained a magnificent large rabbit of old red anchor Chelsea at Van

53. *The Chelsea porcelain tureen in the shape of a rabbit, made around 1755, given to the museum in 1884 by Lady Charlotte Schreiber (I.151).*
54. *A soft paste porcelain plate, made in Bow c. 1755 (I.45).*

53

54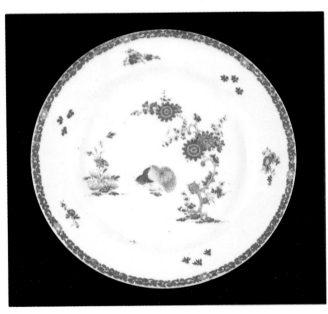

Minden's. Very cheap. Would only it had been perfect — Still, it is a noble piece. He only asked £5 for it and took £4.' This is probably the same rabbit which was advertised in the sale catalogue of 22 March 1755 of the Chelsea factory, no. 43, as 'A very fine tureen, in the form of a RABBIT BIG AS LIFE in a fine oval dish' (plate 53). It is now in the galleries of the museum, for when Charles Schreiber died in 1884 Lady Charlotte decided to give the English part of her ceramic, glass and enamel collection, 1,800 items, to the museum. It compensated for the poor reputation of English ceramics in the department up to that time, and it was especially strong in certain categories: English hard-paste figures from Bristol and Plymouth; salt glaze; some sorts of Wedgwood; certain kinds of Bow (plate 54) and some Chelsea-Derby figures. On 9 May 1884 Sir Philip Cunliffe-Owen led a deputation of thanks to her house and from June to October she demonstrated her remarkable self-taught scholarship in her catalogue which came out as an official museum

56. *Zephyrus and Flora,
Vincennes porcelain of the
mid-18th century, with
ormolu mounts. Height:
11⅜ins. (C356-1910).*

publication the following year. This collection can still be seen as a unit in Gallery 139 on the top floor, and has recently been redisplayed.

The English collection remained weak in certain areas, however, despite some happy acquisitions earlier on. In 1871, for example, it had got the two poignant salt-glazed figures made by John Dwight in memory of his little daughter Lydia who died 3 March 1673. This one (plate 55) cost £31 10s, and the other £158, the remarkable fact about them being that they had remained at the Fulham factory founded by John Dwight until 1862. There was also quite a number of Wedgwood jasper and basaltes pieces bought in the 1850s, and of course the copy of the Portland vase, the Duchess of Portland's unique Roman cameo vase from the Barberini palace, now in the British Museum; one of the only fifty made was bequeathed to the museum by Jones (plate 45). The museum still needed the more robust sorts of English ceramics — medieval pottery, English delft — and then Liverpool, Lowestoft and Caughley porcelain. This lack was made good suddenly by the merging of the unaccountably good collections at the Museum of Practical Geology in Jermyn Street with the Victoria and Albert in 1901, which happened on the occasion of the great division between Science and Art which took place when the scientists moved across the road to the Science Museum, and Jermyn Street moved next door into the Geology Museum. Quite why the Museum of Practical Geology should have collected 4,000 pieces of ceramics since its foundation in 1832 is hard to explain, as that was surely much more than was necessary purely to demonstrate the practical use of geological materials — possibly it simply reflected the chance interests of its curators. In any case, it included good slipware, much Swansea porcelain, another part of the Enoch Wood collection (now united with the pieces bought by South Kensington in 1852), a stoneware jug made by Francis Place of York and which had belonged to Horace Walpole, and another Portland vase. At a stroke a comprehensive basis to the English collections was formed, and thereafter the department has been especially lucky in the number of exceedingly generous donors, notably Herbert Allen, who have seen to it that the gaps have been filled in. Herbert Allen collected deliberately to illustrate the history of English porcelain and included representative specimens of every important factory from the earliest time to the middle of the nineteenth-century; in particular he supplemented the Schreiber collection, which was mainly confined to the eighteenth-century. Thus his collection includes the productions of the later Worcester firms, the nineteenth-century porcelain of Derby, pieces made at Pinxton, Nantgarw, Swansea and Coalport, and the output of the second Josiah

55.   Lydia Dwight: a white-glazed stoneware portrait of his daughter by the founder of the Fulham Pottery, made about 1673. Height: 10ins. (1055-1871).

58. Meissen porcelain goat, about 1732. Height: 22ins. (C111-1932).

57

57. Enamelled delftware dish from the Lambeth pottery, about 1640 (C106-1914).

Wedgwood and other Staffordshire potters. The very large collection was put on show in the museum in the summer of 1915 and bequeathed to it in 1935.

Assistance also came from the National Art Collections Fund which, for example, paid £60 to buy a fine dish of English delft-ware from the Lambeth pottery, *c.*1640, painted with Alexander the Great and his family (plate 57). Then in 1938 the museum was grateful to improve on a white Derby group in the Schreiber collection by a bequest by Wallace Elliot of the painted version (plate 59). This is one of the rare early Derby figure groups made between 1750 and 1752, and known to connoisseurs as 'dry-edge' because the bases of such figures normally appear dry of glaze along the lower edges; in 1977 the department bought the second in this series of the five senses, 'Sight', for £100,000.

The department has always had a close association and friendship with the English Ceramic Circle, which began in 1927 with the name of the English Porcelain Circle as a group of friends meeting in each others' houses to discuss each others' pieces. A founder member, and later president, was Wallace Elliot who was to leave his collection between this museum and the British Museum in an admirably fair manner: he divided it into three parts, one of which was to be sold and the others to be picked over by the keepers from each museum, first one choosing a piece, then the other.

58

59

59. 'Tasting' (right) and 'Sight', from the set of five Derby porcelain figures representing the senses, made in 1750-54 (C103-1938 and C109-1977).

A genial collector, J. H. Fitzhenry, who came to know museum officials so well that his scrawled letters from grand hotels on the continent would begin 'My dear friend' and end 'Fitz', did much to make up the deficiencies in the continental porcelain collections from other factories besides Sèvres. From 1891 onwards hardly a month went by without a consignment of goods arriving on loan, usually converted later to a gift. He was obviously an obsessive buyer, and although porcelain was his principal interest he also acquired wrought iron, architectural fragments, old cutlery, silver, medals, jewellery and textiles, a large part of which also ended up in the museum. He was the ideal kind of benefactor: objects would arrive on ap-

proval from a dealer to be accepted or rejected without fear of giving offence; he cared not at all how his pieces were displayed, leaving it entirely up to the discretion of the keepers; and he would actually ask what the museum wanted and occasionally put large sums of money at its disposal to spend as it liked. He was a friend of Salting, and indeed put up the fountain in the garden in memory of him, but in character he could not have been more different from that mean and cautious man. Numerous pieces of Menneçy and Tournay porcelain came to the department from him, as did the exceptionally fine white ormolu-mounted porcelain group (plate 56) from Vincennes, where porcelain was first made in France. Thus although the museum was not itself in the market it benefited from the last time when the products of these less famous factories were still relatively cheap, the serious price rise coming in the early part of the twentieth-century.

Then in 1951 another collector, Stuart G. Davis, bequeathed another huge collection of very good French faience and porcelain.

This left the German part of the porcelain collections the weakest, and it certainly deserves to be much more representative. Plate 58 is one of the pieces which was snapped up after the sale of duplicates from the Dresden porcelain collection in 1920. It came up again

at Sotheby's in May 1932, and the Murray Bequest provided the £220 10s necessary to buy this important documented piece, mentioned in a report of 18 August 1732 on the state of the completed animals and birds for Augustus the Strong's Japanese palace at Dresden. The Meissen factory working for Augustus was, as we have seen, the first in Europe to succeed in making true porcelain. That report mentions four unpainted goats of which this is one. In the category of Meissen alone, however, more *Commedia dell'arte* figures are needed, as well as those very popular brightly-coloured bird figures.

The glass collections are extraordinarily complete and are one of the many areas where the museum can boast the most representative selection in the world. The department has very fortunately been offered much of it either as gifts or purchases in the form of ready-made collections. The early acquisitions are either of contemporary pieces or of fifteenth- and sixteenth-century Venetian glass, which for nineteenth-century taste was to glass what Renaissance maiolica was to pottery.

Plate 60 shows a splendid and large Venetian goblet and cover, whose form is derived from contemporary vessels in precious metals, and which is decorated with enamel colours. It dates from the late fifteenth-century and was collected by Alessandro Castellani, son of the famous goldsmith. Unlike his highly business-like father, he was an artistic romantic, and spent his inheritance on archaeology and collecting. He had become involved in politics during the period of the unification of Italy, and for a while was held captive by papal forces in Castel Sant'Angelo. While there he translated Shakespeare, which helped establish his connections with England. On 2 November 1870 he wrote a triumphant letter to the director of the South Kensington Museum saying: 'I just arrive from Rome whence I had been banished seven years ago and where I entered on the 20th Sept last with the Italian army on the ruins of the temporal power of the Popes.' He then goes on to offer his collection of classical antiquities, jewellery, glass, marbles, bronzes and terracottas to the museum. A wrangle about the price followed and it was decided on 9 December 1871 to rent the collection from him at 5 per cent of its value per annum and to have it transported by the Royal Navy. Accordingly the collection was brought to England by *H.M.S. Defence* and *H.M.S. Himalaya*, but unfortunately some civil servant had bungled, and this was followed almost immediately by an exchange of increasingly formal and angry minutes between the Lords of the Treasury, the Admiralty, and the Lords of the Department of Science and Art about who should pay the 1 per cent of the total value due in freight charges to the captains and officers of these ships under an old law of George III. The British Museum, which had bought half the collection, paid up almost immediately but the South Kensington museum's debt was only discharged in July 1872.

What happened to this part of Castellani's collection is unclear: whether it was sold piecemeal by him when the leasing agreement with the museum was suddenly broken off is not known, but when he died in 1883 the museum was intensely keen to buy as much of his second collection as could be afforded. This large sale, half of classical antiquities and half of Renaissance and medieval art, took place at Castellani's Palazzo Rosso in via Poli, Rome, in March 1884. The museum had got the grudging permission of the Committee of the Privy Council for Education to let money saved on, say, cleaning services and the joiner's shops to be spent at the sale, up to £11,000. Fortnum, as on numerous earlier occcasions, was sent to deal for the museum, and he wrote back firmly and enthusiastically about the excellence and variety of the objects, recommending precisely which lots should be bought. Unfortunately the Venetian goblet of his choice, lot 405, of blue glass with pictorial enamelling, was one of the four objects to have an export interdict put on it by the Italian government. The museum clearly had to support the authorities, so another selection of Venetian glass was made, £800-£1,000 put aside to spend on it, and the goblet in plate 60 was one of the pieces bought, together with some good maiolica.

61. Jacopo Verzelini's soda glass goblet, dated 1581. Height: 8⅛ins. (C523-1936).

62. A lead crystal goblet by G.Ravenscroft (1618-81). Height: 6½ins. (C530-1936).

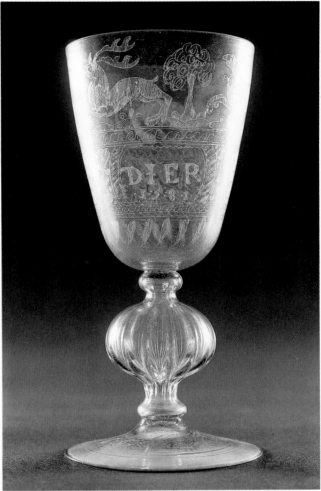

61

62

A great deal of glass also came with the Jermyn Street Museum collections of 1901, including one piece which was particularly appropriate, a water carafe designed by Richard Redgrave (plate 2), one of the judges of the Great Exhibition and the first Superintendent of the Art Museum. This piece was made by the Felix Summerly workshops, the manu-facturing enterprise and alias which concealed Henry Cole, the first director, with his ideas on good design. Decoration had to be suitable to use, and here this is interpreted very literally, with painted green water reeds around the body of the flask. It was not much admired in 1901 but was one of the first Victoran objects to be rehabilitated and shown in the Victorian and Edwardian Decorative Arts Exhibition of 1952.

In 1936 six hundred and sixty-five pieces of glass collected by Wilfred Buckley were given by his widow in memory of him. Mr Buckley and his barrister son had made a formidable duo in the world of glass specialists, both of them collecting avidly and well, and the son publishing prolifically on the subject. One of the greatest rarities in the collection is a goblet by George Ravenscroft the inventor of lead 'crystal' (plate 62), a heavier form of glass with a higher proportion of oxide of lead than that made by the Venetians. It has

remarkable interior fire due to its good light-dispersing character, surpassing even rock crystal in this quality; hence the use of the word 'crystal' to describe it, and now to denote glass in general.

In the same bequest were two other glasses of enviable rarity, both by Jacopo Verzelini (plate 61). Elizabeth I had for some years wanted to encourage the setting up of a glass-making industry in England, and in 1575 Verzelini (1522-1606) was given the privilege to make glass and to teach the art to English apprentices; for as Harris, in his *Description of England* (1586) wrote: 'in these daies wherein gold & silver most aboundeth, (now that gentilitie as lothing those mettals because of the plentie) do now generallie choose rather than Venice glasses both for our wine and beere . . . such is the nature of man generallie, that it most coveteth things difficult to be attained . . .' These glasses are now so coveted that one sold recently to the Birmingham City Art Gallery for £100,000.

Overleaf: 63. St James the Less: a detail from the Winchester College glass, c. 1400 (4237-1855).
64. The figure of Maximilian; Flemish stained glass of c. 1496, from the Chapel of the Holy Blood, Bruges.

65. *A bowl of green and brown glass, made in Nancy in the late 19th century and signed E. Gallé. Height: 10ins. (C599-1920).*

66

66. *This modern bowl by Jacqueline Poncelet (born 1947) was purchased by the Circulation department in 1974. It is of slip-cast bone china, carved and polished, and stands 3¼ins. high (C366-1974).*

The stained glass which the visitor can see set in walls around the museum building (and a great deal more which he cannot see as there is no space for it in the galleries) came to the museum in a steady stream from the earliest years. The great majority of it is continental because the Napoleonic wars and secularisation led to the stripping of works of art of all sorts from religious institutions. The romantic Gothic revival made these spoils, especially ones which could be fitted into the decor of neo-Elizabethan houses, very popular, and so it was that the two large picture cycles of sixteenth-century glass in the cloisters of the monasteries of Mariawald and Steinfeld in the Rhineland found themselves incorporated into the chapel which the architect Wyatt was building at Ashridge. These were given to the department in their entirety by E. E. Cook in 1928. Similarly, the windows from the Chapel of the Holy Blood, Bruges (plate 64) which had been sold by the municipality of the city in 1795, and at some date in the next thirty years shipped over to England, were incorporated with Kilburn Grange from which they were bought for £6,000 in 1918. In the meantime, in 1848, Bruges had had to go to the expense of putting up modern replicas of the old glass. The fifteenth-century English glass from Winchester College chapel (plate 63), on the other hand, seems to have been torn from its setting merely on misguided aesthetic grounds. In 1820-21 a 'restorer' was employed to make a modern copy of the window, presumably with the virtues of a brighter and newer appearance. He sold the old glass to the Rev. W. G. Rowland, the incumbent of St Mary's, Shrewsbury, who recognised a good thing when he saw it, even if the college authorities did not. He installed it in his church where it remained for twenty years before being removed to make way for an 'Albert Dürer'

window from Saxe-Altenburg. Rowland bequeathed it to a Mr Corbet who sold it to the museum in 1855 for £25, a paltry sum for such an important late Gothic work of art. If one shudders smugly at these stories and imagines that such vandalism could not happen again, one should think of the Victorian churches being pulled down almost weekly and consider whether that is not exactly comparable. As with church monuments, the museum cannot provide a home for more than a tiny handful of the windows made homeless, which means that they are smashed up or sold to the highest bidder. The museum has all the less room as it is actively trying to make up for the previous neglect of twentieth-century stained glass. The department owns the *maquettes* for Piper's famous windows at Coventry Cathedral, plus one of the windows themselves (a copy was made at the time); and in 1978 some exceptionally stylish glass by well-known German designers, including Johann Schreiter and Ludwig Schaffrath, was bought from the exhibition at the Royal Exchange in the City. None of this can be seen until there is more display space conjured out of the architecture of the museum, or another building is found to house it.

The department has always been more receptive than some to nineteenth-century and contemporary design: in 1920, for example, it accepted with gratitude a gift of some Art Nouveau glass from Dr John Macgregor (plate 65), and Bernard Leach, one of the founders of the art pottery movement, has always been admired. Both the Circulation and the Ceramics departments acquired some of his rough, homespun pots in the 1920s and 1930s, and this group has since been added to. Indeed in 1977 the museum held a major retrospective exhibition in honour of the great old man on the occasion of his ninetieth birthday.

In the last ten years more and more contemporary ceramics and glass have been bought, and the members of the department now regularly visit graduation shows at the Royal College of Art, the galleries which specialise in modern design, and the shops of commercial firms such as Rosenthal; and they generally keep their ears open for news of any outstanding talent rising above the horizon. Of course the department has also benefited from the many sage purchases of modern work made by the Circulation department over the course of the years (plate 66).

The collections of ceramics and glass are more accessible to enthusiasts in foreign countries, who are unable physically to get to the museum, than those of most other departments, because there are so many catalogues of them, and books about them. The department has, from the late nineteenth-century, when Bernard Rackham entered the museum, been fortunate in having a succession of Keepers, such as W. B. Honey, Arthur Lane and Robert Charleston, who have all been world authorities in their various fields, and who have, as with Arthur Lane and Islamic pottery, laid the foundations on which all later students have built.

*67. The Emperor Rudolf II; a bronze portrait by the
north Netherlandish sculptor Adriaen de Fries (c. 1545-1626),
dated 1609. Height: 28ins. (6920-1860).*

4
Sculpture

Among his other great contributions to the building of the museum's collections, J. C. Robinson laid the foundations of what is undoubtedly the best collection of Italian Renaissance sculpture outside Italy. He was aware, when in 1852 he became Superintendent of the Art Collections, that the British Museum and other institutions were so slavishly devoted to the works of Greece and Rome that they had neglected the Italian Middle Ages and what he called the 'revival period', the Renaissance. He deplored this tendency particularly because of its effect on contemporary sculpture, which he regarded as cold and lifeless, as compared with the fifteenth-century Italian school which was 'inspired by external nature, religious feeling, human character, expression, quite as much as the antique'.

Almost at once Robinson began to build a different sort of collection. It was not an easy job. He was like an explorer in virgin territory, with none of the convenient aids which fill the bookshelves of his modern successors — no photographs, no reference works to organise the material neatly into schools; all he had was Vasari, the sixteenth-century biographer of the artists, and a pioneering work on Italian sculpture by Count Cicognara. Nor could he rely on the support of his superiors, but had to cajole and bully them, often from half way across a continent.

His opportunity came, however, when the Gherardini Collection began to be hawked around Europe. It was not a dramatic-looking collection on which to base a major turning point in the museum's buying policy; indeed the artist's sketch models of which it consisted were unimpressive in size and desiccated in appearance. The attributions, however, were of startling and evocative boldness. At first almost every piece was supposed to be by Michelangelo himself! The legend went that the group had belonged to a member of the Gherardini family, an old priest, who had been unaware of its importance. It appeared rather suddenly in the Casa Gherardini in the Via della Pergola, Florence, and around 1850 sophisticated visitors to Florence were encouraged to go and see this *recherché* collection of masterpieces, all in terracotta or wax. Whether this provenance can be trusted or not is a debatable point; certainly the collection includes some items, like a mid-eighteenth-century English model, which have no business to be in

an old Florentine collection. At the time, however, the story was swallowed.

Shortly afterwards the collection was put on sale and appeared in a number of European capitals. The Tuscan and French governments turned it down as being ridiculously expensive, so Signora Gherardini, the head of the family, moved the collection to London, and it was agreed that it should be exhibited for a month in the Museum of Ornamental Art at Marlborough House, 'with a view of eliciting from the public and artists of this country such an expression of opinion as to their value and authenticity as will justify the purchase or the rejection of the Collection by Her Majesty's Government'. This democratic practice of submitting potential purchases to the approval of the public is something which is now quite unthinkable in an English museum, although in America, where the idea of public accountability is more widespread, it is perhaps still possible. The sum being demanded was £3,000. The public's reaction is unrecorded, although considerable interest was shown; Queen Victoria and Gladstone, then Chancellor of the Exchequer, both visited the show. On 10 April Richard Redgrave, the Superintendent of Art, was summoned to the Chancellor and, after some discussion, the collection was acquired for £2,110. Even at the time, the attribution of all the models to Michelangelo was pooh-poohed, but gradually the true importance of the collection emerged, and it is now clear that among a certain amount of miscellaneous material, it does indeed include a genuine wax model by Michelangelo (plate 70), four very important models by Giambologna, two fine terracotta models by his pupil Francavilla and by Battista Lorenzi, and two works by François Duquesnoy. It is worth lingering over the Michelangelo model, not least because it is the only work in the museum now believed to be by him. Modelled in red wax, it is a preparatory study for the Young Slave for the tomb of Pope Julius II, the full scale version of which then stood in the Boboli Gardens, Florence.

Of course the museum was not buying only Italian sculpture during the 1850s and 1860s. In 1856, for example, it acquired a very fine terracotta of a running fawn by Claude Michel known as Clodion (1738-1814) (plate 68). Although not widely known, it is indisputably a genuine work by an artist who was

68. *A running fawn; terracotta by Claude Michel, known as Clodion (1738-1814). Height: 17ins. (2627-156).*
69. *The Virgin and Laughing Child by Antonio Rossellino. Terracotta. c. 1465. Height: 18⅞ins. (4495-1858).*

69

68   greatly in vogue during the Second Empire and thus had the distinction of being more faked than any other eighteenth-century sculptor. Although a solitary example of this taste in the museum's buying at the time it fitted in with the contemporary commercial vogue for eighteenth-century French art stimulated by the splendid exhibition which had taken place under the museum's auspices at Gore House in 1853.

In 1860 Robinson bought a piece which has been the envy of museum colleagues in Vienna and Prague ever since: for £89 5s, again from an unspecified provenance, Adriaen de Fries's third portrait of the great, melancholy Holy Roman Emperor, Rudolph II, was acquired (plate 67). De Fries was a Dutchman who trained in Florence under Giambologna, worked in Augsburg and then became court sculptor at the imperial court in Prague. From the art historian's point of view it is a very important work because it is not only signed, and dated 1609, but can be traced through the inventories of Rudolph's own personal museum to the collection of Queen Christina of Sweden, whose occupying forces looted it from Prague in 1648.

In 1857, when the museum was transferred from Marlborough House to its new premises in South Kensington, Robinson had more space and scope for adventurous purchases. The great coup of 1858 was to become one of the most popular pieces of sculpture in

the museum: the terracotta by Antonio Rossellino (1427-79) of the 'Virgin and Laughing Child' (plate 69). This was correctly attributed when it was bought by Robinson in Paris, from an unrecorded vendor, for £28. Since then it has been assigned to various masters including Leonardo da Vinci, but the consensus is again for Rossellino. It must have been the model for a much larger figure which seems not to have survived; but the freshness and skill of the modelling and the informality and tenderness of the attitudes gives it great appeal to the viewer.

In 1861 Robinson, again with Gladstone as the benefactor in the government, achieved another great success by being in the right place at the right time and exploiting a difficult political situation. The various states, kingdoms and principalities of Italy were engaged in the upheavals of the Wars of Unification, and the Papal State in particular was being squeezed from north and south. A few years earlier, in the 1850s, the papal authorities had decided to throw into gaol the Marchese Campana, director of the national pawn-broking establishment. His offence was that in the process of acquiring his huge and varied collection of works of art he had embezzled official funds. While he lay in prison his sequestrated possessions were put up for sale by the Papal States in the hope of recovering some of the money. Wild rumours about their sumptuousness flew around Europe and

70

70. *Michelangelo's red wax model, a preparatory study for the Young Slave for the tomb of Pope Julius II (c. 1513). Height: 6½ins. (4117-1854).*

attempts were made, in both England and France, to purchase the collection *en bloc*.

In 1956 the British Museum sent out two representatives, who made the then not ungenerous offer of £34,246 for the classical parts of the collections; but their offer was peremptorily turned down. The South Kensington Museum, of course, was only interested in the Renaissance sculpture and maiolica wares, which had been augmented by items belonging to a Signor Ottavio Gigli, a Roman literary man and dealer, who had had the misfortune to become embroiled in the affair. He had pledged his much finer collection to the pawn-broking establishment when Campana was still at the head of it in the expectation that the Marquis would buy it, but when Campana was imprisoned Gigli found his objects confiscated along with the offender's. In 1859 Robinson was sent to report on this dual collection, and of Gigli's 124 specimens he concluded that 69 were worth acquiring; while of Campana's he recommended only fifteen.

Signor Gigli was understandably rather desperate to extricate himself, and armed with a photographic catalogue of his objects he travelled to Paris and St Petersburg, but without finding a buyer. Meanwhile the war was taking on a savage character. 'One might suppose Rome to be a second Lucknow,' writes Robinson on 4 May 1859, referring to the recent Indian Mutiny, 'and the Campagna outside, hot and dusty and lonely as it is, to be swarming with brigands and sepoys ready to cut the throats of every living soul.' No progress, however, was made with negotiations for the collection and Robinson returned to England. In the autumn of 1860 he was again in Italy, and on 22 November he writes from Naples: 'The Papal Government is at the moment greatly in need of money and would probably make any sacrifice for a lump sum. I have been informed on Cardinal Antonelli's part that they would now gladly treat for this portion of the Campana irrespective of Gigli the ostensible owner . . . No such collection is ever likely to occur again for sale.' In other words, the unfortunate Gigli's separate rights were to be ignored in the deal. Robinson promised 'a letter in an open envelope to Mr Gladstone, which if you think there is any chance of going on with the Gigli affair you may perhaps think proper be forwarded to him. Whatever is done, however, should be done without the loss of a day.' On 7 December Robinson left Naples by stage-coach with an escort of Papal Dragoons, and a revolver ready in his hand in expectation of brigands; and on arrival in Rome he found a telegram authorising purchase. For £5,836 then, £1,134 less than the money owed to the pawn-broking establishment by Gigli alone, an outstanding and unrepeatable collection was brought to the museum.

It included the Arnolfo di Cambio 'Annunciation', the Donatello 'Ascension with Christ giving the keys to St Peter,' the Donatello 'Lamentation over the Dead

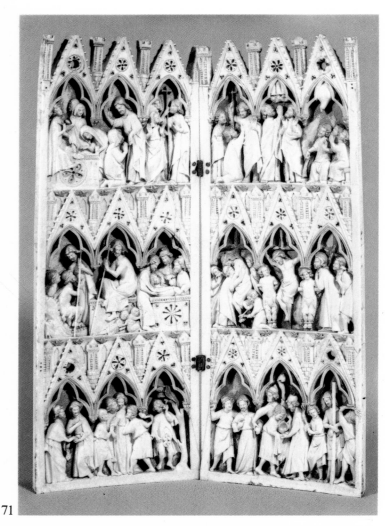

71

72

71.   The painted ivory diptych said to have come from the treasury of the Soissons cathedral. It is just over 1ft. high, and dates from the late 13th century (211-1865).

72.   Donatello's 'Lamentation over the Dead Christ', bronze, c. 1458. Height 12⅜ ins. (8552-1863).

Christ,' the Luca della Robbia roundels of the 'Labours of the Months' from the Palazzo Medici, Verrocchio's sketch-model for the Forteguerri monument, Jacopo Sansovino's model of the Deposition and the so-called 'Cupid,' for many years attributed to Michelangelo. With this material to his credit, Robinson sat down to write his excellent catalogue of the sculpture.

To remind us, however, that the skilled Italian forgers had already begun to anticipate demand, it is interesting to reflect that one of the most popular pieces in the entire Gigli-Campana collection, judging by the number of plaster casts of it sold by the museum in the second half of the nineteenth-century, was a low relief of the Virgin and Child in grey stone in the manner of Desiderio da Settignano: this has since turned out to be an early nineteenth-century fake.

It is at first surprising to compare the prices paid for the Rossellino Madonna (£28) and the relief of Rudolph II (£89 5s), with the relatively vast price of £650 given for the Martelli mirror (plate 73). But this was bought as being by Donatello, with a water-tight history behind it, from Marchese Martelli of Florence. It was offered to the museum in 1857 or 1858 for £800, but there was not enough money to buy it, so in 1863 it was offered again through the dealer W. B. Spence in Florence, and on this occasion the purchase was completed. Robinson thought it so important that it should not be sent by sea, but brought overland by Spence himself or carried by the Queen's messenger. Its appeal in the nineteenth-century must have been its exquisite finish and detail, and the combination of the three colours of metal-working worthy of a fine goldsmith. It is possible also that its mysterious subject with the inscription NATVRA FOVET QUAE NECESSITAS URGET (nature fosters what necessity urges), a platonic sentiment about the association of nature and necessity, tickled the classical awareness of members of the board. Robinson, surprisingly, wanted to bowdlerise its rather gnomic message; and shortly after the plaque's arrival he wrote a minute recommending a craftsman in Jermyn Street who could make a damascene gold figleaf for the Priapus. The attribution to Donatello has long since been set aside, and although no convincing alternative has yet been found it remains one of the master pieces of the collection.

Robinson went on successfully to follow the two Donatellos bought at the Gigli-Campana sale with a third work indisputably by the master. This is the bronze 'Lamentation over the Dead Christ' (plate 72). Robinson must have become aware of it when he was arranging the Special Exhibition of Works of Art, on loan to the South Kensington Museum in June 1862. In this extraordinary display of varied and great works of art winkled out of stately homes and private collections of England and Europe, he made the authorities and the public aware of the range of art objects which might potentially be in the museum, and indeed, he spent much of his energy and literary enthusiasm in the following years trying to get 'Their Lordships' to buy

73

74

73. *The Martelli mirror, made in Italy of bronze, gold and silver in the last quarter of the 15th century. Robinson suggested that the Priapus at the top should be covered with a gold figleaf. Diameter: 6¾ins. (8717-1863).*

74. *San Diego of Alcala kneeling before the Virgin and Child; a painted terracotta sculpture by Luisa Ignacia Roldan, made in Madrid in the last quarter of the 17th century. Height: 20ins. (250-1864).*

exhibits which had been on show. In this case he was successful: the owner was a M Armand Baschet of Paris, who had probably bought it from the Palazzo Mocenigo di S. Luca in Venice. By the curious system then operating the dealer, John Webb, bought it and held it until such a time as the museum could produce the £140. Webb was a very distinguished dealer in works of art, whose role was a semi-philanthropic one, for on more than one occasion he bought objects for the museum, depositing them on loan, in exchange for

suitable payments of interest on the capital sum involved, and then released them when the authorities came up with the money. The relief once had a bronze background, which has been chiselled away, and it is not known what its original function might have been. Stylistically, however, it is related to Donatello's work in the late 1450s on the bronze doors of the Old Sacristry of San Lorenzo, Florence.

After this Robinson was to acquire one more work thought to be by Donatello, the Virgin and Child, of gilded terracotta, the last before the Chellini tondo which the museum so triumphantly acquired by public subscription in 1977.

Robinson clearly enjoyed his 'chase' for works of art, as much as Lady Charlotte Schreiber pursuing her porcelain, and it must have been a relief for him while abroad to be more of a free agent, instead of controlled at every turn by the Lords of the Department. In the autumn of 1863 he was travelling again, this time in Spain, using Madrid as the centre of operations and radiating out from the city to all the important centres — Burgos, Salamanca, Valladolid, Avila, Segovia, Astorga, Léon, Guadalajara, the cities of Andalusia, Saragossa, Murcia, Valencia, Tarragona and Barcelona. His task was to report back on what should be photographed, drawn or reproduced by plaster casting, and his excited letters read like the art historical equivalent of Speke's missives sent back from the journey down the Nile. This task was not easy, however: travel was uncomfortable and time-consuming, and cathedrals so dim and sombre and so frequently used for services that a photographer, even if one could be found, was almost unable to work. It was equally almost impossible to make plaster casts, so Robinson recommended that a few very large ones be made, supplemented by large coloured drawings. He complained of suffering from diarrhoea, and that the air of Madrid caused him 'inflammations'. The British Embassy managed to open certain doors, especially to the Royal Collections, for him, but also caused him one of his most anxious moments: he was, of course, to bring back works of art, but for any item over £100 he had to write back and ask permission, and his letters are full of complaints at the failure of these letters of credit to arrive. In November, just as he had abandoned hope and had got on the train from Cordoba to Madrid, he heard an agitated messenger shout his name on the platform. He barely had time to seize the letter, which turned out to be the long awaited money. Apparently this had been sent *poste restante* care of the Ambassador, Sir John Crampton Bart, and had been languishing for weeks in a pigeon hole under 'B'. In a long minute written in March 1864, after his return, Robinson justified his purchases and produced an interesting apology for what he clearly regarded as a disappointing result. 'It is certainly more difficult there than anywhere,' he wrote, 'to find out and acquire such objects; whereas in Italy, Germany and France, everything is known and noted, where every

75

76

75.   *A rock-crystal cup with silver gilt mounts, engraved by Georg Schwanhardt the Elder of Nürnberg. c. 1625. Height: 8¼ins. (49-1867).*

76.   *The five orders of architecture, made of lapis lazuli mounted in gold, on a base of red porphyry mounted in ormolu. The piece dates from about 1780, and was probably made for Marie Antoinette. From left to right, the orders are: Doric, Tuscan, Ionic, Corinthian and Composite. Height: 11ins.(853-1882).*

town and village has been searched to exhaustion, and the machinery of acquisition, if I may so term it, organised in the most complete and practical manner, in Spain comparatively but little of the kind has been done.'

He shows distinct respect towards the Spaniards for this, putting it down to their innate pride and reserve. 'It is as difficult to obtain information in respect of objects of art in private hand as it is easy in Italy, where, as a rule, all classes are willing to barter their artistic possessions.' Nonetheless, as his three consignments arrived, including much sculpture and ecclesiastical metalwork, and some furniture and jewellery, the lists show a number of impressive acquisitions. The piece of which he was proudest was a Pax by Antonio d'Arphe, the goldsmith who made the great silver monstrance-tabernacle at Compostella; but the third consignment included a polychrome figure of the Moses from the great altarpiece of San Benito el Real at Valladolid, by the greatest of Spanish Renaissance sculptors, Antonio Berruguete, and among the characteristically Spanish painted terracotta sculpture of the seventeenth century was a fine group by Luisa Ignacia Roldan (1656-1704) of San Diego of Alcala kneeling before the Virgin and Child (plate 74).

The following year a number of highly important early ivories were bought; the tenth-century Byzantine Veroli casket for £420; the first leaf of the fifth-century diptych of the Symmachi; and the painted ivory diptych from the Treasury of Soissons cathedral (plate 71). This latter is one of those works of art around which other anonymous works have been grouped by the historians; it depicts eighteen scenes in the Passion of Christ, from Judas' kiss to the Descent of the Holy Ghost, reading from left to top right. It cost £308 and is described, like so many of the distinguished ivories, as coming from the Webb Collection. But as these were all bought over a good many years, no doubt this inscription concealed the kind of holding operation that John Webb had also performed for the Donatello Relief, and he had always been buying with the museum in mind. For example, in 1866 the museum acquired from him three of its most famous ivories, which had come up at the Soltykoff sale, where Robinson would obviously have bought them if he had had the money.

Robinson was nothing if not bold: it is now a forgotten fact that while in Spain he tried very hard, with the assistance of the British Ambassador, to buy some of the Spanish Treasury. He particularly coveted some of the previous mounted stone vessels which were originally part of the Dauphin's collection in France. Robinson had been given access to these and indeed had been allowed to have some of them painted, but he clearly felt they were wasted in the Royal Palace, and came up with a scheme whereby the museum would buy some of the pairs, thus providing the Royal Curator, Señor Madrazo, with the money

77

77.   *The tympanum from the Scuola della Misericordia in Venice, showing the Virgin and Child and kneeling members of the Brotherhood of the Misericordia. It is by Bartolomeo Buon, carved in Istrian stone, and dates from about 1441-51. Height: 8ft. 3ins. (25-1882).*

which he needed to restore the rest. The Ambassador, Crampton, was obviously enthusiastic and promised to raise the matter at the next quiet dinner; but some months later, in March 1864, he wrote that while Madrazo had not actually been insulted by the suggestion, he had not given way either!

The museum still lacks a good array of these earliest of collectors' pieces so prized by the European princes of the fifteenth-, sixteenth- and seventeenth-centuries. In 1867 it paid the large sum of £150 (although cheap by comparison with the Hamilton

Palace Sale (1882), and the Spitzer Sale (1893), when prices reached the thousands) for a standing cup of rock crystal, engraved on the wheel, with figures of Neptune and Amalthea, recently identified as the work of the Nürnberg master, Georg Schwanhardt the Elder (1601-67) (plate 75). At the time it was considered to be Italian, the clear 'N' town-mark of Nürnberg on the silver-gilt mounts being as yet unidentified. From time to time other mounted hardstone vessels have been added to it, the latest being from the Mentmore Towers sale held in 1977, when Baron Meyer de Rothschild's collection was sold up, but the best pieces have always eluded the museum.

In 1882 the John Jones collection of French art arrived in the museum. Its strength lay less in its sculpture than in its furniture and ceramics, but it did include an elegant architectural toy (plate 76),

Venice has taken no steps, or only feeble, perfunctory ones to prevent the destruction or alienation of innumerable archaeological and artistic treasures of the city and when unavoidable demolitions occur, no effort is made to acquire precious architectural fragments and details for the vaunted museum. Thus the ancient Abbey 'La Misericordia', which for years past has stood empty and desecrated has just lost its sculpturesque decorations and these, as they were openly on the market for sale, I have secured for this country . . . the tympanum of the Misericordia is intrinsically a work of high merit and importance, but it had infinitely more significance in its original place. It is indeed a page torn from the book of Venetian art.' The tympanum is the sculptured relief which filled in the central triangular space of the gothic arched doorway above the level of the vertical shafted jambs. Some Venetians, at any rate, shared Robinson's view that it was a disgrace, and *La Venezia,* on 9 April 1882, reproaches the Commission of National Monuments for not even having been aware that the sale by private individuals, into whose hands the Scuola had reverted, had taken place. Robinson had entered on the scene only after the family had sold the fragments to an antique dealer, and he paid the very moderate amount of £157 9s 8d for this chunk of Venetian history, the work of the most important Venetian sculptor of the first half of the fifteenth-century, Bartolommeo Buon.

The loss of J. C. Robinson was a serious one, however arrogant or intransigent he could be, because he was succeeded by a group of art referees including the architect Matthew Digby Wyatt, Alfred Gilbert (best known for his Eros in the middle of Piccadilly Circus) and Walter Crane, the designer, none of whom took his intense personal interest and pride in the formation of the collection, and who made up for their lack of historical understanding by their strong artistic prejudices. They depended too much on the judgment of even remoter third parties, especially dealers, and tended to be wayward and trivial in their purchases.

Indeed at that time a high proportion of fakes entered the building. 1870-1900 were bad years for the museum and it was pipped to the post again and again by the new Berlin Museum under the brilliant directorship of Wilhelm Bode. Worse still, the museum was often not even competing with Berlin, so parochial had its interests become. This makes it all the more welcome to see that in 1893 it bought what is almost certainly its most important late Gothic German sculpture (plate 80), the small boxwood statuette of the Madonna and Child by Veit Stoss (d. 1533). It cost a mere £88 4s which was very cheap compared to the hundreds fetched by northern sixteenth-century sculpture at the Spitzer sale in the same year. It came without any provenance worth mentioning, and it is almost certain that no one in the museum knew what it was; although the German scholars seized on it as early as 1908, and published it as the only small scale work surviving by this great Nürnberg master.

78   illustrating the five orders of architecture from the Doric on the left to the Composite on the right. These represented the elementary ABC of architectural knowledge which every educated person in the eighteenth-century had to know. It stands just 11 inches high and the columns are of lapis lazuli, with gold mounts, while the base is of porphyry and ormolu. A legend always associated it with Marie Antoinette, and very recently the bills for making the case to contain it came to light at Versailles, so unlike so many legends of this sort this one has turned out to be true.

Robinson had, of course, ceased to be an art referee in 1876 (see page 11), but in 1881 he and the museum made it up enough for him to be sent on a purchasing trip in Italy. He returned with a vitally important example of Venetian sculpture, the stone carving which originally stood over the door of the Scuola della Misericordia, one of the great charitable penitentiary lay orders which dominated Venetian life for over three hundred years (plate 77). It is extraordinary that as late as 1881, even after Ruskin had published his works on Venice, and when sightseers were flocking to see the marvels of the city, the authorities should have allowed such an artistically and historically important work to be removed. Robinson clearly thought so as well and wrote a letter to *The Times* on 24 October 1883 explaining how it came to happen. 'All this time the Municipality of

79

80

78.   The bronze 'Shouting Horseman' by Andrea Briosco, acquired by George Salting in the Spitzer sale in 1893. Briosco was active in Padua from 1480 and died in 1532, and this piece dates from about 1505-09. Height: 13¼ins. (A88-1910).
79.   Don Carlos, in coloured wax on glass, by Antonio Abondio (first half of the 16th century). The locket containing it is copper gilt. Height: 5⅛ins. (A525-1910).
80.   The Madonna and Child by Veit Stoss of Nürnberg, carved in boxwood with traces of gilding, and dated about 1520. Height: 8ins. (646-1893).

In the end, however, the catastrophe of the thirty years of bad buying was almost compensated for, at least in the sculpture field, by the generosity of one man, who was scooping up the finest pieces while the museum was fiddling. This man was George Salting. *The Times* in its obituary, on 14 December 1909, called him 'the greatest English art collector of this age, perhaps of any age,' which was putting it perhaps a little strongly, but certainly nearly everything among the 2,500 objects which he left to the museum was of the highest quality. He was born in 1836 in Australia, where his father, a Dane by birth, had made a fortune with large sugar estates and sheep farms. He was educated at Eton and Sydney University and from his thirties came to live in England with around £30,000 per annum to spend, no inclination to marry, and no philanthropic interests. He did, however, have a vague interest in art. He was taken in hand by a collector of Chinese porcelain, H. C. Huth, who taught him about it, as well as giving him more generally a sense of quality. After building up what was for the time an outstanding collection of oriental ceramics, Salting moved on to Renaissance art, probably under the guidance of the dealer Murray Marks, from whom he had also bought much Chinese porcelain. The turning point in his collecting was 1891, when he traded in the famous Red Hawthorn vase, a *famille noire* vase with white prunus blossoms tinged with red, for a

Renaissance bronze. He went over to Paris for the Frederick Spitzer sale, which lasted through April, May and June 1893. He bid there, every day maddening all the dealers, who felt it unsporting of him to spend so much money without employing an agent, and he ended up spending £40,000. Definitely his best purchase was the 'Shouting Horseman' by Andrea Briosco, known as 'Riccio' (plate 78). This taut and dramatic, delicate yet vigorous sculpture, dating from the early years of the history of small bronzes, is more coveted by the connoisseurs than any other in the world. As anyone who has had to deal seriously with *objets d'art* knows, a Spitzer

81. Thomas Baker (1606-58); marble
bust by Gian Lorenzo Bernini
(1598-1680), made in Rome in the first
quarter of the 17th century.
Height: 2ft. 8⅛ins. (A63-1921).

provenance for an object is often not an unalloyed recommendation. As an ex-dealer he was well in with the trade and the restoration craftsmen, and he often improved things which passed through his hands. In this case the improvement is relatively inoffensive and he merely replaced the three legs on which the horse stands, but while it was in his collection, he had some casts made of it which, with a few exceptions, account for all those in other collections today.

Together with this most precious bronze, Salting also left the museum ten cases full of other Renaissance bronzes and reliefs, fourteenth- and fifteenth-century ivories, sculptures of wood, marble, stone and terracotta, and a quantity of very good medals, including the finest examples of Pisanello in the world. The British Museum reacted to this bequest, as it did over Salting's miniatures, in a way most unbecoming of a sister institution and immediately put in a claim to the Director, Sir Cecil Harcourt Smith, that although the will specifically said that Salting left the whole of his collection, apart from the prints, drawings and paintings, to the South Kensington Museum, they had a moral right to the Renaissance coins and medals, because one perfect collection was better than two imperfect ones and Salting had frequently consulted their expertise and even mentioned that he was collecting for them. This suggestion was, of course, strongly resisted by the director and the medals joined the already distinguished group assembled by Robinson in the 1860s (plate 83). On the left, then, is one of Robinson's, acquired in 1886 for two guineas, a rare hand-chiselled and chased work by Antonio Averlino, otherwise known as Filarete, whose most famous work was the bronze doors of old St Peter's in Rome; bottom right, is a Salting piece showing Antoine, Bastard of Burgundy, made by an Italian craftsman at the Northern Court between 1472 and 1480; and top right is one of the most recent additions to the collection, bought in 1976 for £240, a minor masterpiece of the greatest sixteenth-century Venetian sculptor, Alessandro Vittoria.

Also with the Salting collection came a number of those miniature wax sculptures, rather macabre in their realism. Plate 79 is of a particularly important one, also originally bought at the Spitzer sale: the subject, the treacherous son of Philip II, Don Carlos, is a distinguished, melancholy one and it is by Antonio Abonado, the well-known Lombard wax sculptor. Its interest is increased by its original copper-gilt locket, which appropriately shows the disobedient prophet dead under a tree.

After the great windfall of the Salting bequest, the sculpture collection began to improve, largely due to the discrimination of Eric (later Sir Eric) Maclagan, who arrived in 1906 and who was eventually to become director of the museum. He was a tall, gaunt man, who always wore a black double stock, and he had an international reputation as a scholar.

In 1910, the distinct department of Architecture and Sculpture finally came into existence and new work began on ordering and cataloguing the objects. Sums of money which were without precedent were also spent on works of art, as the museum began to take seriously once again the business of building up its collection. For example, £1,563 10s was paid at the Marquess of Anglesey's sale at Beau Desert for the Bernini bust of Thomas Baker (plate 81). Bernini was just emerging from a period of neglect and was now being admired again as the greatest Italian portrait sculptor of the seventeenth-century. It was an especially suitable piece for an English collection: the subject was an English gentlemen, and it was by the same sculptor who did the bust of our greatest royal art collector, Charles I, from the famous triple portrait by Van Dyck.

Thirty years later another member of the department, John Pope-Hennessy, who was also to become director of the museum, added an enormously important monumental sculpture by Giovanni Bologna (plate 82) to the galleries. This too came from an English country house, Hovingham Hall in Yorkshire, whence it was bought for £25,000 with the assistance of the National Art Collections Fund. It had never been intended for a place in the English rain although chance history connected it with the Thomas Baker bust, and with the same royal court of Charles I. It shows Samson and the Philistine, larger than life size, and was made to stand on a fountain in the Cortile dei Semplici of the Casino of Grand Duke Francesco de Medici in Florence. From there it passed as a gift to the Spanish Duke of Lerma, the favourite and chief minister of Philip III, and was erected in the royal gardens at Valladolid. In 1623 it was given — this time without the fountain — to Charles, Prince of Wales (later Charles I of England) who was on his return journey from Madrid after the negotiations for the Spanish marriage. He in turn presented it to his favourite, the Duke of Buckingham, who stood it in his gardens at York House; and in the early years of the eighteenth-century his descendant moved it to Buckingham House, later to become Buckingham Palace. George III gave it to his Surveyor-General of His Majesty's Board of Works, who moved it for the penultimate time to Hovingham House, Yorkshire; and it was his direct descendant who finally sold it to the museum. Like much painting and sculpture of the sixteenth-century the Giovanni Bologna sculpture was tardily but enthusiastically absorbed into eighteenth-century English artistic sensibility. Copies of it, the earliest dated 1691, by Nost, Cheere and others, stand in the gardens of the English stately homes of Chatsworth, Seaton Delaval, Southall and others.

Pope-Hennessy went on to add to all aspects of the sculpture collection, especially the bronzes. Although his first enthusiasm was for the Italian fifteenth and sixteenth centuries, he also appreciated more extravagant examples of the high Baroque such as the

*82. Samson smiting the Philistine with the jawbone of an ass. A marble
by Giovanni Bologna of Florence, dated c. 1565. Height: 6ft. 10ins. (A7-1954)*

83. *Three bronze medals. (Left) Antonia Avelino, with the inscription ANTONIUS. AVERLINUS. ARCHITECTUS. Italian, c. 1451-65. Height: 3½ins. (Above right) Tommaso Rangone (1493-1577), with the inscription THOMAS. PHILOLOGUS. RAVENNAS. Italian (Venetian), c. 1570, by Alessandro Vittoria (1526-1608). (Below right) Antoine de Bourgogne, with the inscription ANTHONIUS. B. DEBURGUNDIA.*

83

pair of purely decorative bronze ewers (plate 84) by the Florentine, Massimiliano Soldani-Benzi. They are exceptionally fine castings, afterwards delicately chased-up, made around 1710, and with their marine monsters, swirling wave patterns and general asymmetry of form they are extraordinarily bold; but despite this they appear to have appealed to an English patron because they have an English provenance and are part of the large quantities of work being made for the English market at this time. The ewers were bought from Rosenberg and Stiebel in New York for $4,000.

Of course the drain of works of art from the greater and lesser English country houses has been constant, and was much accelerated after the Second World War. The museum has tried to pick up the pieces where possible so that they at least remain on show to the public, but the acute problem of redundant and impoverished churches is a recent one, which has led to a change of policy where the collecting of English monumental sculpture is concerned. In the nineteenth-century and the earlier part of the twentieth the curators would have pointed to Westminster Abbey, among scores of lesser churches, if asked where the national collection of British monumental sculpture was (and this remains true today). But someone has to provide a home for works in abandoned, roofless or even demolished churches; so in 1967-68 the museum paid for the removal and re-erection of five monuments from Eastwell church in Kent. This was an isolated foundation, so neglected during the Second World War that its roof collapsed in 1951. Since there was no demand for it as a place of worship nothing was done about rebuilding it, but it contained six tombs, five of which were of considerable artistic merit. They were all connected with the same family, the Moyles who married into the Finches; four of them are sixteenth-and early seventeenth-century in date, while the last is a neo-classical monument to a nineteenth-century descendant, Emily Georgina, Countess of Winchelsea and Nottingham, who died in 1848. These

are all now under the vast barrel-vaulted roof of the English sculpture gallery.

However, just as works of secular art are better seen in the context for which they are designed or collected, and thus it is infinitely preferable that the English country houses should retain their treasures, so monumental sculpture loses a great deal of its historical meaning if taken from the church where it belongs. The museum neither wishes to be, nor is physically capable of being, a repository of works of art from redundant churches all over the country and is encouraging the recent policy of moving sculpture from such sites into flourishing churches in the neighbourhood.

Occasionally art historians, as a result of painstaking research, know that a certain work of art by a great master must exist, even if they have no idea where it might be. This was the case with the Chellini tondo by Donatello, the most important purchase made by the museum in this decade. In 1962 Ronald Lightbown, Keeper of the Library, turned up a fascinating document, a sixteenth-century paraphrase of a statement by the Florentine doctor, Giovanni Chellini Samminiati, (1372-1462), telling how he had looked after Donatello who, in gratitude, had given him a circular bronze relief, sculpted with the Virgin and Child and two angels, and with the outer side concave so that an impression in glass of the same scene could be cast from it. Shortly afterwards, in 1965, Sir John Pope-Hennessy, who because of his distinction in the field of Renaissance bronze had been asked to catalogue the Samuel H. Kress Collection in Washington, described a rather coarse roundel, with the same subject, and connected it with the work mentioned in the document. Three other casts of this roundel, all of different dates, also existed, one in the Museo del Castelvecchio at Verona, another in the church of San Lorenzo at Vicchio di Rimaggio near Florence, and the third at the Sir John Soane Museum, London. This third one was the clue that the piece might be found in England, rather than Italy or any other place in the world. The word circulated round the small number of people in London who could be interested in this problem and, stimulated by this, one day in 1966 a lady decided to bring her bronze roundel into the museum for an opinion. It was indeed the lost tondo, and it was immediately recognised. The visitor was told this and she took it away again. No more was heard of it for ten years. As was later found out, she was the step-daughter of the 10th Earl of Fitzwilliam, who had given it to her as a present. He had inherited it from his ancestor, Charles Watson Wentworth, 2nd Marquis of Rockingham. He in turn had bought the roundel in about 1750 from the last of Chellini's descendants who only had one daughter. The chain linking the piece with Donatello himself was now complete and it was obvious that if it ever came up again for sale the museum would have to exert every muscle to buy it. Unfortunately the roundel was never offered directly to the museum and the first it heard of its imminent departure from this country was when an export licence application was forwarded to the office for approval in the summer of 1975. The price was £175,000, but rumours flew around that an American gallery was offering $2 million for it. It was a bad moment for the museum, even at this bargain price, as the financial year was far enough advanced for the kitty to be almost empty. The Treasury was unprepared to make a special grant as it was floundering in a financial crisis, so the museum found itself with three months in which to raise a very large sum. Dr Roy Strong, Pope-Hennessy's successor, was someone who believed in involving the public, so he launched an appeal to which people responded generously despite the fact that this rather austere religious work of the early Renaissance might not have been expected to have a very general attraction. Then Strong suggested that, since the tondo was intended for replicas to be made from it, then why not make replicas and sell them; so a limited edition of silver casts was made, and these sold out. Finally the National Art Collections Fund and the Pilgrim Trust came up with a large sum of money in memory of Lord Crawford, and just before the three months was up the museum bought the roundel (plate 85). It was a triumph for research and for the museum.

Just as Bernini went out of favour and then came in again, so cameos and intaglios, those small works of sculpture carved on the surface of precious stones, have also suffered an eclipse and a revival. After the mania of eighteenth- and early nineteenth-century collectors there was a distinct decline in enthusiasm for them except as forms of personal adornment. Thus the museum has collected only a handful of these tiny but most durable of works of art. Recently, however, a number of publications on the subject, particularly on individual collections of the past, such as Lorenzo de Medici's, have come out and interest is quickening. Some old dispersed collections are being tracked down

84

again, as in the case of a beautiful onyx cameo of a lady in a veil which two dealers, Richard Falkiner and Thomas Heneage, saw in an auction house catalogued as nineteenth-century. It is indeed in immaculate condition and in a style which the nineteenth-century admired, but they realised that it was in fact a sixteenth-century piece, and on further research identified it as a cameo once in the Duke of Marlborough's collection which had descended to him from one of the earliest of English collectors, the early seventeenth-century Earl of Arundel. This provenance, combined with the obvious quality of the cameo, made it irresistible to the department even when offered at the large sum of £16,000. Fortunately it was the time of year when the museum still had money to spare, so it was bought and added to the small 'treasury' which forms the first room of the baroque galleries.

85

84. One
of a pair of
bronze ewers by
Massimiliano Soldani-
Benzi of Florence,
dated about 1710.
Height: 2ft. 7½ins. (A19-1959).

85. The
Chellini
tondo by
Donatello. It dates
from before 1456, and is
11⅛ins. in diameter (A1-1976).

The department's attitude towards nineteenth and twentieth-century sculpture has been a changing one since Maclagan's day. It is a little known fact that this distinguished Renaissance specialist took a keen interest in modern sculpture. He was, for instance, a great champion of Epstein, and it was he who acquired for the museum the Modigliani and Mestrovich pieces; he presented the museum with a whole collection of Gaudier-Brzeckas, and it was largely because of him that Rodin decided to house his great gift of his own work in the Victoria and Albert rather than in any other British museum.

But the museum's role as a collector of nineteenth- and twentieth-century sculpture has, since an agreement in the late 1930s, largely been assumed by the Tate Gallery. The Modiglianis and Mestrovich's were placed on permanent loan there, and the Rodins were sent out to Bethnal Green along with the other nineteenth-century material. During the next forty years the only department to buy contemporary works was Circulation, and a very representative collection was made over the years, with Henry Moore, Hepworth, Dobson, Paolozzi, and even Kurt Schwitters all included. These pieces have now been transferred to the Sculpture department, and there are plans to bring the nineteenth-century collection back from Bethnal Green. Negotiations with the Tate Gallery are being reopened over who should collect what, because it is obvious that there should be no rivalry; but equally it is illogical that this department alone in the whole museum should fail to show contemporary art. The recently appointed Keeper is straining to take the department into these fresh fields with brand new galleries and purchases, and indeed the bulk of his first year's purchase grant has already gone on twentieth-century purchases.

86. Cabinet in marquetry of various coloured woods, with ormolu
mounts and porcelain plaques, and a top of inlaid marbles. English,
1855. Height: 13ft. 6ins. (548-1867). This and the vase in the foreground
(311-1883) were both shown at the 1862 exhibition.

5
Furniture and Woodwork

The first objects in this department were rather humble, and very much a reference collection for the artisans who were supposed to learn the art of fine decorative carving from them. The first item on the books, bought in 1848, is a carved Flemish mask of the early seventeenth-century. Only 3¼ by 8¾ inches, it is obviously a fragment of some greater, unidentified whole, and the pages of the registers continue to be full of equally anonymous panelling, newel posts, banister rails, bits of choir stalls and reredoses — and continental Gothic and Renaissance furniture, especially Italian marriage chests. While the fragments all cost a few pounds or so, these last were mostly over a hundred pounds and were higher priced because, as J. Hungerford Pollen's first handbook to the collection (1875) said, in Italy 'the best artists of the day did not hesitate to give their minds to the making of woodwork and furniture . . . of the fine Renaissance period'. In other words they were examples of the principle fervently embraced by the nineteenth-century museum that painters, sculptors and architects should involve themselves in the crafts, and they were also very useful for clothing the walls in the rooms which contained the growing collections of Renaissance art. As one turns the pages of the registers one is sometimes amused by how far this buying of 'props' was taken — what can the museum have wanted with twenty-four of those stiff, carved Venetian sixteenth-century hall chairs (incidentally, popular subjects for nineteenth-century fakers) from the huge collection of the Toulouse lawyer Jules Soulages.

Two very important pieces were bought from the 1851 Exhibition at the Crystal Palace, one being Pugin's vast cupboard and the other Lestler's desk for Prince Albert. Both are superb examples of the Gothic revival and were especially mentioned in the reports. Nonetheless woodwork, as opposed to furniture, dominated acquisitions in the ratio of about five to one until the early twentieth-century. The earnest students from the School of Art Wood-carving, part of the Art Schools still housed in the same building as the museum, trooped around with small folding chairs sketching and picking up ideas for design and technique. The museum only unbent enough to buy the fruits of their study once, in 1897, when seven pieces were acquired from the women's work section of the Victorian Exhibition. These were also of a fragmentary sort, one piece being a walnut drawer front, heavily carved with interlacing leaf and money moulding, and obviously based on one of the Italian marriage chests already in the collection.

Much of this woodwork was still the spoils from the Napoleonic secularisation of religious institutions on the continent, imported by dealers catering for the long-lived antiquarian taste for old panelling (plate 88); and from our own church restorers, led by the architect Sir George Gilbert Scott. These were tearing out post-medieval, and indeed some medieval, fittings from churches in a fury of purist restoration which was bitterly criticised even at the time. A particularly fine set of misericords (the carved props on the underside of hinged seats of choir stalls on which tired clerics could rest their bottoms without actually sitting down during the service) came to the museum from St Nicholas's Chapel, King's Lynn, Norfolk, whose church wardens had sold them in 1852. They had then gone to the Royal Architectural Museum in Westminster and were finally bought by the museum in 1921 when that closed down (plate 87).

The second half of the nineteenth-century was also the great period for the redevelopment of the business heart of the Empire, and the old City of London was being rebuilt as fast as Manhattan in the 1930s. That is how the museum came to own the twenty-two feet high front of Sir Paul Pindar's house, erected about 1600 in Bishopsgate Without, and demolished in 1870 to make way for a bigger Liverpool Street Station. The Chairman and Directors of the Great Eastern Railway Company stored it away in their warehouse for twenty years without being able to think what to do with it, and then donated it in 1890.

All this woodwork just mentioned can be seen in the galleries, together with a few other pieces of the same nature, but where, the visitor may ask himself, is the rest? It used to stand in a large Architectural Court which was to wood-carving what the Sculpture Galleries were to stone-carving, but the enthusiasm for antiquity for its own sake and for virtuoso medieval and Renaissance carving has dwindled. It is no coincidence that all the pieces illustrated are ones which have a provenance and consequently an academic interest. After the Second World War, when the Keeper, Ralph Edwards, was confronted with the mountains of stuff brought back from the war-time hiding place in the caves of Bradford-on-Avon, he was naturally aghast

87

88

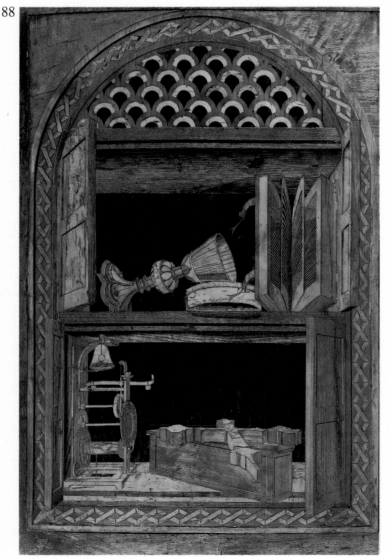

87. *An oak misericord from St Nicholas' Chapel, King's Lynn, about 1415, showing a master carpenter at his bench, and his two apprentices carving away on the left. Width: 22ins. (W54-1921).*

88. *An intarsia panel from the choir-stalls of S Michele in Bosco, Bologna, dating from 1521-25, and dispersed in 1797. Height: 3ft. 7½ins. (150-1878).*

and he took a drastic decision — to get rid of everything which seemed valueless or which was damaged. Many of the larger architectural fragments went into the disused bedrooms at a newly acquired country house, Osterley Park, with the aim of eventually creating a study collection there. A tiny proportion was left on show in the museum, and the remaining pieces were 'boarded'; that is, a group of the curatorial staff formed a kind of tribunal which sat in judgement on the merits of each piece and then decided which could be 'written off' the records. An object was first offered to a sister institution, and if that failed it was sold anonymously, but if it was in such a dilapidated state that no one could possibly wish to buy it, or if a fake, it was destroyed. Fakes, like heretics, were always burned because it was considered unhealthy to release them on the public at large. The serious objection to this lay in the criteria used for defining fakes: many of those destroyed objects would now be regarded benignly as interesting examples of antiquarian revivalism, while some are now known to have been perfectly genuine. There were some tragic losses: for example the handbook of 1875, mentioned earlier, illustrates a pedestal with a base formed as the head and forelegs of an elephant. This was destroyed because it was in poor condition, and now it is thought possible that it was one of the very rare pieces of furniture designed by Inigo Jones. Whether this supposition is right no one will ever know now. All that can be said is that the curators have learned from

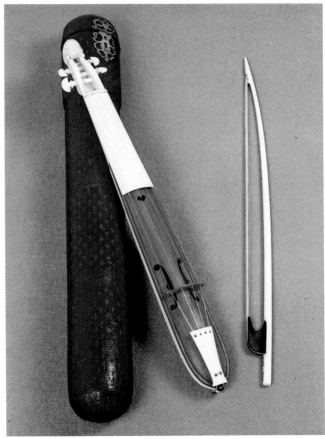

their mistakes and the present generation is very wary of 'boarding' unwanted objects.

There is no doubt that the museum's great early collector, J. C. Robinson, must have found these early acquisitions very pedestrian, and when he borrowed for the 1862 Art Treasures Exhibition at the museum he showed exactly where his, and where expensive English taste had always lain — with the grandest French furniture of the courts of Louis XIV, Louis XV and Louis XVI. He only included one piece of woodwork and all the rest comprised the finest pieces from the greatest collections in the land. In particular he admired Boulle work, the furniture of the court of Louis XIV, with tortoise-shell and brass inlay, and he showed eleven pieces of it, borrowed from the Queen, the Duke of Buccleuch, Earl Grenville and others. Of a marquetry and ormolu *étagère,* said to have belonged to that infinitely romantic figure Marie-Antoinette, he stated that it displayed 'the utmost perfection of design and execution at the culminating period of French art'. The trouble was that his taste in these things was very much the aristocratic one of the period and the Rothschilds, Lord Hertford (who built up the Wallace collection) and other great noblemen were competing for pieces of this kind. Fortunately, unknown to Robinson, a modest, amiable and rich bachelor living in Piccadilly was devoting himself to building up a collection of such pieces, and twenty years later it was all to come to the museum — but that is a story yet to come.

Meanwhile the museum contented itself with buying a magnificent exhibition piece (plate 86) which the judges at the Paris exhibition of 1855 said epitomised the finest qualities of the Louis XVI period. This was extremely expensive, £1,200 (compared to £100-£150 for a Renaissance *cassone),* but patriotic zeal, quite apart from aesthetic considerations, must have swayed the Department of Science and Art. It was designed by a Frenchman, M Eugène Prignot, but made by Messrs Jackson and Graham, the Oxford Street firm. It is a technical triumph, with its marquetry of many-coloured woods, electro-gilt hand-chased mounts, hand-painted Minton porcelain plaques, and a top of inlaid marbles. The exhibition catalogue tells us, credibly, that a total of forty craftsmen worked on it.

Nine years later the museum bought its first original piece of the Louis XVI period (plate 91), influenced by its legendary association with Marie Antoinette. On 8 April 1869 the Department of Science and Art was offered for 60,000 francs (£2,100) a complete room removed from the Hotel Sérilly, 122 rue Veille-du-Temple, in the Marais district of Paris. Sir Matthew Digby Wyatt, a prominent architect and one of the Art Referees, was sent over immediately, and on 22 April wrote back enthusiastically with the romantic tale which had been spun to him. Apparently Monsieur de Sérilly, one of the paymasters of Louis XVI army, married the favourite maid of honour of Marie Antoinette. While he was briefly away from Paris his wife decided to give him a surprise and with the aid of the Queen decorated

the boudoir. The magic of the royal association worked and their Lordships agreed that the room should be bought forthwith. In fact, although there is not the slightest reason to suggest that Marie Antoinette actually had a hand in it, there was a core of truth in the story, since later research has shown that the room was decorated by Rousseau de la Rottière, whose services were almost exclusively monopolised by the Queen and who was at the same time decorating the private apartments at Versailles and Fontainbleau.

The 1870s went by and some eighteenth-century Venetian gilt wood furniture was bought, as well as a great deal of Persian woodwork, much of it sent back together with fine textiles, ceramics and metalwork by Major Murdoch-Smith from Persia in 1876, and an unrivalled collection of Persian sherbet spoons and some fine musical instruments. These, and the many later acquisitions of instruments, were all in store until the late 1960s; then what one research assistant, Willy Thorpe, insisted on calling the 'savage instruments' — that is all non-European ones — were sent to the Horniman Museum while the rest were displayed extremely well in a special circular gallery, with every piece, if not on show in a floor case, in sliding glass-fronted storage cases. They were collected primarily for their decoration but many are of great interest to musicologists who, since it has become fashionable to play music on authentic instruments, come to study their construction in detail. They are also used at

90

concerts in the museum from time to time. An important little kit and bow (that is, a small fiddle used by dancing masters) (plate 89) was bought in 1872 from an aristocratic English clergyman for a paltry £1 10s. It is signed by the Parisian maker Dimanche Drouyn. Its present precise dating to the time of Louis XIV's eldest son, the Grand Dauphin, is due to the hairstyle of the girl at the end, combined with the fleurs-de-lis and dolphin emblematical of dauphins on the leather case.

Rather grudgingly, perhaps, the first acquisitions of English eighteenth-century furniture were made. A number of mahogany chairs were bought, all for low prices, including one described as 'By Chippendale' costing £4. They were flatly lacking in romance and the technical virtuosity of French furniture of the period, and were altogether too recent and too commonplace to arouse great enthusiasm. However, the museum was beginning to show a desire for comprehensiveness in its displays, and so they were bought. An early photograph shows them displayed miserably in bays with fragments of a Gothic carved screen on the walls and brown wooden chairs in rows beneath, knee to knee, without any apparent system behind their arrangement and looking rather like lots in a second rate sale room.

Then, in 1882, the museum had its greatest bequest of the century, and the Sérilly boudoir suddenly had a gallery full of furniture and works or art to keep it company (plate 90). The retiring collector mentioned

earlier, and living at 95 Piccadilly, had been John Jones (1799-1882). His early life is obscure, but he made his own way remarkably successfully. In 1825 he set up a military tailoring establishment at 6 Waterloo Place, close to all the gentlemen's clubs, and after only twenty-five years of business he was able to retire. He made yet more money from the Crimean war which broke out in 1854, since his firm supplied the uniforms for the troops, but his life-style was obviously modest: he never kept a carriage and never married. How he developed his passion for French decorative art is not known, but it was estimated when he died that he spent £250,000 on his collection, which he began in the 1850s when prices were already high, and had one quarter assembled by 1865. He would certainly have visited the important Gore House Exhibition of French decorative arts held by the Department of Science and Art in 1853, and he also travelled to see his favourite styles. He was in Paris for the 1867 exhibition to which Princess Eugène lent pieces supposed to have belonged to Marie Antoinette, and there was caught by the current nostalgia for that ill-fated queen. He bought anything which could plausibly be associated with her: a roll-top desk attributed to Roentgen, a picture, a bust, the miniature model of the Five Orders of Architecture in lapis lazuli (plate 90) and the box with the miniature of the French royal family (plate 25). He also acquired two charming pieces of furniture which had been lent to Robinson's

92. A bracket clock veneered with kingwood and with gilt-metal mounts, made by John Fromanteel of London about 1675 (W7-1926).

1862 exhibition at South Kensington, and which did have associations with Marie Antoinette. They are a reading stand and a work-table (plate 93), both made by M. Carlin and decorated with Sèvres porcelain, which the Queen gave to Mrs Eden (later Lady Auckland) whose husband was arranging a commercial treaty with France. The rest of the furniture includes many pieces which later research has confirmed as being very fine examples by famous makers such as Bernard von Risamburgh, Weisweiler, David Roentgen and Riesener, together with some very good Boulle marquetry. About a third have turned out to be revivalist pieces or partial concoctions of the dealers such as E. H. Baldock who catered for the Boulle-work craze of the first half of the nineteenth-century, but these also have an historical and cautionary interest.

Together with this luxurious furniture came Sèvres porcelain and gold boxes, fine paintings and miniatures. It seems that the museum, knowing that it would never have the collection bequeathed by Lord Hertford to his son Richard Wallace (now the Wallace Collection Museum), made efforts to court John Jones. Cole's successor as director, the charming Sir Philip Cunliffe-Owen, started calling on him in the 1870s to 'advise him how best to dispose of his collection', and when it finally came to the museum in 1882 a grateful handbook was produced almost at once which described the bequest as 'the most magnificent gift ever bequeathed to the people of England'. Alfred de Champeaux in the influential *Gazette des Beaux Arts* (1883) castigated the Parisian museums for not gathering in the debris of their artistic heritage and putting together a similar collection which would be an inspiration to manufacturers. The London journal *The Athenaeum*, however, referred sourly to the bad taste of Louis XV and to 'voluptuous and unintellectual bric-a-brac'. This carping was rightly ignored and the collection was displayed *en bloc* in the Loan Court until 1910 when it was removed to the former Ceramic (now Silver) Galleries. It was arranged by Oliver Brackett, first Keeper of the newly-formed department, and the furniture was shown for the first time out of glass cases, 'in spite of threatened damage from London fogs'. Academically, however, the collection languished: no catalogue came out until 1922, and although a great deal of work has now been done on the pieces in the intervening years, none has appeared since. 1922 was also the year when it was installed in the rooms where it is now shown, although its stylish and imaginative display is due to the present Keeper of the department, Peter Thornton.

The decade 1891 to 1912 brought six of the rooms which are such a memorable feature of the museum. The first was the late sixteenth-century panelling (at a cost of £1,000) from Sizergh Castle in Westmorland; the second, in 1894, the early seventeenth-century panelling and fireplace from the building known as 'The Old Palace' in Bromley-by-Bow, East London, which was being demolished by the School for London; the third,

93

93. Worktable in marquetry of tulipwood and other woods, with ormolu mounts and Sèvres porcelain plaques, made in France by M. Carlin in the Louis XVI period. Height: 2ft. 6ins. (1067-1882).

in 1899, was early Tudor Renaissance panelling from a house in Green Yard, Waltham Abbey, and the fourth (for £666 7s 6d) in 1903, the 1680s panelling of a lawyer's room in Clifford's Inn. In 1910 and 1912 the first two eighteenth-century rooms arrived, for fashion had definitely swung round to that period by then. The first was given by His Majesty's Office of Works from No 5 Great George Street, Westminster, and the second came from a house in Hatton Garden in the City. Interestingly they were both installed with the paint pickled off the woodwork, and must have reinforced the mistaken (and still flourishing) fashion of the 1920s and 1930s for pickled and bleached woodwork. They have, of course, now been repainted as they would have been in the eighteenth-century.

English furniture, particularly of the eighteenth-century, had at last come into its own, and there were plenty of pieces with which to furnish these two rooms. As with the Gore House Exhibition of 1853 for French decorative arts, and the Victorian and Edwardian

94. Perhaps the museum's most famous possession, the Great Bed of Ware. It dates from about 1575, and was made in England of carved oak with painted decoration (only part of which remains). The bed is mentioned by Sir Toby Belch in Shakespeare's Twelfth Night ('...as many lies as will lie in thy sheet of paper, although the sheet were big enough for the bed of Ware in England, set 'em down . . .'); and in Ben Jonson's Epicene: or the Silent Woman. It measures 8ft. 9ins. by 10ft. 8½ins. (W47-1931).

Decorative Arts exhibition in 1952 for nineteenth-century styles, it was a public show which crystallised interest in the subject and gave it official approval. This was the Special Loan Exhibition of English Furniture and Silks held at Bethnal Green in 1896. The outstation there now had a large open space in it since the collection of national portraits had been moved in the summer of 1895 to the new National Portrait Gallery off Trafalgar Square, so Hungerford Pollen and Purdon Clarke, the director, visited over seventy collections all over the country to report on suitable exhibits to illustrate the various styles prevalent in England from the seventeenth century to the time of George IV. As Pollen pointed out in his introduction, the museum was hardly in the avant-garde of interest in the eighteenth-century styles, as 'Queen Anne' pieces, meaning anything from the time of the Georges, had been very

popular in the trade for some while and prices were rising fast. Indeed, foreign museums had already started representing fine examples of 'Chippendale' and his contemporaries, so it was time that the public started to appreciate the beauty of 'these old national productions'. It is worth quickly glancing over the categories into which he divided the exhibits as these

94

and delicate rather than 'full and juicy mouldings'. Hepplewhite got a mention in the same breath, but otherwise Pollen provided little hard information.

From 1900 onwards the writings on English furniture piled up: the periodical *Country Life* was begun in 1897 and immediately started a series of articles, still running, on English country houses and their collections, so that for the first time furniture was published in its surroundings. *The Connoisseur,* a periodical dedicated to private collections formed in recent years by individuals, came out in 1901; Chippendale's, Sheraton's and Hepplewhite's pattern books were reprinted; the Keeper of the department, Oliver Brackett, wrote the first monograph on Chippendale, and Percy Macquoid, the interior decorator associated with the famous firm of Lenigon and Morant, did the first and still memorable sorting into categories with his voloumes *The Age of Oak*, *The Age of Walnut*, *The Age of Mahogany*, and *The Age of Satinwood* (1904-08), which provided the framework for collecting until the 1960s.

Scholarship and taste always follow closely on each other, sometimes one leading, then the other; in this case, they were in perfect accord for nearly thirty years and much of what could be seen in, say, the windows of Mallet's of Bond Street was to end up in galleries. A peppery but invigorating scholar entered the Department of Woodwork in 1926, and from 1945 to 1954 was Keeper of Woodwork: Ralph Edwards. He did much to build up the museum's very large holdings in English seventeenth- and eighteenth-century furniture and also wrote what many, including himself, regarded as the definitive book on the subject: *The Dictionary of English Furniture* (first edition with Percy Macquoid, 1924-27; revised edition 1953). He summed up his own attitude to furniture studies in a review of a new book on Chippendale which he wrote while in retirement. He liked to think that the last word had been said on the subject and was merely being unashamedly repeated again and again with ingenious variations. Edwards certainly laid a solid foundation, but a more precise knowledge was only just beginning to be unearthed by patient research in archives and by looking at the subject in the wider context of architecture and the architects. One incentive to this was the three great architect-designed rooms bought between 1936 and 1955. The first was David Garrick's room from 6 Adelphi Terrace in the Strand, that great and speculative development by Robert Adam; the second, in 1938, was the Music Room from Norfolk House in St James's Square. Both these were the victims of the smash-up of the West End, in particular of the nobility's town houses which took place in the 1920s and 1930s. The third, in 1955, was the Grand Drawing Room by Robert Adam which once formed part of Northumberland House, the great palace of the Percy family which for three centuries stood on the banks of the Thames near Whitehall, until the Metropolitan Board of Works compulsorily purchased it from the 6th Duke in 1873.

must have guided the purchases of curators for the next decade or so. For a start, he aimed to have what he called a complete 'catena' of chairs illustrating their development throughout the period. Chippendale figured largely, but astonishingly Pollen repeats the old mistakes about the date of his pattern book *The Director*, suggesting that he had never seen a copy. However, he does warn sensibly against assuming that all 'Chippendale' chairs are actually from his workshops. Following, rather than leading, a fashion which had been flourishing for the last twenty years, he praises Sheraton above all others. He admires his feel for the colour of woods, the waxy silken grain of satinwood with its colour of red gold, the delicate workmanship and fine graceful structures. Robert Adam he described as a 'projector', presumably referring to his activities as an architectural entrepreneur, and as a designer of fine

95

95. *The Norfolk House music room, designed by Matthew Brettingham for the 9th Duke of Norfolk and completed in 1756 (W70-1938).*

Together with many of the best furnishings it was taken to the Duke's other London house, Syon, and stored in the riding school. After the Second World War the present Duke sold it to the dealer in monumental masonry, Bert Crowther, who rented it out for decor at debutante balls. It was to the great credit of the then Keeper of the department, Delves Molesworth, that he recognised something of great quality when looking at a stack of rather battered and tawdry panels, and persuaded one of the museum's benefactors, Dr Hildburgh, to buy them. The lessons learned from these rooms were reinforced ten times over by the houses administered by the museum: Ham House for the seventeenth century, Osterley for the eighteenth, and

Apsley House for the early nineteenth. Ham House and Osterley Park were given to the National Trust in 1948 and 1949 respectively, and then leased to the Department of the Environment which looks after the fabric, and the contents given to the museum; while Apsley House, the Duke of Wellington's London residence, was accepted by the nation with the museum again as curators by Act of Parliament in 1952, and the present Duke continues to live in part of it.

All of these acquisitions have posed different scholarly problems, in the unravelling of which different skills had to be used. The Norfolk House room (plate 95), with its elaborate plaster-work and gilt woodwork, was clearly the product of more people than just the architect of the whole building, Matthew Brettingham. Archival research showed precisely what a complex bit of collaboration it was, with plaster-work executed by Thomas Clarke, and carved and gilded woodwork by the French craftsman Jean Cuenot. The bills show to the last penny how much each was paid and consequently how important each was considered in the overall scheme of things. Perhaps most important of all, as a result of the department's studies of social history over the last ten years, it is now understood how a room like this was used. These studies have been greatly encouraged under the Keepership of Peter Thornton, and the ceremonial of life in the English nobleman's house has been worked out in great detail. The museum now tries to arrange the furniture as it would have been seen in the appropriate period and to get rid of the mistaken 'furnishing with antiques' effect which its rooms once gave. Thus the rather austere effect of the chairs and stools lining the walls of the Norfolk House room is perfectly correct, an expression of the fact that this was a formal state room where formal manners were displayed.

The Adelphi ceiling, on the other hand, was a restoration problem. It arrived with all but the central roundel and four rectangular panels painted over with layers of creamy white. It remained like this, giving an entirely false and enfeebled idea of Adam's decorative schemes, until 1972 when scrapes were made of various parts of the ceiling and then examined in the conservation laboratories. Under magnification these showed that the main colours were pink and green with areas of vivid blue, porphyry red and grisaille. It was known that the walls were originally hung with damask, and in the process of restoring the upholstery of a documented Adam chair from the room a fragment of original green silk was found, so this was copied, the walls hung with it and the chair upholstered *en suite*, and the ceiling carefully scraped down and part-restored to its original state. There is no doubt that this now authentically decorated room looks infinitely more interesting even to the casual visitor, and has taught a great deal to the curators and all who have to deal with old buildings.

Another lesson learned partly through the general interest in restoration and correct decoration, but also because Peter Thornton began his career in the Textiles department, is the importance to the appearance of furniture of correct upholstery. This can completely change the appearance of an eighteenth-century chair, and was the most expensive part of a decorating budget in the seventeenth and eighteenth centuries. Usually the most expensive piece of furniture, because it involved most upholstery, was the state bed. The Melville bed in its almost perfect state of preservation is

96

96.   *The headboard of the Melville bed, of white Chinese silk damask and red velvet, with the initials of the 1st Earl and his wife Catherine. The whole bed is 7ft. long, 8ft. wide, and 15ft. 2ins. high (W35-1949).*

therefore especially fascinating (plate 96). It came to the museum in 1949 as a result of a correspondence between Lord Leven and Ralph Edwards. Lord Leven had written for advice about what to do with the bed, as Melville House was about to be pulled down, and Edwards wrote back saying that there would be very little commercial demand for this fifteen-feet high construction as the Americans had stopped collecting state beds. No one in Scotland appeared to want it, so Lord Leven gave it to the museum; but after it had been publicised in an article by Edwards there was a great outcry from the Scots demanding its return, and words like 'rape' were hurled at the museum. Lord Leven, however, stuck to his gift and it has remained at the museum ever since. Made in the 1690s by Huguenot immigrant craftsmen, to the designs of the Dutch designer Daniel Marot, of white Chinese silk damask and red velvet, it is one of the finest of surviving state beds, a symbol of the 1st Earl Melville's pro-regal role as King William III's representative in Scotland. His pride is flaunted in the initials G C M (his own and his wife's) in the headboard, surrounded by earl's coronets. It is now preserved with the utmost care in a darkened corner so that the fabrics will not fade and rot, and under glass, which protects it from the constant 'fall-out' of dust brought in by the thousands of visitors in the galleries, and from the constant fingering which all exposed upholstery in a museum inevitably attracts.

Although the galleries began to acquire examples of early nineteenth-century furniture, particularly in the 1930s, collecting had tended to stick at the point where neo-classicism began to diversify into the full range of nineteenth-century styles after the 1820s. Indeed much of the nineteenth-century furniture

97

98. A panel from the back of the lift in Selfridge's store in Oxford Street, designed by the French artist Edgar Brand about 1922, in bronzed wrought iron and beaten tinplate (Circ 719-1971).

already in the museum, including pieces mentioned earlier, was put into store, probably after the First World War, and it was only the 1952 exhibition of Victorian and Edwardian decorative arts which persuaded people that a gallery had to be created for it. This in turn begins now to look over-weighted in favour of untypical designer pieces such as plate 97, and prejudiced against high-quality commercial productions which closely imitated earlier styles and were more commonly found in nineteenth-century houses. For example, some pieces of Sheraton revival by Wright and Mansfield which were bought in the 1880s, have only gone on show again in the last year. It did not occur to anyone that, quite apart from their interest as examples of late nineteenth-century taste, they could help train the eye to distinguish between the real eighteenth-century style and its later imitations or fakes.

The exile of twentieth-century furniture has been even longer, and stems back to an aesthetic scandal which took place in 1901, up to which date the museum had regularly, if not frequently, bought contemporary pieces. It is worth going into it in some detail for the insight into how some eminent figures in the English artistic world regarded themselves, and into the passion which questions of artistic orthodoxy could arouse.

In 1900 there was a vast Universal Exhibition in Paris of the sort which had become common in Europe since the Crystal Palace show of 1851. Prizes for merit were to be awarded and a Bond Street dealer and friend of the museum, George (later Sir George) Donaldson, was among the foreign jurymen. The museum had intended to buy a token number of pieces but Donaldson wrote to Purdon Clarke, the director, saying that he considered the furniture on show to be so important that a larger selection should be acquired and then circulated around Britain. In his opinion 'the new Art Movement has taken a firm hold in Europe and in most cases superior ingenuity and taste are displayed than that shown in our productions'. By this of course he meant what is now known as Art Nouveau, with its flowing asymmetrical lines, which has been so popular in the last fifteen years or so. Donaldson went on to say that he was therefore prepared to offer several thousand pounds for the acquisition of pieces, and so furniture from the firms of Emile Gallé, Majorelle Frères, M. Chenue, Ed. Ianousky, A. Perrault, Bing's 'L'Art Nouveau' (the shop where it all started in the 1890s), Edmund Farago of Budapest, and J. J. Graf of Strasburg, were shipped over to London. A certain quantity of glass, pottery and porcelain, metalwork and textiles, was bought at the same time by the museum.

It all came to rest in the Tapestry Court which had earlier been arranged by Professor Middleton and William Morris. Almost immediately an astonishing letter was sent to the director by the museum's Advising Council signed by its members, Walter

97.   A washstand of carved, painted and gilt wood, with top, bowl and soap-dishes of marble, and the bowl inset with silver fishes and a butterfly. The back and water-tank are set with mirrors, and the taps and fittings are of bronze. The piece was designed by William Burges (1827-81) (W4-1953).

Crane, the designer and illustrator, Sir William Richmond, the portrait-painter, T. G. Jackson, the architect, and Onslow Ford, the sculptor. This utterly condemned the collection, implying that it would actually harm students because of the false principles which it epitomised with its pictorial treatment of the inlay, the concealment of the constructional form by the lines of the design and the character of the wood-carving. Then a whiff of chauvinism comes across with the letter of complaint to *The Times* of 15 July 1907. Signed by, among others, John Belcher, Reginald Blomfield and Mervyn Macarthy, it says 'it represents only a trick of design which, developed from debased form, has prejudicially affected the design of furniture and buildings in neighbouring countries'. 'Vulgar' and 'shameful' were other adjectives bandied about in the press and the museum authorities crumbled in the face of this attack. They immediately had a manifesto printed which, like the warning on cigarette packets, was to accompany the exhibits and warn consumers of

99. Pine cabinet veneered with marquetry of various woods and with tortoiseshell and pewter inlay, made in Würzburg in 1716, and emblazoned with the arms of von Hohlach (W23-1975).

the danger of contamination: 'It is therefore necessary that students inspecting the examples in this collection should be guided in forming an opinion as to their merits and obvious faults, by instructors who have given attention to such subjects as Historical Ornament,' The editor of the *Magazine of Art*, on 17 August 1907, was the only brave voice to attempt a defence, and even he admitted to the pieces' 'imperfect design and illogical construction', but said that they were clearly in search of something fresh and fine, and that it was a case of the old struggle between purism and revolution. This had no effect, however, and after eight years circulating in the British Isles, when the collection returned to South Kensington, the official decision was not to show it, 'for by doing so the Board would be giving the sanction of its authority to objects of very doubtful educational nature'. Anyone wanting to see these 'shameful', 'vulgar' examples by some of the most famous names in the history of Art Nouveau has still to go to the Bethnal Green outstation in the East End of London. It is almost as though the episode broke the museum's nerve, and when the separate departments emerged in 1910 after the reorganisation, it was no longer in their brief to buy contemporary design; that role was confined to the Circulation department.

Suggestions that the museum should accept certain examples, even as gifts, were met with ridicule and contempt as recently as the 1970s. For example, in 1971 the splendid bronzed lifts at Selfridge's, the Oxford Street store (plate 98), were offered to the museum as a gift, and the then director, Sir John Pope-Hennessy, who is famous as a connoisseur of Renaissance art, wrote the following crushing minute to the then Keeper of Metalwork, Basil Robinson, a mild and distinguished orientalist, who had felt that at least an open mind should be preserved on such matters: 'I am frankly astonished at this proposal. It will be in order for Circulation to accept, as a gift, a specimen panel for use in a travelling exhibition but I cannot reconstruct the reasoning which leads you to conclude that Metalwork should accept a representative selection of the pieces of the grille and doors, paying for their removal, far less the acquisition of a complete lift car, with perhaps a set of outer grille and gates. If specimens of this garish (and anonymous) stuff are preserved in the Circulation Department and in the London Museum this should surely suffice. The possibility of exhibiting an elevator, and even an elevator gate, from Selfridge's in the foreseeable future is nil.'

One of the panels from the back of a lift now occupies an honoured place in the new Twentieth-Century study collection, having entered by the usual 'back-door' of the Circulation department in 1971. This shows the danger of making predictions of this sort. One suspects that the outrage expressed by the director was as much at the vulgar associations with trade as at the style of the pieces. The charge of

anonymity is obviously illogical, as that would have disqualified many of the antiquarian objects in the galleries already, and in any case this has been put right by the briefest research which has shown them to be by none other than Edgar Brand. The design repeats that of a plaque entitled 'Les Cicognes d'Alsace', first shown at the Salon des Artistes-Décorateurs in Paris in 1922, and again at the Paris Exhibition of 1925.

The change of heart towards modern design was already beginning to be felt in the Woodwork department when the new director, Roy Strong, gave it strong encouragement by finding at least a temporary space for a twentieth-century gallery, setting aside certain proportions of the purchase grant for twentieth-century purchases and forcing the collections of the Circulation department to be distributed among the relevant departments for exhibition to the public. The Keeper, Peter Thornton, already an admirer of much modern work, welcomed this new departure and has been bringing the collections up to date as fast as possible.

But the bulk of the purchase grant in the last five years has gone on antiquarian continental pieces, either with full documentation already, or of such obvious splendour that it is clearly only a matter of time before their mysteries are solved. They demonstrate painfully how much the museum has suffered financially from the chauvinism of the earlier generation, for such pieces could have been bought for a fraction of their recent prices right up to the 1960s, when foreign buyers with an eye for the superlative were not yet packing out the London sale rooms, and prejudice among English dealers and collectors against all but French furniture was still entrenched.

One piece has an especially endearing story attached to it (plate 99). At Christmas 1967 the grandchildren of the last owner were playing with a very fine marquetry cabinet inlaid with tortoise-shell and pewter, when they dislodged a moulding and found a yellowed piece of paper beneath it. It was written over in a rather difficult German hand, but the museum, to whom it was brought, deciphered it. It turned out be a letter addressed to posterity by the craftsmen, Jacob Arend of Koblenz and Johannes Wittalm of Vienna, who were working on the cabinet in 1716. They told how they were employed by Servatius Arend, the court cabinet maker to the Prince Bishop of Würzburg and that it was a time of war against the Turks, when conditions were hard: they ate too much cabbage and not enough meat, and the vines had made sour wine that year. Whoever found the letter was to drink their health, 'and, if we are no longer in the land of living, then may God grant us rest and eternal salvation'. It need hardly be said that a bottle of wine was immediately drunk in the department to these men, working two hundred and fifty years ago on this very grand piece. The last owner then generously lent the cabinet to the museum in 1971 and in 1975 it was bought.

100. Cabinet of ebony with gilt bronze figures and mounts, made in France about 1630, and traditionally associated with Marie de Medici (1573-1642) (W64-1977).

A magnificent rococo bureau made for Augustus III of Saxony (plate 101) and a seventeenth-century cabinet made for Marie de Medici (plate 100) were the only pieces of furniture which the museum was able to salvage from the dispersal of the great early Victorian collections of Baron Meyer de Rothschild at Mentmore Towers. This huge country house, designed by Joseph Paxton specifically to house Rothschild's magnificent collection, was offered to the nation for £3 million (plus the three and half million owing in death duties) by Lord Rosebery. The offer came during one of Britain's economic troughs and the government felt it was inexpedient to be seen to be spending money on such frivolities; so despite much lobbying by preservation societies such as 'Save' and the National Trust, and covert pressure by members of the museum, the sale by Sotheby's went ahead. Curiously, although it was a national disaster it was treated as a great social occasion, almost on a level with Ascot, and the grand total at the end was £6,389,330, showing at once what a bargain the nation had missed.

This bureau and cabinet were given to the Treasury according to a new law which permits the State to acquire objects of national importance in lieu of tax owing to it; but there is no doubt that, had the museum been forced to bid for both pieces at the sale, their price on the open market would have approached a million pounds, a ruinous sum considering that the entire purchase grant for the year has only gone up recently (1979-80) to £950,000.

Nonetheless, there is a general feeling that it is the museum's duty to step in and buy whenever any important piece is about to leave the country, and if the destruction of country houses and the dispersal of their collections continues at the rate of the last five years, then the burden on the museum will be intolerable, from both the financial and the spatial point of view — the galleries are already almost full.

Another even more important consideration is a consequence of the new direction taken by furniture studies in the last decade. Because the department suddenly had to think of how to present three historic houses to the public, its viewpoint was immensely broadened. It became clear that furniture, indeed all the works of art in a fine historic building, are much better understood together *in situ* than in a museum gallery. Thus the department has made the radical new suggestion that objects accepted in lieu of tax might be allowed to stay where they belong so long as they are reasonably accessible and protected. For example, the department has recently acquired four great gilt settees and six armchairs designed by 'Athenian' Stuart for the Painted Room at Spencer House, one of London's great unknown noblemen's residences, in the hope that if it were ever made accessible to the public again they could once more stand in the curved alcoves for which their curved form was designed.

Furniture and Woodwork, as the department was renamed in 1966, has a complex future, with much more than a curatorial and scholarly role to play. Of course, the national Furniture Archive of photographs built up in recent years will continue to grow; the Furniture History Society will continue to have its base, and many of its most active members, in the department; and catalogues, exhibitions and articles will be produced. But the department has made itself too useful to outside bodies to be able to restrict itself to a purely museum role. The Department of the Environment which has in its care buildings as diverse as Windsor Castle, one of the Queen's residences, the Foreign Office, a mid-Victorian building with a wide range of nineteenth-century furnishings, Audley End, an Elizabethan country house, and the Houses of Parliament with their neo-Gothic splendours, has called heavily on the department's advice in matters such as archival research, scientific analyses, social history, upholstery, architecture, and sheer connoisseurship.

The department's reputation for a wide range of interests and a willingness to give advice has meant that backwoods squires with tumble-down country houses as well as public organisations now feel that they can come to it with requests for help in preserving this country's very fragile architectural and artistic heritage.

*102. Detail of the 15th century Flemish tapestry
The Boar and Bear Hunt (see also plate 113) (T204-1957).*

6
Textiles and Dress

The visitor to the Museum of Practical Art in Marlborough House in the 1850s would have seen relatively little in the way of textiles, but he would have been confronted with a kind of negative display, the 'Chamber of Horrors' in which Cole had put examples of the kind of industrial design which he was convinced should be avoided, and large numbers of contemporary textiles in particular seemed to fall into this category. He and his co-judges at the 1851 Exhibition, Owen Jones, Richard Redgrave and Pugin, all believed that ornament should avoid excessive naturalism, that it should be adapted to the form and function of the object being ornamented, and that above all it should be flat, not three-dimensional and illusionistic. The glazed chintz in plate 104 was on show at Marlborough House entitled 'False Principle in design: Direct Imitation of Nature. No. 10, and clearly sins against two of these rules, although to our eye it now looks a perfectly inoffensive and rather characteristically English piece of design. There is no doubt that Cole and his colleagues must have hated some of the specimens later presented to his museum, such as the Swiss silk cloth woven in black and white, with the figure of Queen Victoria (plate 103), given by the manufacturer after being displayed at the London International Exhibition of 1862, together with a similar cloth showing Wilhelm Tell's chapel on Lake Lucerne.

But this negative display only lasted a year, until 1853, because protests from the manufacturers and mockery from the press closed it down. Charles Dickens, never an admirer of Cole's, published a satire by Henry Morley upon the 'False Principles' in his periodical *Household Words* in 1852. Mr Crumpet of Clump Lodge, Brixton, laments that up to the middle of October he had always been a happy man, but then he acquired some Correct Principles of Taste after a visit to the Museum at Marlborough House. 'I had heard of a Chamber of Horrors there established, and I found it, and went through it with my catalogue. It was a gloomy chamber, hung round with frightful objects, in curtains, carpets and clothes, lamps and what not. In each case the catalogue told me why such and such a thing wasn't endurable and I found in the same place also, on equally good authority, in black and white, a few hints on what the correct principles of decoration are in each class of ornamental art. I could

have cried, sir, I was ashamed of the pattern of my own trousers, for I saw a piece of them hung up there as a horror . . . I saw it all; when I went home I found that I had been living among horrors up to that hour. The paper in my parlour contains four kinds of bird of Paradise besides bridges and pagodas.' The unfortunate Crumpet is invited to dine at a friend, Frippy's, house where he sees one offending object after another and eventually suffers a collapse at having to drink out of a tea-cup with a butterfly painted inside the bowl. He is taken home in a cab and Frippy whispers to him in a soothing manner, what was probably Dickens' own view of the matter: 'My dear Crumpet . . . I shall go where you have been and take the lessons you have taken; but I shall not bolt them in a lump as you have done, and get a nightmare for my troubles. A little precise knowledge of some true principles of design is wanted just now, quite as much by the manufacturers as by the public. The schools of design connected with that department of Practical Art and its museum in Pall Mall will lead, I have no doubt, to great improvement hereafter . . . in the meantime we must live happily in the endurance of worse daily sights than check trousers and clumsy paper-hangings.'

So apart from the modern Indian textiles, mostly silk ribbons shot with silver and gold thread, bought at the 1851 exhibition, the museum had relatively few textiles in its collections. In 1857 Prince Napoleon presented it with a neo-classical Gobelins tapestry depicting Arria and Paetus, after the painting by François André Vincent (plate 105). The museum had moved that year to its new premises at South Kensington and, knowing how dear it was to Queen Victoria's and Prince Albert's heart, the tapestry was probably something of a diplomatic gift. The border with its bees was added by Napoleon Bonaparte, so its provenance is a highly distinguished one.

The serious collecting of textiles began in the 1860s and in this, even more than with Renaissance bronzes, the museum was ahead of fashion.

Although collectors like Ralph Bernal, and the Frenchman, Jules Soulages, had been buying almost every sort of decorative art during the 1830s and 1840s, and the museum ultimately benefited greatly from this, neither had thought of buying textiles to any great extent. The Bernal sale catalogue includes none; J. C.

*105. Arria and Paetus; a Gobelins
tapestry dated 1785, and given
to the museum by Napoleon III.
Height 12ft. (6733-1857).*

104

103.   Swiss woven silk cloth, about 1862 (374-1864).
*104.   English glazed chintz dating from about 1850
(T8-1933).*

103   Robinson's catalogue of the Soulages Collection when
it was put on show at Marlborough House, has only
one small section of eleven textile items, all of which
Soulages obviously used as decorating pieces in his
house. They included rich Genoese velvets, a German
embroidered table cover dated 1598, two fifteenth-
century Flemish tapestries and some silk and gold
brocade. Robinson's attributions are tentative and
traditional. 'Arras?' he says of the tapestries, that
being the name associated for centuries with the
production of Flemish tapestries. The museum bought
all of them, together with the rest of the Soulages
collection. Then in 1860 it made its first of a number of
large purchases of woven and embroidered fabrics
from Dr Franz Bock, Canon of Aachen Cathedral.
Bock, who also sold to the Museum für Kunst und
Industrie in Vienna, could be dubbed the Scholar with

the Scissors, because while going around the treasuries
of churches in the Rhineland and elsewhere in Europe,
he would cut chunks out of vestments and altar
frontals which interested him. This is not to suggest
that he was dishonest: since he knew about the objects
and the local sacristan and clergy did not, he probably
felt that it was only right that he should own didactic
samples, and he probably had the permission of the
local clergy to do so. In one case he was perhaps acting
as an agent for a willing church, as when he sold the
museum whole vestments and silks from the Treasury
of St Mary's, Danzig, in 1863-64.

Bock was an ecclesiologist, that is someone who
took an antiquarian's interest in the outward trappings
of the church, and as such he had a lot in common with
the English architect and designer Augustus Welby
Pugin. He was the author of the first studies on silk

105

and brocade weaving in the Middle Ages, including one book, which came out in 1860, illustrated by 800 pieces from his own collection. He also wrote on the contents of the treasuries of much of the Rhineland between Aachen and Cologne. Robinson, who was still buying for the museum until 1867, had enough respect for his knowledge to commission him to find out more about the great twelfth-century Eltenberg reliquary bought at the Soltykoff sale, and frequently called upon his advice. Indeed the museum relied upon his knowledge of textiles during the 1860s and 1870s, much as it relied later on William Morris.

Sometimes this could be embarrassing, as when, in 1871, Bock was asked to comment on four damasks bought on the recommendation of one of the art referees, the distinguished architect Sir Matthew Digby Wyatt, and all four were totally dismissed by

him. Later, he produced a printed list of descriptions of the brocades, silks and damasks in the museum.

In 1862 the museum held the great exhibition of art treasures from private collections, and in the catalogue there is a small section (the only one on textiles) written by the English scholar, Dr Rock, entitled 'Ecclesiastical Vestments Tissues and Embroideries'. Most of these were borrowed from the Catholic hierarchy and institutions, including the great 'Syon' cope (plate 106), which belonged to Bishop Brown of Shrewsbury. This fine work of English late medieval embroidery was bought for the collections in 1864. Robinson wrote to the Board saying that it was a most important and beautiful work of art in itself, and the finest surviving example of English ecclesiastical embroidery, but also of considerable historical interest. He therefore suggested offering £150, but

*106.
The 'Sion'
cope, which
once belonged
to the Bridgettine
Convent of Syon. It is
linen embroidered with
silk and metal thread in split
stitch and underside couching,
and dates from 1300-20 (83-1864).*

keeping £300 in reserve. In any case he urged the Board to buy it without delay 'as there is always a danger of works of art such as this kind, in the possession of Roman Catholic ecclesiastics, with whom pecuniary considerations are often of no special moment, ultimately becoming, by bequest or otherwise, the property of Ecclesiastical Corporations such for instance as Stonyhurst College, from whence it is then very difficult to extract them again.' The cope was duly bought, and became the foundation piece in a very distinguished collection of the celebrated English embroidery, *opus anglicanum,* which was exported in the later Middle Ages to cathedrals all over Europe. Indeed, the museum collection of English embroidery from all periods is, as one might expect, very good, with quite outstanding examples of Elizabethan and seventeenth-century embroidery, such as the four pillow covers, embroidered with coloured silk and silver-gilt thread with biblical scenes, and acquired in 1928, and the embroidered gloves and scarf given by Sir Edward Denny, Bt, in 1882 (plate 109).

The Primary Galleries display several dozen, mostly ecclesiastical, examples of continental embroidery, and plate 107 shows one of them, a mitre made probably in 1518 for the Flemish abbot, Willem van der Molen of Heylissem (1507-44). Although Robinson was no longer on its staff by the time it was offered to the museum in 1880, nonetheless he was called upon to recommend its purchase.

For the acquisition of Persian textiles, as for so many other branches of the decorative arts, the museum was indebted to Major Murdoch-Smith who was in Persia supervising the building of the telegraph line linking Europe with India. He collected for the museum from 1873 to 1885 and his greatest single coup

was the Jules Richard collection. Richard was a Frenchman who had been tutor at the Shah's court and so had had many opportunities to buy very well. The museum reacted enthusiastically to suggestions that the collection should be bought *en bloc*, and £1,778 7s 3d was paid for it in 1875. It arrived in sixty-two cases on Christmas Eve that year, and in April 1876 was shown to the public in the newly opened Persian galleries, explained by *The Handbook of Persian Art* by Murdoch-Smith himself. Plate 110 shows one of the items from the Richard collection, a piece of Persian white work of muslin embroidered with silk, one of the numerous examples of fine needlework. The *Handbook* includes a chapter on textile fabrics which runs through the subject of carpets, veils, saddle cloths, patchwork, and printed calico. Murdoch-Smith records with regret that European designs and fashions had been having a strong effect on local styles over the previous twenty years. Of the type of white work shown in the illustration, he notes that it was used to embellish the edges and network of ladies' veils.

The following year there were more consignments of textiles from Persia, including a group which came as a gift from the Shah. This was also the result of Murdoch-Smith's efforts; in 1875 he wrote that he had managed to excite the interest of Nasiruddin Shah in the subject of what was on show at the South Kensington Museum. Murdoch-Smith then had a number of interviews with the Amin al Mulk, and was sent an assortment of fourteen carpets and twenty-four pieces of Resht embroidery, since they wanted to represent all the principal textiles of Persia. As he wisely observed, 'In choosing one class of objects and that textiles, H.M. (the Shah) is following the

107. An embroidered Flemish mitre, probably made in 1518. The figures are St Barbara and St Leonard, and on the carpets the apostles Peter and Paul. Above are the arms of the Abbot of Heylissem (203-1881).

107

suggestion I made last year to the Emin el Mulk . . . my reasons for making the suggestion were first the idea of a present of modern textiles would probably commend itself to His Majesty's mind as an indirect means of increasing the trade of his own country, and secondly that whatever sum His Majesty might devote to the purpose would be better expended on one class of objects than if it were frittered away on many'.

These Persian textiles, like the examples of Indian, Middle Eastern and Far Eastern crafts at the Great Exhibition of 1851, aroused great admiration in the new generation of designers in England, particularly from the Arts and Crafts school, partly because they came from a living craft tradition and so were unsullied by post-industrial commercialism, and partly because they accorded with the criteria for a good design laid down at the beginnings of the School of Design; the decorative motifs were stylised, rather than floridly naturalistic, the colours rich and subtle, and above all the designs were flat not illusionistic. Sometimes, of course, the fragmentary state of knowledge about Persian art led to mistakes being made. For example, in 1877 and 1879 a number of carpets were bought from Arthur Lazenby Liberty's 'eastern bazaar' in his new Regent Street shop, which was in revolt against high Victorian taste. These were all

108. William Morris's 'Rose and Lily'
pattern, designed about 1885 and
made of woven silk and wool
(7122-1953).

thought to be Persian at the time, but many are now
known to be Caucasian or Turkish, and some Spanish
or Indo-Portuguese.

In order to make the study of the textiles easier the
museum frequently commissioned paintings of them
(these often costing more than the objects themselves)
which spared the textiles too much handling and made
the design much clearer. There is no doubt that the
collections were much studied and some of William
Morris's works, especially after 1876, when he began
to design woven fabrics, can be traced back to the
specimens on display. For example, the silk and wool
tissue called 'Rose and Lily' (plate 108) and dating
from about 1885 is based closely on a seventeenth-
century Italian woven silk bought in 1877 by the
museum; and the only figure tapestry designed wholly
by Morris, the 'Orchard', woven in 1890, has a number
of details which can be related directly to the two
tapestries of pastoral scenes in the Soulages collection
mentioned earlier: the flowering and fruit-bearing
trees in the landscape background seem to have
provided the inspiration for the trees in Morris's work
which was bought by the museum two years after his
death in 1898. This was a case of a relationship between
institution and artist which was mutually beneficial
and wholly productive.

We have seen (Chapter 1) that Cole was so taken
with Morris's work that in 1865 he commissioned his
company, Morris, Marshall, Faulkner and Co, to
decorate the West Dining Room. In 1884 Morris was
asked to join the first formal committee of art referees,
and he served on this until his death. Among his first
fellow committee members were Sir Frederick
Leighton, G. F. Bodley, Alma Tadema, J. H. Pollen
and E. J. Poynter. Morris's opinion was most
frequently consulted on carpets and tapestries, and
during the 1880s and 1890s he sent in detailed and
scholarly reports. The first carpet to be bought on his
advice was the famous Ardabil carpet (plate 111). This
is one of the greatest masterpieces in the museum, one
of the most famous carpets in world, and the earliest
securely dated example (1540). It was in the Mosque at
Ardabil until the late 1880s, when it was bought by a
Manchester firm directly from the mosque and
shipped to England. Morris wrote in a letter dated 13
March 1893: 'no reasonable man who understands the
subject would think it (£2,000) an extravagant price for
such a remarkable work of art. For my part I am sure
that it is far the finest Eastern carpet which I have

109

110

109.   These early 17th-century leather gloves were given by
James I to Sir Edward Denny, afterwards Earl Norwich,
who as Sheriff of Hertfordshire received the king on his
journey from Scotland. They are embroidered with gold
and silver thread, and the cuffs are decorated with silver lace
on a crimson silk ground, and fringed (150 & a-1882).
110.   19th-century Persian muslin with open embroidery in
white silk, 18ins. square (2363-1876).

111. The Ardabil carpet, one of a matching pair formerly in the mosque at Ardabil, Persia. It is dated 1539-40, and measures 34ft. 6ins. by 17ft. 6ins. (272-1893).

111   seen . . . For firstly it must be remembered that this one has no counterpart, whereas the finest carpets hitherto seen like the famous ones at Vienna belong to a class of which there are many examples. Next . . . the design is of a singular perfection; defensible on all points, logically and consistently beautiful with no oddities or grotesqueries which might need an apology, and therefore most valuable for a museum the special aim of which is the education of the public in Art . . . Lastly the fact that it is dated is of real importance . . . as it gives us an insight into the history of art, and a standard whereby one may test the excellence of the palmy days of Persian design. In short I think it would be a real misfortune if such a treasure of decorative art were not acquired for the public.' He was right about its special interest to the public but would probably have been distressed if he had seen the reduced versions of its principal design, the lobed medallion radiating sixteen double-ogee panels filled with

arabesques and floral stems, which has become a cliché of carpet designers since the late nineteenth-century. The price was made to look small very soon by the £16,000 which the American Charles T. Yerkes was said to have paid for the companion to the Ardabil in 1892.

Morris also advised on the buying of tapestries, something for which his medievalism admirably suited him. The museum had acquired Gothic tapestries since its earliest days and for very moderate prices, because until the late 1870s there was almost no domestic demand for such things. For example, in 1856 it paid £10 for a late fifteenth-century German panel, 11¼ feet long and representing the soul in search of redemption from the life of a female saint. At the Soulages sale the most expensive tapestry was £25, but by 1886 the museum was asked to pay £1,600 for the 'Troy' tapestry from a famous series first mentioned in 1472 and depicting scenes from the Trojan wars. It had been

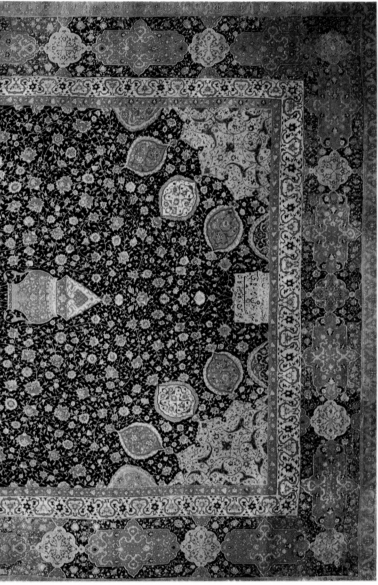

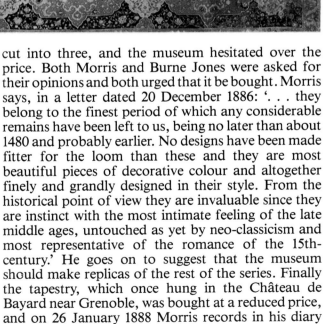

112

112.   A fragment of tapestry from the tombs of Upper Egypt, 6th to 9th centuries AD. The pattern originally consisted of four roundels similar to those that survive, showing a man alone and a man with an animal. The piece measures 9ins. by 4ins. (179a-1891).

cut into three, and the museum hesitated over the price. Both Morris and Burne Jones were asked for their opinions and both urged that it be bought. Morris says, in a letter dated 20 December 1886: '. . . they belong to the finest period of which any considerable remains have been left to us, being no later than about 1480 and probably earlier. No designs have been made fitter for the loom than these and they are most beautiful pieces of decorative colour and altogether finely and grandly designed in their style. From the historical point of view they are invaluable since they are instinct with the most intimate feeling of the late middle ages, untouched as yet by neo-classicism and most representative of the romance of the 15th-century.' He goes on to suggest that the museum should make replicas of the rest of the series. Finally the tapestry, which once hung in the Château de Bayard near Grenoble, was bought at a reduced price, and on 26 January 1888 Morris records in his diary

with glee, 'went to South Kensington yesterday to look at the Troy tapestry again since they bought it for £1,250. I chuckled to think that properly speaking it was bought for me since scarcely anyone will care a damn for it'.

The collection of tapestries has since grown until it includes over two hundred pieces, with more at Ham House, and a room of eighteenth-century Gobelins with matching upholstery, after designs by Boucher, at Osterley Park. From the 1880s onwards some of the most ancient textiles in existence were beginning to emerge in large quantities from the Egyptian graves of the Graeco-Roman and Christian period in the sand hills beyond the limits of the Nile inundation. Such stuff had been coming to light for almost a century, but it was only after the British and French expedition of 1882 that they were produced as a result of a systematic excavation. The formidable Franz Bock acquired some in Upper Egypt in 1885-6 and in 1886 the

113

foundation of the museum's collection was laid by the acquisition of about 300 pieces from Akhmim in Upper Egypt, on the right bank of the Nile, 315 miles above Cairo. In ancient times it had been one of the chief seats of linen manufacture for which Egypt was famous, and the pieces include tapestry-woven ornaments, patterned woollen stuffs, embroidery, resist-dyed linens and some garments, all with their colours remarkably preserved. This collection continued to be added to (plate 112) until it now numbers between 1,500 and 2,000 pieces. In 1887 the first director's son, Alan Cole, produced the first catalogue, and from 1920 to 1924 a series of catalogues by the former Keeper of the department, A. F. Kendrick, was published.

One of the very first pieces of lace to come to the museum was a collar of Belgian seventeenth-century pillow-made lace which the director's wife, Mrs Cole, gave to the museum in 1853. Since then the collection has grown until it is now one of the largest in the world, with over 2,500 pieces, ranging from lace covers of the sixteenth-century to complex machine-made laces of the twentieth. A large proportion of the collection was acquired in the nineteenth century, a great deal of Irish contemporary work arriving in 1855 for example, and much antique lace in 1868, 1872 and 1875. Mrs Bury Palliser, one of the art referees, wrote a catalogue of it

in 1871 and this went through three editions with a supplemental volume. The reasons for the intense interest in the subject were that in the first place, lace-making was still a living tradition in a number of countries such as Belgium, and secondly, attempts were being made to revive it in many more. Mrs Bury Palliser talks enthusiastically about the lace schools being started in France, Belgium, Germany and Bohemia, 'where the Archduchess Sophia was making a special success of it' (plate 116). She clearly hoped that her book would stimulate the interest necessary for such schools to be founded in England as well, but the lace revival did not last long enough for this to happen.

Among other technical rarities the department also owns some very early knitting, such as the seventeenth-century Venetian jacket, knitted in silk with silver gilt thread (plate 114). The history of woven textiles from a very early date onwards can be studied here; not only are there Egyptian textiles, several dozen of which date back to 3000-1000 BC, but also about a hundred pieces made in Peru before the Spanish conquest. The collection of medieval woven fabrics is also one of the most important in existence. Morris, being a medieva-list, had of course been principally interested in early silks and velvets, and he recommended numerous pur-chases of these. Occasionally, however, a seventeenth-

113. *The Boar and Bear Hunt, one of a series of Flemish tapestries of 1430-35. It measures 33ft.6ins. by 13ft.3½ins. (T204-1957) (see also plate 102).*

114

114. *Jacket of knitted silk with silver gilt thread, made in Venice in the 17th century (106-1899).*

century silk would slip by, mistakenly described as fifteenth-century. He especially disliked eighteenth-century silks of the rococo period, despite the fact that the museum owned a large number of English manufacturers' designs for them, still housed in the library in his day. Much recent research, however, has been devoted to the identification of English eighteenth-century textiles, both printed fabrics and also the silk fabrics made at Spitalfields.

There had been a tendency until around 1960 for any fine silk to be called French, as English design was thought to be provincial and inferior. Then, by the simple step of getting the designs for the English silks out of the Prints and Drawings department (see plate 180) and comparing them with the museum's holdings, it became clear that some of these very fine silks were in fact English. Furthermore, a new bias towards economic history was making people more aware of what industries were flourishing where, and at what period, and the picture emerged of this flourishing luxury trade, just east of the City of London. Then the upholstery fabric manufacturers Warner and Sons, whose centenary in 1970 was approaching, invited two members of the department down to their factory at Braintree to look into their archives as they were planning a commemorative exhibition. In a damp, rat-infested cottage the two curators found volume after

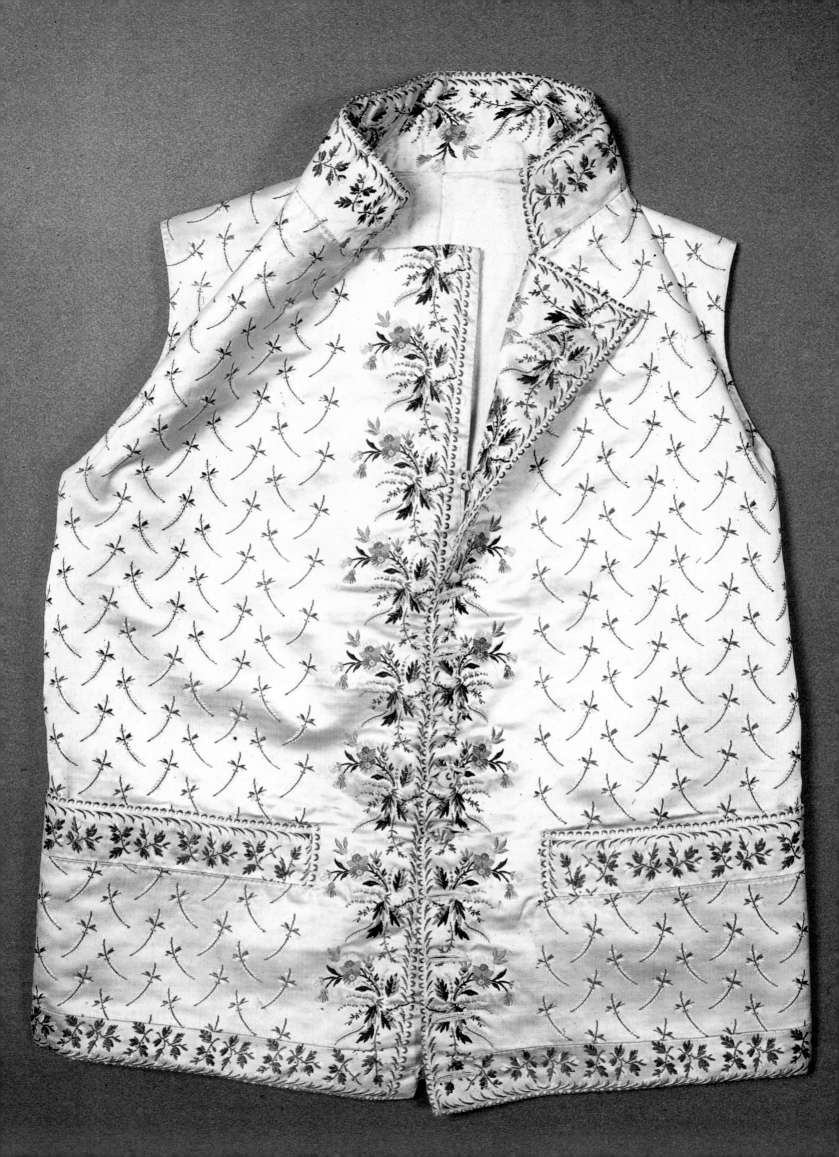

115. *A waistcoat made at Spitalfields in 1789 of woven satin with flush pattern, and with cotton lining and back (T676-1974).*

116

117

116.   *A sampler in English needlepoint lace from the first half of the 17th century (76-1910).*

117.   *A page from Maze and Steer's pattern book for winter 1789 (T384-1972), showing the material used for the waistcoat in plate 115.*

volume of pattern books belonging to the firms which had been taken over by Warners and its predecessors, so that a very precisely dated evolution of design from the early eighteenth century right into the twentieth could be traced. Warner's then put the whole lot up for sale at Christie's in 1972, where most were bought by the museum, against stiff opposition from other museums and manufacturers eager for designs to copy. Plate 117 shows one page of the 1786-89 pattern book of Maze and Steer's workshop, showing samples of 'Fancy Vestings and Handkerchief Goods'. The particular silk pattern shown is for winter 1789, and by great good fortune a waistcoat made of this material came on the market two years later (plate 115) and was bought at once. It is by these methods and by this broader outlook that a much more precise knowledge of the different aspects of the collections is being acquired. The fruits of these researches on Spitalfields silk will probably be published very soon and will be most interesting, especially for the many American museums, such as Boston and New York, which have even bigger collections because of the eighteenth-century export trade to America.

The department changed its name to Textiles and Dress in 1978 in recognition of the importance of the costume collections. These began to be built up from 1864 onwards when a cleric named Brooke presented his collection, and now they include over a thousand complete outfits divided between the museum and its outstation at Bethnal Green. These outfits are nearly all the kind of clothes worn by townsfolk or the nobility, but the museum also has a few peasant costumes from various areas of Europe.

The museum's holdings had a great boost in 1913 when the Chelsea portrait painter Talbot Hughes put his collection of about 150 costumes from the Stuart to the Victorian periods, about 300 boots and shoes, and about 300 embroidered and bead purses, up for sale. He was asking £8,000 for it, and the American owner of a department store was said to be negotiating for it with a view to showing it in his store and then presenting it to the Metropolitan Museum in New York. The then director, Cecil Harcourt-Smith, thought that Harrods might be persuaded to perform the same role, which — with the incentive of much free publicity — they did. The director clearly thought it important to secure the collection because what the museum already held was being used constantly by students of literature and drama, and also by the dress-making trade, as revivalist fashions were in vogue. Harrods, indeed, became so enthusiastic about the whole project that they added another fifty outfits, mostly of the late nineteenth century, but also including two rare Stuart costumes. The collection continued to grow and in the 1960s the vast hippodrome-like hall, which Aston Webb had included in his plans, was converted to house it by putting in a mezzanine and dividing the area below into shop-windows, in which the costumes stood on headless mannequins in informal groupings.

In 1970 a member of the department found what is now the collection's finest eighteenth-century

118. Waistcoat of English Spitalfields silk, c. 1755, brocaded in coloured silks, silver and silver gilt thread (T181-1979).

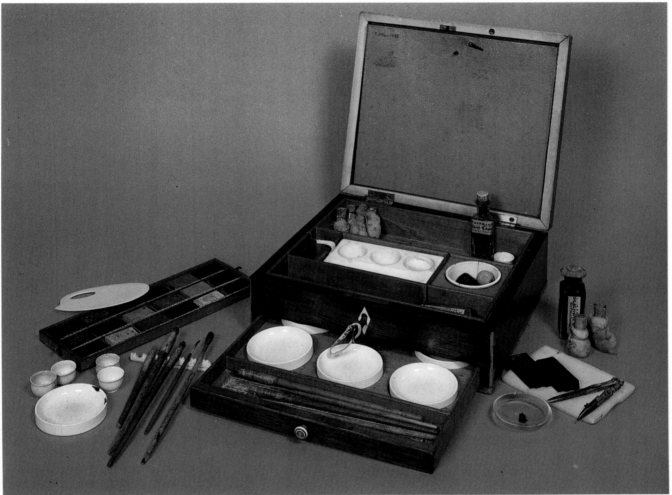

119

119. A wooden box containing paints for painting on velvet. It was made by Reeves and Woodyer around 1814 (T294-1975).

woman's costume in the spare bedroom of Lord and Lady Cowdray's house in Inverness. In grandeur it outdoes even Catherine the Great's engagement robe at the Hermitage in Leningrad. Its original owner is unknown but, extraordinarily, the names of the embroideresses who worked on it have come down to us because it is signed underneath the embroidery on the hem. The signature is in the form of a receipt from Marie Madeleine Garneron to Madame Leconte, both Huguenot ladies. Lady Cowdray had worn the dress at her daughter's coming-out dance in the 1920s, its line somewhat altered to make it more like something out of Watteau; and the present Lord and Lady Cowdray generously presented it to the museum. With immense care and skill the textile conservation staff remade the dress to its original shape and cleaned the tarnished silver wire so that it looks almost as fine as when it was made.

The department's holdings of twentieth-century textiles of every sort, already extensive, are increasing apace. Where early twentieth-century costume is concerned it had a fortunate wind-fall when the vast wardrobe of Heather Firbank, sister of the novelist Ronald, was presented in 1960 by her nephew and niece. Heather Firbank had an exquisite and restrained

taste — her tailored suits are especially good — she also had dozens of hats, gloves, items of underwear and accessories all of which were beautifully cared for during the period when she was wearing them, from about 1908 onwards. Then, in 1921, they were carefully packed away in mothballs until they were offered to the museum thirty-nine years later, and gratefully accepted (plates 121 and 122).

Another donor, this time an obviously slightly obsessive collector, filled the gap in the twentieth-century footwear collection. He was Lionel Ernest Bussey, and he lived in Streatham. For over fifty years he collected very stylish women's boots and shoes, mostly in rather small sizes, and kept them wrapped in tissue paper in their boxes. The first the museum heard of him was a letter from his executors, informing the department that these had been bequeathed to it. Fifty pairs covering the period 1908 to 1960 were gratefully accepted. They include the pair shown in plate 123 said to have been Mr Bussey's favourites.

120. A French fan dated c. 1758-60. The leaf of vellum is painted in water-colours after Jean-Baptiste Pillement, and the sticks are of mother-of-pearl. The fan is 10⅞ins. long (T154-1978).

120

Then, in 1971, the museum held a very stylish exhibition of twentieth-century fashion put together by Cecil Beaton. Every dress was by a famous designer such as Balenciaga, Givenchy or Schiaparelli. The lenders, who then became donors, were mostly bywords for glamour, like Baroness Elie de Rothschild and Princess Stanislaus Radziwill. Nearly every exhibit was given to the museum after the show closed, and they set the standard for the future collecting of contemporary costume.

Besides textiles and costume, the department also knows about and collects accessories, such as buttons and fans. The foundation of the fan collection was laid in 1883 by Sir Mathew Digby Wyatt, the distinguished architect but less distinguished Art Referee, and his wife, who presented the museum with five hundred

121

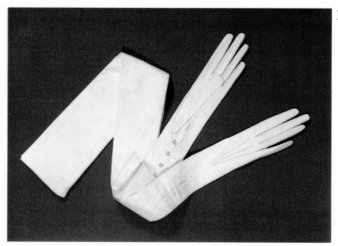

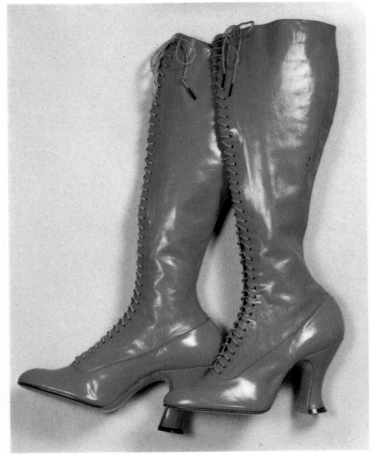

fans; nowadays the ones which are bought are mostly documented in some way, such as plate 120, which is based on dated designs by the Frenchman, Jean-Baptiste Pillement. Recently the department has also bought a neat wooden box containing all the equipment necessary for the lady-like hobby of painting on velvet, so popular in the late eighteenth and early nineteenth centuries (plate 119).

123

The penalty, if indeed it is a penalty, of covering such a wide range of subjects, from the high art of *opus anglicanum* vestments and tapestries after designs by the great masters, to Edwardian underwear and Victorian ladies' hobbies, is that this department receives probably the largest number of enquiries and visitors. After all, there can hardly be a household in the country which does not have its bit of lace, or a bead bag. It is a conspicuous virtue of the members of the Textiles and Dress department that, despite all their scholarly activities, they never got bored by the innumerable objects they are shown for opinion, and they are happy to share their expertise with every visitor.

122

121 and 122. Some of the accessories from Heather Firbank's wardrobe, dating from about 1910. Far left: a pair of kid gloves; left: a pair of garters (T79, 61 – 1960). 123. A pair of dark rose-pink glacé kid boots; Belgian/English, about 1925 (321-1970).

124. The Sānchī torso (representing the Bodhisattva Avalokitesvara), from the temple at Sānchī in central India, dated around AD 800-850, and carved in sandstone (IS184-1910).

7
The Indian Section

By a mixture of *force majeure* and the agreement of the local potentates, the Honourable East India Company ruled over Bengal in the second half of the eighteenth century. This rule was by no means completely exploitative and the Company included enlightened men who saw the importance of governing India according to its customs, which of course required that these and its languages should be studied. Warren Hastings in particular extended his patronage to all branches of scholarship with special emphasis on Arabic, Persian, Bengali and Sanskrit literature; and with his encouragement Sir William Jones, the father of English academic orientalism, founded the Asiatic Society of Bengal in 1784 with its journal *Asiatic Researches*. Within twelve years the curiosities, the gifts from durbars, and the antiquities had accumulated to such an extent that space had to be found to house them. At about the same time the Court of Directors in London was becoming worried that the oriental manuscripts collected by its employees were in danger of being neglected, 'and at length in a great measure, lost to Europe as well as to India'. They decided therefore to create what they called an Oriental Repository at the Company's new building in Leadenhall Street in the City, and it was natural that the objects should join the library material there. In 1801 a day book was started, and among the earliest entries is one which suggests the scope of the collection: three Elephant Heads, a Persian manuscript and six brass images representing Hindu gods.

This museum could not have been founded at a more favourable time. Interest in India was greater than ever before for a combination of reasons. The first was philosophical: the majority of the philosophers and antiquarians of the eighteenth century who were debating the question of the origin of human culture believed that it had one source, but they disagreed hotly among themselves which this might be. Some, taking the Bible literally, supposed it to be the Hebrews, others supported the Egyptians or the Chaldeans, and yet others, of whom Voltaire was the most famous, thought it to be India. This idea of the extreme antiquity of Indian culture was supported by the knowledge of the gigantic cave temples at Elephanta and Kānheri, which, the pro-Indian camps decided, must be immensely old. Some indeed, like Pierre Sonnerat, the famous traveller, natural his-

torian and author of a profusely illustrated work *Voyages aux Indes Orientales,* published in 1782, even risked some precise dating in the case of the temple of Jagannātha in Orissa which, from ancient texts, he decided was 4,883 years old.

Even if you did not believe that India was the cradle of the universe it was still a thrilling and romantic place for the generation which was travelling further and further afield in search of the picturesque and sublime if not necessarily beautiful. While Indian architecture might not have found many who would plead that it was beautiful in the classical sense, it certainly had the power to arouse fear, amazement at its strangeness, admiration of its vast size, and melancholy at its usually ruinous condition. In other words, it was ideal material for the Romantic artist who wished to move the emotions of his audience. In the last quarter of the eighteenth century a series of English artists went to India where, under English protection, they could travel with relative safety and produced engravings, paintings, drawings and aquatints of picturesque sites. The most successful and influential of these were Thomas and William Daniell, uncle and nephew, who arrived in Calcutta in 1788 and set up a workshop with the aim of transporting back 'picturesque beauties of these favoured regions'. With a large staff they travelled from top to bottom of the sub-continent, making extremely accurate drawings, partly with the aid of the camera obscura, of the great Indian sites. When they had enough material they returned to England, and between 1795 and 1808 their work appeared in a number of splendid volumes called *Oriental Scenery.*

These volumes were immediately successful and had a very large circulation. They had the honour of being plagiarised by the French orientalist Langlés, and influenced the architect Humphrey Repton into using Indian motifs in his proposed design for the Royal Pavilion at Brighton. Turner himself said of them that the artists had succeeded 'in increasing our enjoyment by bringing scenes to our fireside too distant to visit and too strange to be imagined'. India had caught the public imagination and was no longer the preserve of scholars and antiquaries. In 1843 the Surrey pleasure-garden in London announced 'Dawson's new stupendous Panoramic Model al-Fresco of the far famed TEMPLES OF ELLORA, the

125

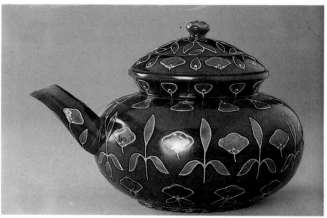

126

125. Tippoo's Tiger, made of painted wood and containing a miniature organ. It was made in Seringapatam, Mysore, about 1790, and measures 5ft. 10ins. in length.
126. A Mughal spinach-green jade wine vessel, ornamented with red enamel encased in gold. 17th century. (02594 IS).

greatest wonder of India', the locale of 'Pyro-Scenic Spectacles, illustrating the splendours of a Burmah Tamashah, or Hindu Festival introducing extraordinary Allegorical Tableaux de feu'; and the East India Company museum, despite its inadequacies (one had to wind through several passages in East India House and ascend a long stairway to arrive in half-a-dozen gloomy rooms with the objects stacked on high dark shelves), was being visited by 40,000 people a year in 1850.

Certainly the most popular exhibit in these rooms, and still one of the most famous in the Victoria and Albert Museum, is Tippoo's Tiger (plate 125). It is the painted wooden model of a tiger devouring a European, and the body of the tiger conceals a barrel-organ mechanism which, if the handle is cranked, produces a most horrible groaning and shrieking sound. It deserves its fame, not just as a curiosity but because of its historical associations. Any army is happiest when it defeats a worthy opponent; and Tippoo Sultan, ruler of Mysore in southern India from whom the British army took it, was certainly an heroic and blood-thirsty enough enemy. He was heard to say that he would rather live two days as a tiger than two hundred years as a sheep; his own name 'Tipu' means tiger, his throne was carved with tigers, and he kept chained tigers in his palace courtyard. He was also determined never to

give in to the English who had whittled away his kingdom. It seems likely that the French, who were united with him in their hostility to the English, were responsible for the mechanism of this spiteful and sadistic toy, which would be rolled out after feasts to amuse him. In 1799 Seringapatam, the capital of Mysore, fell in dramatic fashion to the British: Tippoo was slain, General Baird and his second-in-command (none other than Col Arthur Wellesley, later to become the Duke of Wellington) extended a pleasing mercy to Tippoo's sons, and some fine booty, including Tippoo's gold tiger throne, was sent back to England. Selected scenes from the battle were depicted by numerous English artists, including Sir David Wilkie, and Tippoo's Tiger arrived in the East India Company Museum.

With the Great Exhibition of 1851 a completely different interest in Indian art was aroused. This had nothing to do with the historical, ethnological or

*127. Chair of state from the palace of
the Maharajah Ranjit Singh (1780-1839),
covered with embossed gold (2518 IS).*

127

romantic preoccupations which existed before, but was based on, among others, Henry Cole's and Richard Redgrave's aversion to the state of manufactures in contemporary Britain. The exhibits in the Indian Court at the exhibition became the focal point in the theoretical discussions on design. It seemed to the reformers that Indian craftsmanship, because it was not industrialised, showed a natural fitness of ornament to form. It avoided 'illusionism,' the word used in a derogatory sense to mean inappropriate three-dimensional ornament (like the large roses which started out at one from some contemporary British textiles). It was marvellously 'flat', and as the *Catalogue of Ornamental Art,* published by the South Kensington Museum, said: 'Orientals always decorated their construction but never constructed decoration.' If Cole was the practical man behind this aesthetic movement, Owen Jones (1809-74) was its theorist and in his *Grammar of Ornament* (1856) he defined and enlarged upon these ideas. It is irrelevant that Cole, Redgrave, Owen Jones and the other supporters of the movement really knew very little about Indian sculpture, architecture and painting. Their vision of it was given the rosy glow of anti-industrial romanticism which is most apparent in George Birdwood's writing. He was employed in 1880 to write a work on the Indian collections entitled *The Industrial Arts of India.* Here he criticised the British government for upsetting the centuries-old balance within the Indian manufacturing industries by trying to mechanise production, and he paints a ravishing picture of Indian village life, with the potter at his wheel, the looms at work in blues, scarlet and gold, the frames hanging between the acacia trees, the yellow flowers whose petals drop on to the webs as they are woven, the feasting and music at nightfall, and the simple ablutions and adorations performed in the open air at daybreak next morning.

128. A 19th-century Tanjore vessel of copper encrusted with silver (3024-1883 IS).

128

This was all in violent contrast to what occurred in 1857 when wide coverage was given in England to the terrible atrocities perpetrated on British residents in the Indian Mutiny. The British Government immediately took over the functions of the East India Company and in 1858 found itself responsible for its museum as well. This was transferred first to Fife House in Whitehall, formerly Lord Liverpool's residence and then a tea auction house. The building had been remodelled in an Indian fashion by Digby Wyatt (later one of the South Kensington Museum's Art Referees), and housed ethnological specimens in the entrance hall, mineral products in the library, stuffed birds in six bedrooms, silk and bejewelled costumes in the drawing room, and so on. Among its exhibits was the gold-covered throne of Maharajah Ranjit Singh (plate 127), captured from the Sikhs. Unsuitable as this building was as a museum, the public had an unlimited taste for gazing and wondering, and during the first two years it received 175,000 visitors. In 1869, however, it was moved once again to the newly built India Office wing in the vast Foreign Office complex in Whitehall, and there the collections became seriously inaccessible. The first, as we shall see, of many plans to provide a proper home for them was made, with the suggestion that a new building be erected next to the Foreign Office with room for the Museum Library, Geographical Department and Asiatic Society. The government, however, was too parsimonious for this, and for the subsequent suggestion that a building be purchased near the new South Kensington Museum.

Cole, characteristically, was beginning to cast greedy eyes at this collection, and in 1874 Lieutenant Henry Cole, his eldest son, wrote a *Catalogue of the Objects of Indian Art*. Exhibited in the South Kensington Museum. Plate 4 shows one of the objects listed, a sword with enamelling on gold, from Rajputana. This is a typical foundation piece in the collections. Exhibited at the Great Exhibition, it was clearly highly prized and £52 10s was spent on buying it. It was singled out, both in the 1853 catalogue and this one, as an example of 'that happy art to which Eastern nations have arrived by centuries of study and experience, of adapting the ornament so perfectly to the form or space to be ornamented'. But the small section at the end of the book was clearly the important one, intended to nudge the authorities into action. Having listed the museum's collection Cole includes a brief account of the objects in Whitehall, including this spinach-green jade wine vessel ornamented with red enamel encased in gold (plate 126), clearly a Mughal piece, and from the collection of Colonel Guthrie purchased by the Secretary of State for India. He concluded by deeply regretting that this unexampled collection should be so inaccessible and so unworthily treated, 'for in truth the Indian Museum is but a Durbar Store Room'. Immediately below this sentence is a section entitled 'Deficiencies in the Collection of Indian Objects in the South Kensington Museum', and one is not surprised to find that some of these overlap neatly with the objects listed as being in the Indian Museum. This unsubtle hint worked, and the government decided to lease the Eastern Galleries, a two-storey complex in Exhibition Road, parallel to the museum, which had been part of the buildings put up for a series of international exhibitions held in 1871-74. From there it was an easy and natural step to amalgamating the two collections. A certain amount of rationalisation took place, with the natural history collections going to Kew or the new Natural History Museum, and the finest sculpture, including the Amaravati marbles, to the British Museum.

Caspar Purdon Clarke, the architect of the Indian Court at the Paris Exhibition, was sent to India to make up deficiencies in the collections, and also to try to find out a little more about the origins of many of the items already part of them, because curators and students were equally in the dark about many. He sent home some 3,400 objects, of which this silver-encrusted copper vessel is one (plate 128). The most important thing, however, which Purdon Clarke brought back was a great part of the illustrations to an

129

129. *An illustration to the Hamzanama, painted on prepared cotton fabric between 1562 and 1582. The painting is 3ft. 9ins. square (1512-1883 IS).*

epic called the Hamzanama painted under the third Mughal, Akbar (plate 129). He found them in a coffee house in Srinagar, Kashmir, and paid no more than a few shillings each for them. These vast illustrations are right at the beginning of the Mughal tradition of manuscript illumination. Like most early Mughal painting, they are narrative; indeed the very size of each of the pictures, combined with the fact that the story is written in Persian on the back, suggests that they were for a story-teller to hold up and show to the assembled company as he told his tale. Here, Hamza's enemy Iraji is tied in a tree, while the witch Ankarut in the other tree offers to free him if he will become her lover.

In July 1883 Clarke was made the first Keeper of the Indian Section. He subsequently became director of the whole museum (1896), and in 1905 Director of the Metropolitan Museum, New York.

At this point it is worth pausing to look at the museum's holdings of Indian art. It had quantities of nineteenth-century artefacts of all sorts, particularly

*132. Sāntinātha, the Finder of the
Ford, a western Indian bronze dated
1168. Height: 3ft. 9ins. (930-IS).*

130

131

*130.   Hanuman, the Monkey God, given to the museum by
William Morris. It is a bronze of the late 13th century from
south India (the Chola dynasty), and stands 2ft. 6½ins. high
(275-1869).*
*131.   A head of the Buddha in the Romano-Buddhist style,
from the 4th to 5th centuries AD. It is of lime composition
with traces of red on the lips, and came from Gandhāra
(IM3-1931).*

those demonstrating technical virtuosity, and a great
many fine silk textiles. Arms and armour and textiles
preponderated in the old East India Company
collection because these were what tended to be given
at *durbars* (audiences) with local potentates. There
was a notable lack of miniature painting, which had all
stayed with the India Office Library. With the
departure of the Amaravati marbles to the British
Museum, there was a complete lack of significant
architectural sculpture. William Morris, one of the
more level-headed admirers of Indian art, had given
the museum a small bronze of Hanuman, the Monkey
God, in 1869 (plate 130). It was the museum's first
important piece of sculpture, but was neither admired
nor acknowledged at the time. Now it is recognised as
belonging to the Tamil tradition of bronze-casting
which flourished in Ceylon and South India, and it is
dated tentatively to the thirteenth or early fourteenth
centuries. It stands in the Primary Galleries, where it
deserves to be. It is not known how Morris came to
own such a piece, since he had no connections with
Ceylon, but he was a friend of Wilfred Heeley who
joined the East India Company Service in 1855, and

Morris and Co was associated with the Sir Jamsetj
Jijibhari School of Art in Bombay, to which it sent
samples, while importing and selling Indian wares.

Again, when the marvellously fine bronze of
Sāntinātha, the 16th Tirthankara (plate 132), dated
AD 1168, was transferred to the South Kensington
Museum in 1880, the register described it succinctly
and disapprovingly as 'Idol'. In fact he represents an
object of meditation for Jain followers, a tranquil
figure, his birth to a King of Hastinapur having
brought peace to the land and respite from plague. The
obstacle to its appreciation at the time is summed up by
Birdwood's remark in his 1880 handbook. 'The
monstrous shapes of the Puranic [i.e. Hindu] deities
are unsuitable for the higher forms of artistic
representation: that is possibly why sculpture and
painting are unknown, as fine arts, in India.' This was
a backward step from the attitude of famous late
eighteenth-century collectors such as Richard Payne-
Knight, and Charles Towneley of the Towneley
marbles fame, who were quite happy to own examples
of Indian monumental sculpture, and even from the
romantic interest of the Daniells' readership. It had

come about through an evangelical conviction, which arose in the English middle classes, that the material superiority of the west was the consequence of its Christianity and that the idolatrous and savage nature of Indian religions held India in bondage. There was a total failure to look at Indian mythology according to its own terms, and so a Monkey god like Hanuman seemed irreverent, and degrading to any man who worshipped it. This was not of course an entirely logical attitude for Birdwood to hold, for it was precisely India's primitive industrial scene which he admired, but the barbarous nature of Indian religion seemed to have been confirmed by the atrocities of the 1857 Mutiny.

Besides this philosophical prejudice, there was a deep-rooted aesthetic obstacle to the true appreciation of Indian representational art. If, however unconsciously, the eye was attuned to the Greek ideal of beauty, then without a special intellectual re-adjustment Indian sculpture was bound to appear grotesque, bizarre and discordant. Significantly, the first Indian sculpture to attain respectability was that which most resembled the familiar Greek canon, the sculpture of Gandhāra, in the north-west Himalayas, produced from the fifth century BC to the fourth century AD under Greek, or later Roman, influence (plate 131). This provided a standard by which all other Indian sculpture could be judged, and the less like a Gandhāra piece it was the less it was admired. In other words, the great majority of it was still inadmissible.

Thus it was that one of the star pieces in the collection, the Sānchī torso, (plate 124) was completely misunderstood when it first came to the museum in 1886. It then belonged to William Kincaid, retiring political agent to the State of Bhopal, to whom it had been given by Her Highness the Begum of Bhopal. He recommended it to the museum as a good specimen of Indo-Grecian art of the third century BC despite the fact that it came from the great ruined temple at Sānchī in central India which was never reached by Hellenic influence. The loan was accepted, but it was ignored for some decades until in 1909 one curator, spectacularly missing the point of it, published it as an illustration to a series of articles on Indian jewellery, not as the masterpiece which it is in its own right. But by this time the climate of opinion towards Indian art was changing; old George Birdwood (now Sir George), for so long the resident expert on the subject, showed himself to have been drastically left behind. The distinguished scholar Havell was lecturing at the Royal Society of Arts in January 1910. Birdwood presided and afterwards produced the comment on a Javanese image of Buddha that 'a boiled suet pudding would serve equally well as a symbol of passionless purity and serenity of soul'. This so disgusted a number of people present that an India Society, was founded. Its aims were declared in a letter to *The Times* : 'to promote the acquisition by the authorities of our national and provincial museums of works

representing the best Indian art.' It went on to say that, 'We find in the best art of India a lofty and adequate expression of the religious emotion of the people, and of their deepest thoughts on the subject of the Divine'. The names at the end were those of prominent artists and intellectuals such as the playwright Lawrence Housman, the illustrator and designer Walter Crane, the architect W. R. Lethaby, A. E. Russell and Sir William Rothenstein, the artist and later principal of the Royal College of Art. At the same time the director of the Victoria and Albert Museum was being petitioned by private individuals over the heads of the Indian Section staff to buy the Sānchī torso. The Board of Education's apathy was finally jogged into putting up the money (£80) when a rumour reached them that a leading continental museum was after the pieces as well. Gradually the dating of the torso began to be reconsidered: almost at once the fourth or fifth centuries AD were suggested rather than the Hellenic third century BC. In 1949 it was proposed that it did not come from Sānchī at all but rather Bengal, and that it was an eighth- or ninth-century work. Finally in 1970 John Irwin, then Keeper of the Indian Section, came up with the true answer, largely by going back to what was already known but forgotten before Kincaid lent the piece to the museum.

The site of the Buddhist monastery at Sānchī had been abandoned by the thirteenth century and was already in a state of decay. It was rediscovered, as were so many of India's archaeological sites, by a British officer serving the East India Company in 1818 while on a military campaign. With characteristic enterprise and thoroughness a succession of army officers first published the ruins, then made site drawings and measurements, then photographed them (1862), made casts of part of them, and cleared the site and reconstructed as much as possible (1881-82), again taking photographs.

This second batch of photographs was to provide the key to the problem. In 1970 the 'pair' to the torso was found in two sections in a warehouse near the archaeological museum at Sānchī. Three months later Mr Irwin was working through the old photographs when he found one which showed both of these sections in rather better condition than they were now. By lucky chance the glass negative of this photograph still existed, and on being enlarged it revealed that the sculpture represented the Boddhisattva Maitreya, in other words, one of the pair of 'about-to-be-Buddhas' who are in attendance on Buddha himself. This meant that the museum's torso must represent the Boddhisattva Avalokitésvara, and all that was necessary now was to find the Buddha originally flanked by this pair. In one of the temples John Irwin found him, his face hammered into formlessness by Moslem iconoclasts, but with the same lotus petals on the base as on the Maitreya, and of the same purplish-brown stone. Dating them all was not so easy, as the particular temple in which they once stood is a hotch-

133

134

potch from various centuries, but the ninth century AD was finally decided upon by comparison with other Buddhas at other parts of the temple.

It was a worthy beginning to what is now one of the most distinguished collections of Indian sculpture outside India, and the shiny polished appearance of the sensuous and delicately modelled torso is proof of how people have felt impelled to caress it with their fingers.

At about the time when the torso was bought the second of the many plans to construct an Indian museum was hatched. Designs were even drawn up for a vast Delhi Durbar kind of building next to County Hall on the south bank of the Thames, but this, like George V's plan for a new museum opposite the Victoria and Albert, came to nothing. Meanwhile objects continued to pour in. In 1916 an ex-missionary called Miss Jessie Joseph gave a large collection of nineteenth-century folk bronzes from an area where she had spent much of her life (plate 134). They were cast by the lost wax process in copper by the Kutiya Koudh hill tribes of northern Madras. Basically they are toys, carried in the marriage procession to amuse the bridegrooms, who were usually about ten years old.

In 1927 the death occurred of Lord Curzon of Kedlestone, the former Viceroy of India, and a discriminating preservationist collector of Indian art and patron of museums on Indian soil. He left the Victoria and Albert Museum two hundred and seven pieces. A large proportion of these were artefacts of every sort, almost certainly presentation pieces which he had accumulated during his years there, but a select group of sculptures, many of them bronzes, must have been his own private collection. Among them is the Shri Devi (plate 133), a fine fifteenth-century cast bronze statuette of this most powerful and complex of the Hindu goddesses, here shown in her beautiful womanly form.

Important sculpture continued to come into the museum, despite the fact that sources of direct supply from India dwindled fast, first as the British authorities prohibited further spoliation of the temples, and then after the country became independent in 1947. But pieces surfaced from unlikely places, like Ireland and Edinburgh, where they had been for many decades.

One Durga, a pair to a stele showing the Sun god Surya, was bought from Powerscourt, Enniskerry County, for £3,500 in 1965 (plate 135). Viscount Powerscourt described in his autobiography (1903) how he acquired this piece at the end of the last century. While hunting in Mysore he greatly admired

---

133. Shri Devi, the consort of Vishnu; a bronze from Madras State, in the Chola style, 11th-12th centuries. The figure and base stand 8⅜ins. high (M137-1927).
134. A bronze hunting group from northern Madras. 19th century (IS115-1916).

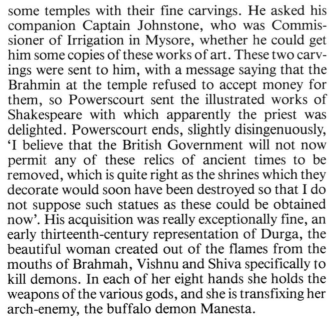

135.   Durga, the demon-killer, carved in limestone in the Hoysala style. Mysore, early 13th century (IS77-1965).
137.   A betel-nut container shaped like a goose, and made of gold set with semi-precious stones. It was part of the Burmese regalia (246-1964).

135   some temples with their fine carvings. He asked his companion Captain Johnstone, who was Commissioner of Irrigation in Mysore, whether he could get him some copies of these works of art. These two carvings were sent to him, with a message saying that the Brahmin at the temple refused to accept money for them, so Powerscourt sent the illustrated works of Shakespeare with which apparently the priest was delighted. Powerscourt ends, slightly disingenuously, 'I believe that the British Government will not now permit any of these relics of ancient times to be removed, which is quite right as the shrines which they decorate would soon have been destroyed so that I do not suppose such statues as these could be obtained now'. His acquisition was really exceptionally fine, an early thirteenth-century representation of Durga, the beautiful woman created out of the flames from the mouths of Brahmah, Vishnu and Shiva specifically to kill demons. In each of her eight hands she holds the weapons of the various gods, and she is transfixing her arch-enemy, the buffalo demon Manesta.

Thus the collections grew in sophistication, but they also continued to grow in breadth, for as traditionally the East India Company Museum had covered much more than just India, so the Indian Museum had to continue as a catch-all institution for Ceylon, Tibet, Afghanistan, Nepal, Burma, Indonesia, Vietnam, Thailand and Malaysia. This, together with India, embraces a quarter of the world's population, countless languages, at least three major religions, and vast cultural differences — an impossible task for a staff the same size as that of the Ceramics department. In 1905, for example, the artefacts brought back from the Younghusband expedition to Tibet arrived in the museum. The eighteenth-century lacquered gold and painted book cover (plate 136) was one of these.

A gold, emerald and ruby-set goose (plate 137) is also a memorial to the imperial past. In 1886 the Burmese regalia formed part of the material requisitioned as indemnity at the end of the third Burmese war. It was returned to Rangoon in 1969 and as a ges-

136.   This gilt, lacquered and painted wood book cover was bought from a large monastery at Gyantse, Tibet. An accompanying letter in the register records carefully that it was paid for at the price demanded by the lama, £15, with the consent of the British Staff Officer at Gyantse, for there were strict orders in force against looting and everything had to be purchased. The object is 2ft. 4½ins. long (540-1905).

136

ture of goodwill this nineteenth-century betel nut container was presented by the Burmese authorities.

For lack of any more suitable department to look after it, the Indian Section is also in charge of Persian painting. This, indeed, is rather suitable, as it was so vital to the Mughal Court style of illumination and a great deal of it must have found its way to India. A peculiar album which came into the collection in 1964 was presented to Clive of India. It must have been put together shortly beforehand, some time between 1750 and 1775. It consists of 102 folios of Indian and Persian miniature paintings, Islamic calligraphy and European engravings (plate 141).

The realistic, expansive and yet minutely detailed and decorative Mughal miniatures had always appealed to western taste. Charles I of England, for example, had owned an illuminated manuscript sent to him by the great Shah Jehan, an almost legendary figure in the west, and Rembrandt had a famous Mughal collection auctioned in 1656-7.

When the fusion took place in 1880 of the old East India Company Museum and the South Kensington

137

Overleaf: 138 and 139.   The tiger hunt from the Akhbarnama, painted in tempera, about 1590. These are two facing pages (2-1896 IS).

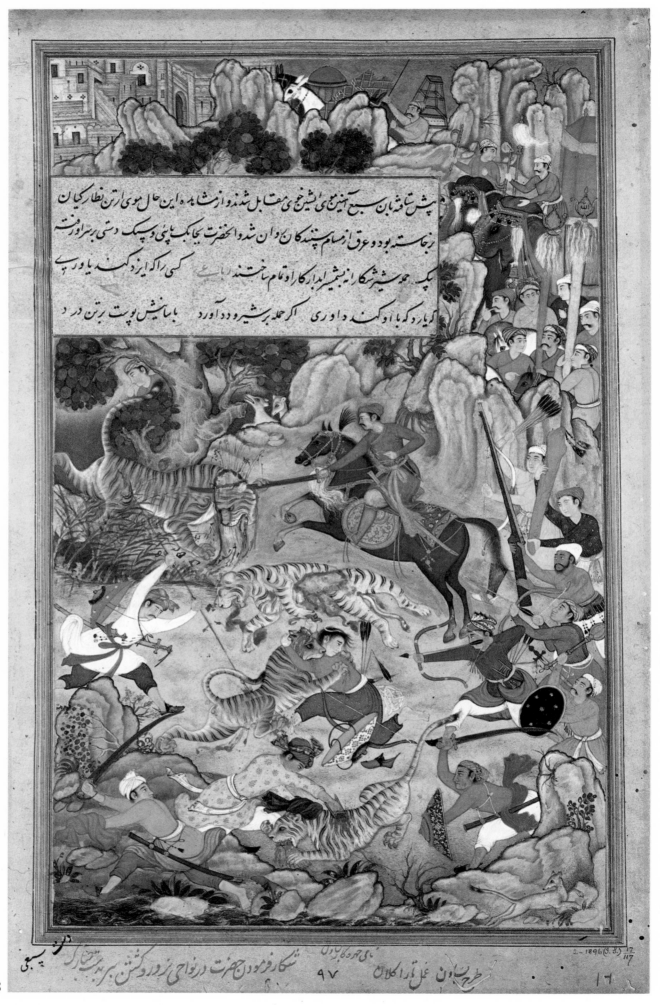

طرح باسادن عمل برون

140. A portrait of one of Jahangir's ministers, Malik Ambar Habshi of Ahmad-Nagar, painted by Mīr Hāshim, from the Earl Minto album (IM21-1925).

Museum, the manuscripts of course remained with the India Office Library; but as has already been mentioned, Purdon Clarke set about remedying this lack with the very fortunate purchase of the Hamzanāma folios. These are early Mughal, from the court of the rather feeble ruler Humāyūn. His son, Akhbar, who ruled for fifty years, was the one who really established the dynasty, and in 1896 the museum bought for a mere £100 one hundred and six illustrations and one illumination of the great history of his reign by his senior minister, the historian and mystic Abůl Fazl. Plates 138 and 139 show two facing pages of a tiger hunt in the crowded, fast-moving narrative style of earlier Mughal art. Akhbar can be seen on the left riding his horse, and cutting off the head of a tiger. The inscriptions are in Persian script.

From the next reign, that of his son Jahangir, the museum has the album bought from Earl Minto's collection in 1925 (plate 140). This was divided between A. Chester Beatty and the museum, so that it ended up with twenty-one pages, just one half of it. It was painted between 1610 and 1614 and shows the late Mughal manner, more static, with large-scale figures in spacious backgrounds. The energy which would once have gone into a turbulent composition is spent on detailed borders like this one with its echoes of fifteenth-century Burgundian manuscripts.

These are just three of the world-famous Mughal albums in the Victoria and Albert Museum, but of course there are many more. The collection also looks beyond the easily comprehensible Mughal art with its blend of Indian, Persian, and even western traditions, to more truly Indian art, the painting of the Rajput states, the independent principalities which were relatively unaffected by Mughal traditions. Plate 142

141

comes from the tiny principality of Basohli in the Punjab, where from about 1680 until the middle of the eighteenth century there flourished a school of painting which was vividly coloured, stylised, but not at all unsophisticated. The scene represents an episode from the fourteenth-century Rasamanjari, a treatise on the different states of loving, where the beloved explains away her lover's scratches on her body by blaming it on the household cat, seen to the left on the roof. In its colouring, its lack of shading and its perspective, this is completely un-Mughal, but it has been influenced enough to show precision of outline and a liking for fine decorative pattern, as in the carpet on which the ladies sit. It was bought from the estate of Sir William Rothenstein, the same who wrote the angry letter to *The Times* in 1910 about Sir George Birdwood. It was probably acquired by him through the great critic, scholar, and mystic Ananda Coomaraswamy, whose writing about the spiritual message of Indian art did so much to raise Indian art above the level of mere curiosities or, at best, archaeological documents, for western viewers.

East India Company art has also found its way into the department. This is the term for the cultural hybrids made for Europeans living in India or for export to Europe. Plate 143 is a chair from a set of furniture, made by an Indian, who veneered it with the local luxury material, ivory, but took its shape from a pattern book such as Hepplewhite's *The Cabinet Maker and Upholsterer's Guide* of 1788. Such furniture would have stood in the comfortable, and very English, houses of the East India company officials. This was for local consumption; but chintzes, the painted and dyed cotton cloths, were specifically for export to Europe. These originally captured the European market because their brilliant colours were the only ones which lasted. During the second half of the seventeenth century the East India Company merchants introduced European motifs such as the spreading tree and the acanthus leaf and other motifs from Chinese art, which, of course, was greatly admired at the time. The adaptable Indian craftsmen, who operated principally on the western, Coromandel, coast, came up with patterns which were equally exotic to Indian and western eyes.

Simultaneously with the expansion of the collection, an academic commitment to Indian and eastern culture was made by the founding in 1917 of a school of oriental languages as part of London University; in 1938 this was enlarged to become the School of Oriental and African Studies. Hopes for a comprehensive Museum of Asiatic Art and Antiquities, however, were constantly raised and then dashed. In 1929 the Royal Commission on National Museums and Galleries proposed amalgamating the British Museum's and the Victoria and Albert Museum's collections; two years later the same proposal was being discussed; thirteen years later in 1944 it was still being discussed.

Then India was granted independence and the whole political scene changed; far from a new and better museum being set up, even that which existed was taken away. The galleries closed during the war were gradually being reopened when in 1956 the Keeper was told that his building was going to be demolished to make way for the expansion of the Imperial College of Science. The culture of the ex-colonies would definitely have to take second place to science in the modern world. The towering plaster-cast of the gateway at Sānchī, made with vast labour eighty years before by Lt Henry Cole, was smashed up. The greater part of the collection was inconveniently put into store miles away from the museum, but light was supposed to be just around the corner — a new building would be provided within ten years. It is now nearly a quarter of a century later and there is still no prospect of a new building. In the meantime popular interest in Indian art has flowered again with the mystical yearnings of the 1960s, the Third World grows yearly more important on the international scene, the Asian communities in this country grow bigger and more influential — and there is still nowhere where Asian culture, in all its diversity, can properly be seen.

142

143

142.   An episode from the 'Rasamanjari', an album from the kingdom of Basohli, c. 1680 (IS20-1958).
143.   Wooden chair veneered with ivory, made for the East India Company market about 1790 (IS20-1958).

*144. Chinese 18th-century jade vase and cover,
18⅛ ins. high (C1920 & a-1910).*

8
The Far Eastern Department

For centuries, ever since the East Indies Companies had begun to trade on a large scale with China and Japan, Europe had had a quaint, exotic, 'willow-pattern' vision of the East. Although a familiar vision, it had no great depth to it, and 'chinoiserie', as its artistic manifestation was called, was considered a light, frivolous style, suitable for ladies' bedrooms and garden pavilions.

The reality of China did not begin to dawn until the Opium War of 1839 (Japan was regarded as culturally indistinguishable from China at this stage). This brought a great deal of publicity in the English newspapers, and a readiness for more hard information in the public. A rich Philadelphian tea trader called Nathaniel Dunn thought that he would supply this need. Being a Quaker and morally opposed to trafficking in opium, he had gained Chinese official sympathy during his twelve years in the East, and had been allowed to bring back a much better collection than his contemporaries. He put these 1,341 items on show in a two-storied green and vermilion pagoda built for it at Hyde Park Corner. This had its chinoiserie, brightly-lit lanterns, but it was also the first glimpse of the real China. One man who visited it, John Timbs, reported that there were life-sized groups of idols, a council of mandarins and Chinese priests, soldiers, men-of-letters, ladies of rank, tragedians, barbers, shoemakers, blacksmiths, boat women, servants etc. among set scenes and furnished dwellings. There was also a two-storied house from Canton, and shop fronts, 'and altogether such a picture of Chinese social life as the European world has never seen before'. This show flourished for two years until 1843, and then toured the provinces with equal success.

At the same time, since the Treaty of Nanking in 1841 at the end of the Opium War, China was more open to trade than ever before. Nonetheless, the government of the Emperor Hsien Fêng (1851-61) failed to send its exhibits to the Great Exhibition at the Crystal Palace in 1851, which then had to make do with what the Board of Trade, English merchants, and collectors could produce instead. This was not, on the whole, impressive. Compared to the section for India, which filled six pages of the catalogue, China (embracing the whole of the Far East) filled two and a half, and the illustrations show a kind of oriental emporium, hung with paper lanterns and stacked with vases.

Exhibits included those tedious ivory balls, each holding twenty smaller balls, reclining bamboo chairs, ladies' shoes, gongs, silver filigree card cases — in other words, modern commercial export wares.

The British consul in Shanghai sent one identifiably old piece, a cloisonné enamelled vase, curiously and inaccurately described as an 'antique vase of enamelled and mosaic brass', but the registers of the museum also show that among the small numbe. of items bought after the Exhibition closed, there were a few which have turned out to be older than expected. For example, from the merchants, Hewitt's, there was a blue-and-white porcelain vase, thought to be Japanese and modern, but in fact Chinese early seventeenth century. Nonetheless, it is clear that the 1851 Exhibition did not play the same important role as it did for the Indian collections. There was no immediate chord struck in the English artistic world by its exhibits, and for a while the museum just seemed to follow fashion in what it bought. In 1858, for example, it acquired an excellent cloisonné dish on a stand for £100 (plate 147). Cloisonné enamelling was just beginning to become fashionable, especially in Paris where, during the following decade, prices soared and firms like Barbedien made skilful reproductions.

In October 1860 an Anglo-French military force committed a real barbarity: it forced its way into the Yüan Ming Yüan, the Summer Palace outside Peking, to which the Emperor and his court had fled. The palace was ransacked and razed to the ground, and as the loot reached the West connoisseurs realised that for the first time they were seeing the art made for the elevated tastes of the Imperial Court instead of the Western export trade. The 1861 and 1862 sales in Paris established the rarer forms of Chinese art as something for which the richest collectors competed.

The museum bought at neither of these sales, but picked up a number of pieces as they came on the market for the second time: in 1876 it bought a cloisonné enamel ice-chest supported by two kneeling figures, and two large cloisonné basins from the Henry Bohn sale; and in 1883 it paid the large sum of £325 for two large curved lacquer vases with dragons chasing pearls (plate 145).

Porcelain and pottery were continuously coming into the collections, rarely, however, by such a round-about route as the eighty-three oriental pieces bought

146

145.   One of the pair of coral lacquer vases of Soochow. They were made for the Emperor Kontsoung of the Ch'ien-Lung period of the Tai-Tsing dynasty (1736-96), and were formerly in the Summer Palace, Peking. They stand 3ft. 1½ ins. high (10-1883).
146.   A porcelain jar from Arita, Japan, made in the second half of the 17th century. Height: 19¾ ins. (1736-1876).

145   in Persia by Major Murdoch-Smith. These appeared in 1875 as part of the large collection formed by Jules Richard, the Frenchman who had been tutor at the Shah's court (see page 46). That these pictures were in Persia at all is not surprising, as there had always been a strong trade link with the Far East, and indeed, Persian and Chinese ceramics had mutually influenced each other. Major Murdoch-Smith revealed a certain confusion in his mind about this in his *Handbook of Persian Art,* published for the museum in 1876, suggesting that the very Chinese looking marks which he had seen on some pottery in Persia must have been made by Chinese potters brought to work in Persia, or by Persians copying the marks on Chinese porcelain. Clearly he was unaware that the Chinese made pottery. Not surprisingly, a number of the pieces brought back were quite wrongly described at first, one greenish-glazed earthenware bottle with a bulbous body, short neck and two handles being Siamese, thirteenth-

century, not Persian, eighteenth-century as originally thought; and a green-glazed earthenware jar with applied flowers, Chinese, about 1600, rather than Persian, sixteenth-century. A very fine Japanese piece from this collection is plate 146, a porcelain jar from Arita in Japan, bought for £5, and of a type much admired and copied in the west since the eighteenth century. Curiously, even this familiar style was identified at the time as Chinese.

The confusion between the two cultures, let alone the even less familiar ones such as Korea and Siam, continued. Indeed as late as 1906 the ex-director of the museum, Purdon Clarke, then director of the Metropolitan Museum New York could say robustly, 'it is all nonsense to attempt to distinguish between Chinese and Japanese art', and by that time he had no excuse for such ignorance.

From the 1860s there was an overwhelming fashion for 'Japanism', much of which, in fact, was for a

147

147. A Chinese cloisonné enamel dish, 18th-century. Its diameter is 26½ins. (4785-1858).

particular kind of Chinese object, the blue and white porcelain painted with prunus blossom of the K'ang Hsi (1662-1722), Yung Chên (1723-38) and Ch'ien Lung (1736-95) reigns. An eminent dealer of the time, Murray Marks, provided the connection between the leading exponents of Japanism, Whistler and Dante Gabriel Rossetti, the South Kensington Museum and two collectors who later on were greatly to benefit the museum. Marks was one of the very first to import blue and white, and as he was of Dutch extraction he had no difficulty in getting good examples from Holland, where it abounded, while it was still cheap. He displayed it to great advantage against the neo-Queen Anne interior of his Oxford Street shop, designed by Norman Shaw and painted entirely in cream, which was revolutionary at the time. In this shop Rossetti introduced a collector called Huth to him, and he became one of his best clients. H. C. Huth it will be recalled (see page 81) was the early

artistic mentor of the Australian millionaire George Salting, who of course was the museum's greatest benefactor of the early twentieth century, bequeathing it practically his entire collection in 1909, among which were over two hundred pieces of blue and white bought from Murray Marks. The other collector friend of Marks was W. C. Alexander, the friend and patron of Whistler, whose name will appear later in a different context. Blue and white became a kind of symbol of the whole aesthetic movement and eventually percolated so far in society that every suburban home had a few cheap pieces.

But Japanism did have an important Japanese side to it, greatly encouraged by the forcible opening up of Japan to the West by Commodore Perry in 1852. This not only meant that trade with Japan increased a hundred-fold but that travellers could now visit the country and describe it to an information-hungry European public. The 1862 Exhibition in South

148

149

Kensington had a separate section devoted to Japan, with exhibits collected together by Sir Rutherford Alcock. This was regarded as a turning point by contemporaries such as Christopher Dresser, the author of extraordinarily spare, elegant designs decades in advance of his time, and one of the early teachers at the Schools of Design which gave birth to the museum. In 1876 he was sent to Japan via Tiffany's of New York, by the oriental importers Charles Reynolds and Co. His mission was to take English goods from Minton, Royal Doulton, Elkington and other manufacturers to the Tokyo museum, and to report on how the Japanese made their goods and bring back specimens. Like George Birdwood writing about India, he was most struck by the romantic image of the perfectionist craftsman, happy in his work and respected by all for his skill. He was also very impressed by the local uninterest in expanding production, however much he guaranteed the potters an increased demand for their wares. (How different he would find modern Japan!) This helped to make Japanese goods morally as well as aesthetically appealing to the Arts and Crafts movement in England. The South Kensington museum played an important part in spreading the familiarisation of Japanese art. The Japanese were planning to exhibit at an international show for the first time with the Philadelphia Exhibition of 1876 and at the same time the museum decided that it should improve its representation of Japanese ceramics. It was therefore decided to ask the Japanese themselves what should be acquired. Negotiating through Fritz Cunliffe-Owen, a relative of the director in the Japanese service in Tokyo, it was agreed that the Japanese should send interesting ceramics from each area to its pavilion at the exhibition, and that the museum would then buy the lot. Four years later, in 1880, a report was compiled on them by Augustus Woollaston Franks, later director of the British Museum. He lent heavily on the text of two Japanese experts, a Mr Shioda and a Mr Asami, and the book provided the first approximately accurate information in the West on Japanese ceramics.

Franks was well aware of this and allowed himself a rather strong paragraph in the introduction on the errors of the French authorities Jacquemart and Le Blant, pointing out that their Korean pottery was in fact old Japanese, that their Chinese *chrysanthemo-paeonienne* ware was likewise Japanese, and that their Japanese eggshell and mandarin vases, on the other hand, were unquestionably Chinese. For the first time, also, the Japanese tea ceremony was described; and indeed a number of pieces used for this purpose were included (plate 148).

This kind of rough finish must have come as a revelation to an English public used to admiring smoothness and translucency in oriental ceramics, and again it struck a chord with the growing Arts and Crafts movement which was in reaction against

148.   A pair of Japanese (Seto) earthenware fire pots, painted with brown foliage and covered with white crackled glaze. They are possibly 16th-century, and stand 3½ ins. high (178 & a-1877).
149.   A woodcut protrait of the actor Arashi Rikan II playing the part of a samurai in the Kabuki Theatre. It is signed Aigadō-Ashi-yukiga, and dates from about 1820 (E2843-1886).

150. *A Japanese 17th-century coffer of black and gold lacquer inlaid with gold, silver and mother-of-pearl. It was once the property of Napoleon, and the key is carved with the arms of Cardinal Mazarin. Height: 22¼ins. (412-1882).*

150

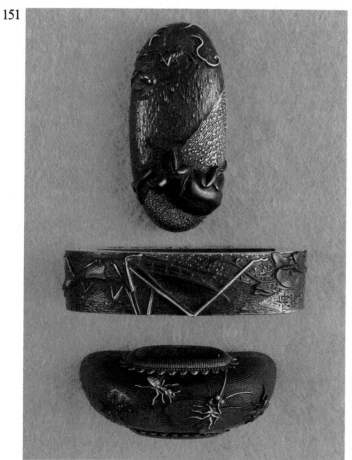

151

151. *Knife mounts made in Mito, Japan, in 1859. They have combined grounds of copper 'ishime', 'shakadō', 'nanako' and copper-gilt with a 'cat-scratch' surface, and an 'iroye' incrustation of plants and insects (467 & a & b-1916).*

tedious machine-made perfection in objects. As Christopher Dresser wrote: 'I have before me some specimens of Japanese earthenware which are formed of coarse brown clay, and to a great extent without that finish which most Europeans appear so much to value, yet these are artistic and beautiful . . . we get finish without art, they get art without finish.'

Another vital aspect of Japanism was the revelation which the Japanese woodcut represented to western eyes. The legend about how they reached Europe is that in the 1850s a consignment of goods arrived in Paris from Japan and a small volume of prints by Hokusai was found among the packing material. This changed hands a number of times before reaching the engraver, Felix Braquemond, in 1856. He reacted with enthusiasm to them, and in 1862 Madame de Soye and her husband opened an oriental shop called 'La Porte Chinoise' in the Rue de Rivoli. There Braquemond, Manet, Fantin-Latour, Tissot, Baudelaire, the de Goncourts and Whistler all came to buy prints. The South Kensington museum was slow to join them, but the present collection of 30,000 prints (in the care of the Prints and Drawings department) got off to a flying start when one day in 1886 a horse drawn cart loaded with 12,000 woodcuts drove up to the back door of the museum and they were offered for a very small sum indeed. The deal was settled at once, of course, and many very good examples were found to be among them (plate 149).

True to its policy of being a craft educator the museum was also buying didactic specimens for English craftsmen, such as the fifty-nine lacquered split bamboo baskets acquired in the same year from Arima, Japan, for £25. This was to help support the findings of the report made a few years earlier on the

152. A detail from a Chinese 18th-century screen of lacquered, painted and gilt wood. It measures 21ft. in length and is 8ft. 10ins. high (130—1885). Left: the entire screen.

lacquer industry in Japan by the acting British consul at Hakodate (1882).

Japanese lacquer had, of course, been admired in the West for centuries (plate 150), but examples of metalwork, especially sword fittings, had only recently become known and appreciated. The crucial event behind this was the edict of 1876 which prohibited Japanese noblemen and their retainers from carrying swords. This meant that the finely worked mounts, objects of such prestige to their owners, began to be exported to the West, often in shipments of thousands at a time. W. C. Alexander was one of the people to buy them up (plate 151), and in 1916 his collection was presented to the museum in his memory by his daughters, the Misses Alexander (one of whom is the little girl in the white dress and Alice-band in the famous painting by Whistler). Interest in both lacquer and metalwork was confirmed by the exhibition held at the Burlington Fine Arts Club in 1894.

Although the climate of opinion over the last thirty years of the century favoured Japanese art, the museum did not, of course, cease to buy Chinese objects, such as the spectacular eighteenth-century lacquered, painted and gilt screen which was bought in 1855 for the considerable sum of £1,000, and which now dominates the centre of the Primary Galleries (plate 152).

Then, in 1909, George Salting's collection which had been on loan to the museum for twenty years, finally came to it by bequest. Oriental ceramics formed by far the greatest proportion of the bequest, with twenty-nine museum cases full of it, as against ten of Italian maiolica and ten of Italian bronzes. The account in The Times, on 22 December 1909, quoting a museum spokesman, said that this oriental collection rivalled the royal one at Dresden, and singled out the blue and white pieces mentioned earlier as being especially praiseworthy. The most notable rarities, however, were considered to be the large famille noir vases (plate 153) which are now regarded as infinitely

153. *A Chinese lantern of porcelain painted with enamelled colours, dating from the reign of Ch'ien Lung (1736-95). Height: 13¼ins. (C1435-1910).*

less important than an austere early celadon such as the Ju-ware cupstand (plate 164). George Salting had been bidding for these ornate, enamelled pieces in the 1880s and between himself, the American millionaire James Garland and, slightly later, J. Pierpoint Morgan, a boom in *famille noir,* and to a lesser extent *famille verte* and *famille rose,* was created. These wares date from the eighteenth century and were imported in relatively large numbers to Europe, where at first, unless they were of unusual size, their price was rather moderate. Then in 1862 Jacquemart and Le Blant coined the terms for them, and around the same time, probably in harness with the collecting mania for the decorative arts of the French eighteenth century, their price began to rise. They suited interiors with ornate inlaid furniture and Gobelins tapestries, especially when mounted in ormolu. By the 1890s good specimens, especially whole garnitures which could be used to decorate a chimneypiece, fetched up to £10,000. The rarest of the three types and consequently the most expensive was the *famille noir* rumoured to be the favourite of the Empress Dowager, the last effective Ch'ing ruler of China in power from the 1860s until the revolution of 1911.

Nearly all this porcelain of Salting's can be seen in a room on the top floor of the museum, displayed together by the terms of the bequest, and embodying a vanished taste in collecting. Among other oriental pieces in his bequest was much fine jade of the more elaborate eighteenth-century sort (plate 144), some ivories including the foundation of a very impressive collection of *netsuke* (plate 154), a great deal of lacquer, and twenty-five *tsuba* (Japanese sword guards).

It is ironical that so far every great leap forward in western understanding of the Chinese had been preceded by a show of military strength: first the Opium War of 1839-40, then the ransacking of the Summer Palace in 1862; and in 1900 the suppression of the Boxer Rebellion by allied forces, followed by another sacking of Peking. The Boxer Rebellion in 1899 was an attempt by fanatical Chinese traditionalists to rid China of western influences. A massacre of foreigners in 1900 compelled the western governments to react sharply, and after the rebellion was stamped out more and more foreigners came to live in China. The shaky imperial government invited the western companies to build a network of railways covering north and west China, and in the process of their building numerous ancestral tombs were cut open and their treasures revealed. In particular, the lines nearing Sian and Lo'Yeng cut through the vast necropolis which surrounded the twin capital cities of the T'ang Empire (AD 618-906). These tombs were filled with bronze vessels and bells, ceramics and statuettes of horses and retainers symbolising the actual ones which during the very ancient Shang dynasty (15th-11th century BC) used to be slain and buried with the king or nobleman.

154

154. *A Japanese ivory 'netsuke' of Gena Sennin and his toad, dating from the first half of the 18th century. Height: 5⅜ins. (A762-1910).*

Most of these finds were shipped back to Europe with, for the first time, the hard archaeological information which dated and identified them. This ancient Chinese art came as a revelation to an artistic world ripe to receive it. Japanism had been a sign of the reaction against western academic art, and by 1900 many people were prepared to make the effort to understand an alien aesthetic, such as Byzantine or Indian art. In the Victoria and Albert Museum the lobby group which formed itself to campaign for the acquisition of the Sānchī torso is an illustration of this. Ernest Fenellosa's book *The Epochs of Chinese and Japanese Art* (1912) was a crucial work for the understanding of Chinese art and culture. It was the first to put forward the idea that the Far East had a high culture, with the Sung dynasty (AD 960-1279) as its apogee, equal to the great days of Greece and Rome. This idea was reinforced by the physical proof emerging from the East of the awe-inspring antiquity of its civilisation.

155

155. The Akita armour, made of gold lacquered small plates, gilt-copper brown lacquer plates and scarlet. The suit was assembled in 1741 for Akita daimio, Lord of Miharu, but includes a late 12th-century helmet. It was given by the Mikado to Sir John Macleary Brown, Chinese Commissioner of Korean Customs and financial adviser to the Korean government (M979-1928).

156

156. A Sung dynasty (AD 960-1275) porcelain Chunware vase. Height: 8⅖ ins. (C936-1935).

The quaint, willow-pattern vision of China had at last had its day, and instead a reverential image arose of the Chinese man of sensibility who lived, not for crass material pleasures, but 'to feel, and in order to feel, to express, or at least understand the expression of all that is lovely in nature . . . a rose in a moonlit garden, the shadows of trees on a turf, almond bloom, scent of the wine cup and the guitar' (as Goldsworthy Lowes Dickinson wrote in his imaginary *Letters from John Chinaman).*

At first Chinese painting was considered to be the supreme expression of its culture, but rapidly the emphasis shifted to ceramics. In 1910 the Burlington Fine Arts Club held an exhibition 'Early Chinese Pottery and Porcelain'. W. C. Alexander, who had been in advance of his time in collecting Sung monochromes, and George Eumorfopoulous, who was to be crucial to the formation of the museum's collection of eastern art, both exhibited here. Then in 1921 the Oriental Ceramics Society was founded, with the Keeper of Ceramics Bernard Rackham as one of the three museum members, and Eumorfopoulous as president. All the great lovers of Chinese art belonged to this society which of course does not confine itself to ceramic studies but in its name pays tribute to the importance of ceramics in oriental art.

By 1923 Rackham could write that no collector was happy without his T'ang and Sung wares, although he recalled when the mere names were remote and difficult, and the awestruck excitement caused by the

157. *Limestone sculpture of Bodhisattva, probably of the Sui dynasty (AD 581-618). Height: 3ft. 1¼ins. (A8-1936).*

arrival of thirty specimens of supposedly Sung pottery bought for the collection by Salting (most of which had since turned out to be archaistic and not even Ming). The academic members of this society had a breadth of interest which perhaps was lacking in the other museum orientalist, Albert Koop, Keeper of Metalwork in the 1920s and 1930s. He was mainly a meticulous student of the Japanese sword and during his time practically nothing was acquired for the Department except sword fittings and a magnificently documented suit of armour assembled in 1741 for Akita daimio, Lord of Miharu (plate 155). His excursions into the field of Chinese bronzes were less successful and many of these acquisitions have since been discredited.

In the meantime oriental museums were being formed in other parts of the world: in 1912 Charles Freer, the great steel magnate and a follower of Fenellosa, gave his collection to the Washington Museum; another collector, Denman Ross, created the Department of Eastern Art at the Boston Museum with 11,000 objects, among which were 4,000 pictures, and after the First World War the Metropolitan in New York and the Chicago and Philadelphia museums all had East Asian departments.

In 1935 a crucially important exhibition of Chinese art was held at the Royal Academy. It received support at the very highest level, with the Chinese government sending over treasures from the Peking Palace Museum and the British Navy transporting these in *H.M.S. Suffolk*. The King and Queen gave their patronage, and Leigh Ashton and Bernard Rackham from the museum sat on the executive committee. It was a show which reverentially displayed a vast range of every art from the earliest Shang-Yin dynasty (1766-1122 BC) to the Ch'ing (1644-1912). In fact it was a kind of celebration of the West's recent realisation of the creative power of the Chinese; the prestige of Chinese art was for a while unassailable, and so when George Eumorfopoulous offered his collection to the nation the proposal was considered by none other than the Prime Minster.

Eumorfopoulous (affectionately known as Eumo) had made a fortune in the firm of Ralli Brothers and eventually became doyen of the Baltic Exchange. His hobbies were art and archaeology and he used his money to surround himself with beautiful and interesting objects. He started by collecting English ceramics but very soon became a devotee of Chinese, especially early Chinese art. He was one of the first to realise the importance of the Han, T'ang and Sung wares (plate 156) which appeared after the opening of the tombs. He then turned his attention to still older bronzes (plate 159) and jades (plate 158) and then sculpture (plate 157), painting, miscellaneous metalwork, lacquer and glass until his collection covered every known aspect of Chinese art. His intention had always been to bequeath all this to the national museums, but in 1934 the trade depression

160. A Chinese embroidered silk robe (K'ossu) of the K'ang Hsi reign (1622-1723) (T190-1948).

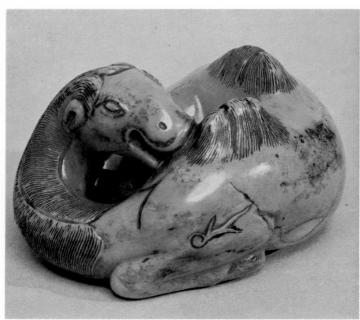

158

159

158.   *A jade dromedary of the Sung dynasty, 3⅞ins. long (A28-1935).*

159.   *This bronze wine-vessel is probably from the Chou dynasty (1122-255 BC). It stands 13½ins. high (M6-1935).*

forced him to sell it instead. The sum he was asking, £100,000, was very fair considering the distinction of the collection, but was beyond the financial range of the British and Victoria and Albert Museums combined, so both institutions mortgaged their future purchase grants to raise about half and made a public appeal for the rest. To stimulate interest in it an exhibition of the whole collection was held in the North Court of the museum in 1936. Sir George Hill, director of the British Museum, and Sir Eric Macglagan, director of the Victoria and Albert, said in a progress report on the appeal fund (*The Times* , 2 January 1936): 'A man who has never seen a Chinese work of art may have a prettier paper on his wall or a less ugly cup and saucer for his tea because in Bloomsbury and South Kensington or elsewhere, there are priceless things of exquisite beauty by which designers and students may enrich and refine their invention.' How interesting to read this pious harking back to the founding principles of the V & A, at a period when neither museum could have been less interested in contemporary design. Begging letters were sent to every figure in the establishment known to be interested in art, from the Archbishop of Canterbury to Sir Robert Witt. There was a great fear that, if the money were not raised, the collection would be bought by Japan or one of the American museums, but by 1936 the appeal had succeeded, with donations from the National Art Collections Fund, the Universities China Committee and many private benefactors, including Queen Mary who gave £25. At a stroke the oriental collections of this museum and the British Museum became quite outstanding, particularly in the field of ceramics.

Then, after the Second World War, again with the help of the National Art Collections Fund, another collection was bought *en bloc* for £2,000. This was of course much more limited in scope than the previous one, but it did make the museum one of the most important institutions for the study of Far Eastern textiles, particularly of the later period. The collector, Bernard Vuilleumie, was a Swiss living in Lausanne, who had bought his first imperial robes in 1933. He quickly assembled a very large collection, which was put on show successively in Paris and London before the war, and it was his activity in this field which really made Chinese embroidered textiles a subject worthy of serious study. They were certainly the passion of the museum's first post-war Keeper of Textiles, George Digby, who subsequently added to the Vuilleumie collection (plate 160).

For a long time it had been obvious that it was illogical for the Far Eastern collections to be scattered between the different departments. It was clear that the prospect for a Central Museum of Asiatic Art, which was being discussed at the time of the campaign for the Eumorfopoulous collection, was very dim indeed, and so the director, John Pope-Hennessy, decided that a separate department on the lines of the

161

162.   A stoneware bowl with wax-resist decoration, by Suoji Hamada at Bernard Leach's studio, 1923. Diameter: 7¾ ins. (C106-1924).

Indian Section should be set up. This occurred in 1970, with the new Keeper John Ayers being recruited from the Ceramics Section. His staff was very small, with just one research and one museum assistant, but it was later augmented by the addition of Basil Robinson, former Keeper of Metalwork, a large, genial, pipe-smoking specialist in Japanese art; and the department is now at last approaching the size of the longer-established offices.

Since 1970 some very distinguished purchases have been made, such as the very rare scroll painting on silk with the Bodhisattva Samantabhadra, acquired for $20,000 from the American Buddhist Academy in 1979 (plate 161). It is Korean, of the thirteenth or early fourteenth century, and reminds one that the Far Eastern department covers China and Japan, Korea and anywhere in the Far East under Chinese cultural influence. The newly formed department has also been extremely fortunate in its friends, to mention only a few. The first object in its books is the extraordinarily rare and valuable Ju-ware cupstand (plate 164) given by the late Sir Harry Garner, who had made a wartime reputation as a specialist in aero-dynamic problems, and a peacetime reputation as a connoisseur of oriental art. He became president of the Oriental Ceramic Society and then gave the museum some of its finest lacquer in 1979.

Sir John Figges, a considerable linguist and student of Japanese culture, who for many years was Counsellor at the British Embassy in Tokyo, gave a superb thirteenth-century Japanese Buddha in 1972 (plate 163), and the next year an anonymous benefactor gave £50,000 to be spent as the Keeper thought fit, and with this two early pieces of lacquered furniture were acquired.

Sir John Addis presented the museum with some elegant Ming furniture and a large group of the burial pots exported from China to South East Asia in the

161.   A silk scroll painted in colours and gold with the Bodhisattva Samantabhadra, from Korea in the Koryo period (13th- or early 14th-century). Height: 85½ ins. (FE51-1976).

*163. A Japanese lacquered and gilt
wood carving of Buddha (Amida Ayorai),
from the Kamakura period (13th-
century). Height: 17½ins. (FE5-1972).*

163

164

*164.   Ju-ware cupstand of the early 12th century. There is
an inscription within the foot, reading 'Hall of Perfect Old
Age'. Diameter: 6½ins. (FE1-1970).*

thirteenth and fourteenth centuries, thereby filling a
large gap in the collections. Export wares were given by
Clement Ades, who also donated the very important
pottery from Gurgan to the Ceramics department, and
by Mr P. Cooke in 1978.

All that this department and so many others, but
the Indian section in particular, must now hope for is
the space in which to show their marvellous
collections. There is a scheme to turn the old
Circulation department court into galleries for both
the Eastern departments, so long as public expenditure
cuts do not lead to its being axed. In the meantime the
collections are being sorted, catalogued and
researched, and objects of every sort continue to be
acquired. In particular, the department is trying to
keep up to date in contemporary art. In the past it had
always acquired the select pieces of the day such as a
bowl by Shoji Hamada (plate 162), the Japanese friend
and adviser of the great English art potter Bernard
Leach, but it is now widening its scope to include more
everyday examples, especially of Japanese crafts.

*165. A design in pen and ink and watercolour picked out with gold,
perhaps by Jacopo Ligozzi (1547-1626). It was in the collections
of Sir Thomas Lawrence and Count Moriz von Fries (4785).*

9
Prints, Drawings, Photographs and Painting

In 1857, in the same year as the South Kensington Museum was established, a National Gallery of British Art was founded there with a core collection of 233 oil paintings given by John Sheepshanks. This was the origin of the paintings, watercolours and miniatures side of this department. At the same time, however, the reference library of the fledgling museum was collecting engravings, photographs and other pictorial sources for the students at the School of Design, and this was to develop into the side of the department which deals with prints and graphic art of all sorts, with drawings and photographs.

John Sheepshanks (1787-1863) gave his collection of oil paintings to the South Kensington Museum because, as he said, he wanted them to be 'in an open and airy situation, possessing the quiet necessary to the study and enjoyment of works of art, and free from the inconveniences and dirt of the main thoroughfare of the metropolis'. (One must remember that in 1857 South Kensington still consisted of pleasant green fields.) Sheepshanks was the son of a wealthy Leeds clothing manufacturer who devoted himself in later life to the appreciation of art, particularly of contemporary British art. He was not alone in this in the 1820s and 1830s, because many English collectors were becoming wary of the often third-rate Italian 'masterpieces' which had flooded over during the period of the Grand Tour. The *Art Journal*, moreover, had been running scare stories on fakes, and buyers were beginning to feel a duty to contemporary art. Sheepshanks kept open house every Wednesday evening, entertaining the wide circle of artists whose works he collected and from whom he often commissioned paintings. These were for the most part genre-works, often with a literary theme and intended to play on the emotions of the viewer. Among the artists were Thomas Duncan, Sir David Wilkie, William Mulready, Sir Edwin Landseer, Frith, and Richard Redgrave, who was much involved in the early days of the museum and was the first curator of the Sheepshanks Gallery. Another friend of Sheepshanks's was John Constable, and the gift includes six works by him, four of them bought at the Executors' sale of 1838. Plate 166 shows one of them, the famous finished oil painting of Salisbury Cathedral, signed and dated 1823.

These were the beginning of what was to become the most complete collection of Constable anywhere. Two full-scale oil sketches, for 'The Haywain' and 'The Leaping Horse', were to arrive on loan in 1862 from the Rev. Henry Vaughan, and were finally bequeathed in 1900, but the great bulk of the material came in 1887 as a gift from Constable's only daughter, Isabel. In 1887 she wrote to R. A. Thompson, one of the two Assistant Directors, saying that she would like to present the museum with 'some landscape sketches by J. Constable R. A.', and regretting that they were not in frames. Then 390 items arrived, most of the contents of her father's studio, and in the following year her death brought another three oil paintings and two watercolours. In all, the museum was richer by 95 paintings, 297 drawings and three sketchbooks which gave a wide insight into Constable's working practices and style (plate 167).

Sheepshanks was also responsible for founding the National Collection of British Watercolours with the 298 examples which came with his paintings in 1857, and while the Victoria and Albert Museum ceased to collect paintings in 1908 when the Tate Gallery was founded, this watercolour collection is being added to all the time. Because nineteenth-century watercolours were highly finished and framed like oils in heavy gilt surrounds, these are classified as paintings, but more sketchy works or monochromes are classified under Prints and Drawings. The distinction is less valid now than a hundred years ago, but as a general rule if something is of exhibition quality then it will still come under Paintings.

The major artists of the British Watercolour School are represented, including Paul Sandby, J. R. Cozens, Thomas Girtin, Turner, Cotman, William Blake, Samuel Palmer, Thomas Rowlandson, and John Varley (plate 168).

There was no systematic policy for collecting foreign paintings, which theoretically should have been the preserve of the National Gallery, but since eight were part of the Jules Soulages collection, when the complicated deal was made to buy it in instalments,

Overleaf: 166. 'Salisbury Cathedral' by John Constable (1776-1837), signed and dated 1823 (FA69).

167

168

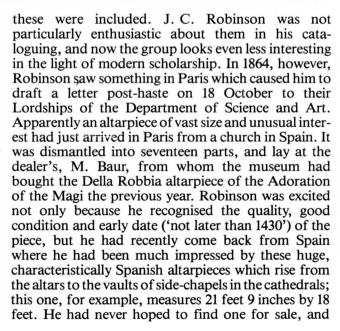

167.   'Salisbury Cathedral'; pen and bistre ink and water-colour, by John Constable (227-1888).
168.   'View of Snowdon'; pencil and watercolour, by John Varley (1778-1842) (P52-1924).
169.   The altarpiece of St George which J. C. Robinson first saw in Paris in 1864. It is tempera and gilt on pine, of the Spanish school, and attributed to Marzal de Sas who was active from 1393 to 1410. It measures 21ft. 9ins. high by 18ft. wide (1217-1864). Plate 170 shows one of its panels.

these were included. J. C. Robinson was not particularly enthusiastic about them in his cataloguing, and now the group looks even less interesting in the light of modern scholarship. In 1864, however, Robinson saw something in Paris which caused him to draft a letter post-haste on 18 October to their Lordships of the Department of Science and Art. Apparently an altarpiece of vast size and unusual interest had just arrived in Paris from a church in Spain. It was dismantled into seventeen parts, and lay at the dealer's, M. Baur, from whom the museum had bought the Della Robbia altarpiece of the Adoration of the Magi the previous year. Robinson was excited not only because he recognised the quality, good condition and early date ('not later than 1430') of the piece, but he had recently come back from Spain where he had been much impressed by these huge, characteristically Spanish altarpieces which rise from the altars to the vaults of side-chapels in the cathedrals; this one, for example, measures 21 feet 9 inches by 18 feet. He had never hoped to find one for sale, and

justified its purchase for the museum saying: 'Although this work is essentially pictorial, considering its architectural and ornamental character it would, I apprehend, fall quite within the province of the Kensington Museum.' This, of course, is pure sophistry, covering his urgent need to possess this very fine work. The competitors were, potentially, the museum in Madrid and the Louvre in Paris, for apparently the Spanish origin of the Empress Eugènie had stimulated an interest in things Spanish. Robinson was authorised to offer £500 and to his great distress was brusquely turned down, so he left Paris, with the dealer John Webb charged to look after the museum's interest if Baur should change his mind. This he must have done, because in December there is a minute from Robinson discussing how it should be cleaned, and recommending the lightest sponging with water and perhaps turpentine.

At that time the altarpiece was believed to come from a church of the Knights Templar, probably a garbling of the truth, which is that it came from a con-

171. Jean François de Troy's 'The Alarm' or 'The Faithful Governess', dated 1723 (the frame is contemporary), (518-1882).

fraternity of civic militia in Valencia dedicated to St George. Robinson was right about its good condition, but the light sponging did nothing to remove the darkened varnish and centuries of candle-soot, which were cleaned off in 1969-72 to reveal the marvellous bright gilding and crisp colours (plates 169 and 170). The vast work now dominates the main staircase area and Gothic primary galleries of the museum.

The idea of a teaching museum to help inspire good design, which stands at the beginning of the museum's history, did of course germinate at the height of the enthusiasm for the work of the painter Raphael. The ornamental work of Raphael was particularly singled out at the Schools of Design as being worthy of copying. Perhaps as a consequence of this, Robinson was offered some supposedly contemporary copies of the great Raphael cartoons. He turned them down on the grounds that they were in oil and therefore quite unlike the originals. He suggested that distemper copies be made because these would at least give the same effect as the originals. Perhaps Queen Victoria came to hear of this, or

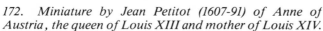

172. Miniature by Jean Petitot (1607-91) of Anne of Austria, the queen of Louis XIII and mother of Louis XIV.

173. Petitot's miniature of the Cardinal duc de Richelieu (1585-1624) (704-1882).

perhaps she was moved by the pious memory of the late Prince Albert's interest, both in Raphael and in the fledgling museum, for a year later she decided to lend it the originals from Hampton Court, and they have hung in the same large gallery ever since (plate 174).

The bequests of the Rev. Chauncy Hare Townsend (1869), a real magpie collector, who also bequeathed the museum a large collection of gem-stones, and of J. M. Parsons (1870), were responsible for the majority of foreign paintings in the galleries. Then, in 1882, John Jones died. This quiet bachelor, who had made a fortune out of military tailoring, had fallen in love with the art of the French Court under the three Louis, XIV, XV, and XVI. Plate 171 is of a typical example of his taste in pictures, bought as being by Watteau because of a later forged signature, but now known to be by Jean François de Troy. Jones's main competitor for this kind of French art was the immensely rich Lord Hertford, father of Richard Wallace and accumulator of the treasures in the Wallace Collection. Nonetheless Jones outbid him on a number of works, including this miniature by Petitot (plate 172). Jean Petitot (1607-91) was the most famous seventeenth-century miniature painter on enamel and did numerous portraits of Louis XIV, his family and court, a number of which are in the museum. This, and plate 173 of Cardinal Richelieu, are just two of a large group by Petitot collected by Jones, which taken together are a high point of the European miniature collection.

As was customary with donations and bequests to the museum up to the First World War, Jones stipulated that his collection should be kept together, not scattered around the relevant departments. This has its disadvantages, preventing the works of art from being put into their proper artistic context with other works of the same period, but as the years go by these individual collections become more interesting precisely as groups of objects epitomising the taste of the day. This has also happened with the collection bequeathed by Constantine Alexander Ionides (1833-1900). It consisted of 1,156 items — 300 drawings and watercolours, 750 prints, and 90 paintings. There was obviously no question of having the drawings, watercolours and prints on permanent display together, but the 90 paintings had to hang as a collection, according to the terms of the will, and this stipulation has been obeyed.

Ionides was the son and grandson of a successful Greek textile merchant who had settled in England. His father, Alexander, was already an enlightened art patron: his house, No 1 Holland Park, was decorated by Philip Webb, William Morris and Walter Crane (all three of whom were, of course, also involved with the

Overleaf: 174. Raphael's cartoon of the Miraculous Draft of Fishes. It is one of seven tapestry cartoons painted in 1515 and 1516, and lent to the museum by gracious permission of H.M. The Queen.

175

museum). In this house Ionides entertained G. F. Watts, Whistler and Rossetti as well as many other artists of the day.

His son Constantine, the museum's benefactor, worked in Greece and Turkey as a young man, looking after Alexander's business interests, then settled in England in 1864 and became a stockbroker. He was a tough energetic man — it was typical of him that he had a lathe at which he worked 'until his knuckles swelled' — and he had many interests besides art, such as astronomy. Most of his collecting was done during the years 1878 to 1884, and although he was not a very rich man he bought exceedingly well and from a wide range of schools. Predictably, he bought the works of family friends, G. F. Watts, Burne-Jones and Rossetti. Indeed, were it not for his bequest, the museum would have nothing by the Pre-Raphaelite school since it failed to buy anything on its own account. The collection also includes a work which belonged to Rossetti in the 1860s, Botticelli's portrait of Smeralda Bandinelli (1470), and an important work by the late fourteenth-century Italian artist, Nando di Cione. Seventeenth-century Holland and Flanders are well represented with an early Rembrandt (plate 175), an outstanding landscape with peasants by Louis Le Nain, and works by other artists such as Ostade, Brouwer and Terborch. There is one eighteenth-century work, a sketch by Domenico Tiepolo for the ceiling of San Lio in Venice (1783).

Ionides' close friend was Alphonse Legros, the French painter who became Professor at the Slade School of Art, and who taught him about French nineteenth-century painting. On his advice, Ionides bought, among many others, Delacroix's 'Shipwreck of Don Juan', Millet's 'Wood Sawyers', painted at Barbizon in 1850, and Dégas' 'Ballet Scene' from the opera *Robert le Diable* (1876). Thus, although his collection is relatively small, it is choice, and the authorities were very happy to waive the rather theoretical rule that they should only acquire works of art which were useful to the study of ornament.

George Salting's death on 12 December 1909 brought to practically every department of the museum the most distinguished collection of decorative arts to be formed in England at the end of the nineteenth and the beginning of the twentieth century. *The Times* obituary of 25 December said, 'he was the most striking instance in England of the collector *pur sang*. He gave his life up to collecting; he had scarcely another interest except that he sometimes allowed himself a few days shooting'. He regularly spent £7,000 a year on buying works of art, which was only £3,000 less than the museum's entire purchasing budget at the time.

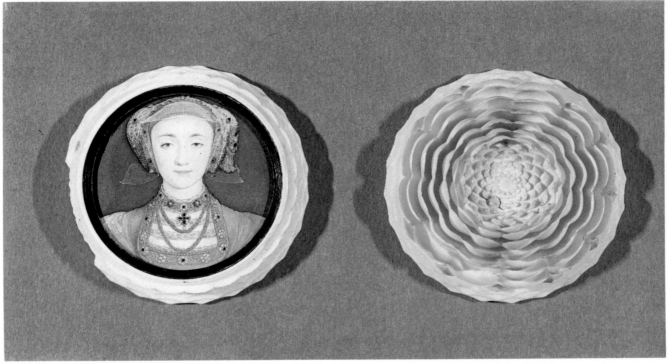

176

His collection included paintings, prints and drawings, besides decorative arts, and his will specified that the former should go to the National Gallery and the latter to the British Museum. This gave the director of the British Museum, Sidney Colvin, the opportunity to rush in with a letter on 23 December saying that in his opinion the miniatures, of which there was a very distinguished group, were drawings, not paintings or *objets d'art*, and that therefore they should go to his museum. Clearly, as over the medal collection, the British Museum was in an unsisterly mood. The Victoria and Albert Museum's director, Cecil Harcourt-Smith, emphatically rejected this suggestion. By 26 January, the exchange had become so acrimonious that Salting's executor entered the ring as referee, to separate the opponents, with a letter to Harcourt-Smith, saying that discussion with the British Museum authorities was 'not only useless but also calculated to affect your mutual relations to the benefit of neither of you — discuss it with me as much as you like — but take my advice and decline to discuss it with anyone else'.

In the end the matter had to go to law, and the Law Officer's Department, which included the famous lawyer, Rufus Isaacs, later Marquess of Reading, decided that the miniatures should go to the Victoria and Albert Museum, as clearly intended by Salting, on the sensible grounds that he was a connoisseur and presumably therefore knew what was what.

This collection consists of 85 miniatures, mostly English, and including a number of extremely famous ones. Plate 176 shows Anne of Cleves, one of only nine miniatures agreed to be by Holbein himself. It was painted in 1539 for Henry VIII who was looking for a

fourth wife and needed to know what his prospective bride looked like. Holbein was sent out to Düren, near Cologne, to paint a full-scale portrait, now in the Louvre, and this was probably done at the same time. Its history is well known back to 1739, when it belonged to the Barretts of Lee Priory. There it was seen by Horace Walpole, the antiquary and man of letters, who recommends to his friends the Misses Berry (28 September 1794) that they ask Mr Barrett to get it out for them, but 'It will be a great favour, and it must be a fine day, for it lives in cotton and clover, and he justly dreads exposing it to any damp'. In the 1830s it was bought by Francis Douce, the antiquary, who bequeathed it with other curiosities to Sir Samuel Rush Meyrick of Goderich Court. It was shown by his descendant Colonel Meyrick at the Manchester Art Treasures Exhibition in 1857, and finally by bequest came to belong to Miss Eleanor Davies who was persuaded to sell it to Salting for £3,250 in 1904. Interestingly enough, it had always been paired with a miniature of Henry VIII, but in 1901 the Meyrick household was burgled and this was stolen; at the time it was considered to be the more important of the two and it turned up a short time afterwards in the collection of the great American tycoon, Pierpoint Morgan. In 1953 it was sold, and then in 1975 chance reunited the two by the bequest of Mrs Hirschorn, although by now the Henry VIII has been demoted to 'after Holbein'.

177

177. Nicholas Hilliard's miniature 'Young Man Among the Roses', painted around 1588 in watercolour on vellum. The inscription around the top reads 'Dat poenas laudata fides'. Height: 5ins. (P163-1910).

The other stars of the Salting bequest are the miniatures by Nicholas Hilliard, Queen Elizabeth's 'limner', and easily the most famous English artist of the period. This full-scale study of a young man leaning against a tree among the rose-bushes (plate 177) embodies the spirit of the languishing love poetry of the day, although the exact message of the painting, with its inscription, is still being debated. So also is the identity of the young man, whom some think to be the Earl of Essex, others William Hatcliffe, possibly also the W. H. of Shakespeare's sonnets. Partly because it is so enigmatic and not just a beautiful work of art, this

is definitely the most popular of the museum's nine Hilliard miniatures, and has even moved some viewers to write poetry about it. Unlike the Anne of Cleves its previous history is unknown, but there is some evidence that it had previously belonged to a Dutch family for some generations.

The miniature collection continues beyond the sixteenth century to include representative examples of all the centuries during which they were painted until the collapse of the art form around 1860. There was a spectacular expansion in its popularity after the middle of the eighteenth century, so obviously only a tiny proportion of these later ones is on show. The Reserve Cabinet houses no fewer than forty drawers of them, but these are available for anyone to see who presents himself at the Print Room. The Print Room, being the descendant of the Art Library, which from the first was intended to be of practical use to students of design and art, has a tradition of welcoming visitors with the minimum of formality. Unlike at the Print Room at the British Museum, all that a prospective viewer needs to do is turn up, sign the book and order whatever print, drawing, engraving or photograph he wants to see.

Prints were originally collected by the library in the nineteenth century because they reproduced the work of great masters, such as the Raimondi engravings after Raphael, or because they were designs to be carried out in other media. Drawings were also collected for the same practical purpose, although quite a large fine art collection was accumulated despite repeated expressions of disapproval by the authorities. For example, in 1863 the Lords of the Committee of the Council on Education said, 'Future purchases should be confined to objects wherein Fine Art is applied to some purpose of utility . . . and works of Fine Art not so applied should only be admitted as exceptions and so far as they may tend directly to improve Art applied to objects of utility'; and in 1909 the Committee for Rearrangement said the same. This was to be the essential difference between the Victoria and Albert Museum's Print Room and that of the British Museum, which collects prints and drawings as examples of fine art.

One of the best collections of drawings to enter the museum was that of the Rev. Alexander Dyce (1869). He had connections with it through his cousin, the painter and administrator of the arts at South Kensington, William Dyce, R.A. He had been educated at Edinburgh and Oxford, and settled in London in 1825. His life's major work was the production of scholarly editions of English sixteenth- and seventeenth-century literature, but he was also an amateur flower and insect painter of some distinction, and a discriminating collector. His bequest included his whole literary library, some good watercolours, such as the museum's finest examples of Cozens and Gainsborough, some engravings, and about two hundred drawings. When the pen and bistre drawing in plate

179

180

179.   Design for a candlestick by G. M. Moser (1706-83), in pen and ink and brown wash, dated about 1745. See plate 32 (E4855-1968).

178 was in his collection it was thought to be by Antonio Pollaiuolo, but has now been reattributed to Bernardo Parentino (1437-1531).

The Keeper of the Library from 1868 to 1890, Robert Soden Smith, was also responsible for many of the Old Master drawings in the collection. Like Robinson, he was a compulsive collector, and if he saw something of quality he felt obliged to acquire it, even if it lay outside the museum's preserve. During his years in charge he added greatly to the 'art of the book' side of the library, buying fine bindings, manuscripts and examples of fine painting. 350 Italian drawings were also bought during his Keepership, of which only 150 are designs for ornament. He got this past their Lordships by simply failing to mention the fine art drawings when he made his annual report on acquisitions. Plate 165 is of one of his decorative art drawings, a design for arms, armour, horse trappings etc, for a pageant or triumph, originally thought to be by the great goldsmith Cellini because of its meticulous detail and finish.

So the drawings collection grew until in 1908 it numbered 50,000 works, and by now it must have

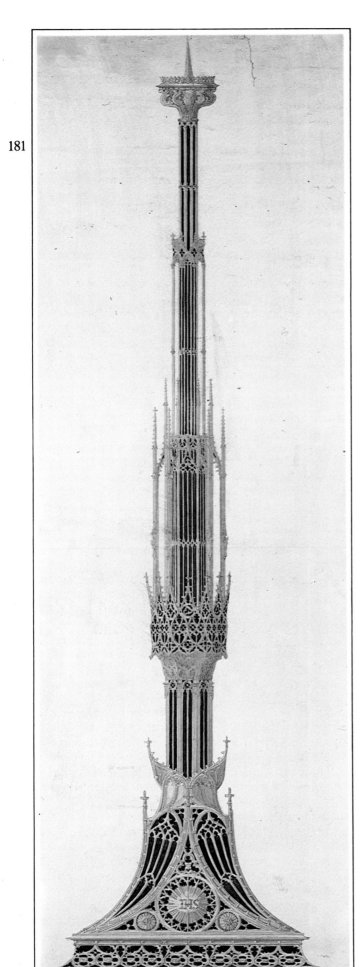

181

182

181. Design for an altar candlestick, by A.W. Pugin (1812-52) (E725-1925).
182. A page from 'Modelles Artificiels de divers vaissaux d'argent et autres oeuvres capricieuses' (Utrecht 1650), a book of engravings by Theodore de Quessel. It shows Adam van Vianen's design for an ewer (24334-1870).

doubled. Many, of course, are really working designs, of continuous use to the curators in other departments who often find the key to some art historical problem by searching through the material in the Print Room. In the 1960s, for example, the Textiles department reclassified a large group of eighteenth-century silks as English, when previously they had been thought to be French, by studying the silk designs in the Print Room. These are in two groups; the smaller includes 82 designs, of which the earliest is dated 1717, and the larger has 766, the latest dated 1756. For the most part they are the work of three people, James Leman, Christopher Baudouin and Anna Maria Garthwaite, and they give a fascinating picture of changing fashion, season by season (plate 180). Many of them also give technical instructions on how the design was to be carried out, and the names of the weavers and mercers who bought the designs, so they answer practically every question which could be asked about the Spitalfields silk industry. A number of the actual silks woven from them have been traced, including five in the Textiles department.

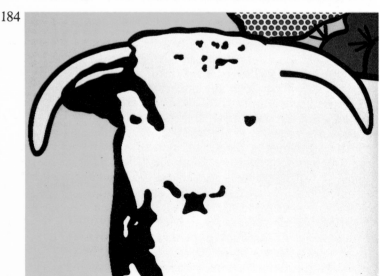

183

184

183. 'Discussing Dress' by John Banting, a collage and watercolour signed and dated 1937 (P16-1971).
184. 'Bull Head I. 1973' by the American artist Roy Lichtenstein, from a series of three such studies in colour lithograph and line block (E416-1976).

The presence of the Moser design for a candlestick (plate 179) also meant that when a set of four splendid candlesticks after that design turned up in the auction rooms in 1977, unmarked and unattributed, the Metalwork department made the connection, and, knowing the identity of the maker, carried the candlesticks off at the sale.

Other designs provide a record of the stages in the development of an artist's style. The pen, ink and watercolour drawings of an altar candlestick by Augustus Welby Pugin (plate 181) is a case in point. It dates from 1833, when he was only fifteen years old, so it shows his very earliest style, and it is *en suite* with designs by him for two chalices, a flagon, and an alms dish commissioned by Rundell, Bridge and Rundell, the King's Goldsmiths. It thus shows how highly his work was regarded, even at that tender age.

The working drawings are, of course, supplemented by thousands more prints. Soon after engraving was invented the medium was being used, in the second half of the fifteenth century, to reproduce ornamental designs for use by craftsmen. They were intended for goldsmith's work, woodwork, embroidery, jewellery, ceramic decoration, paintings on fans, in short everything which was decorated, which was practically everything. The museum has one of the largest collections in the world of these prints, comparable in size with those in Paris, Vienna and Berlin, and practically every stage in the development of the language of ornament is illustrated. A very great number was bought in the 1870s, 1880s and 1890s from the firm of Parsons at 35 Brompton Road. Soden Smith was also a regular buyer of fine bindings and drawings from these dealers, who went on selling to the museum into the 1930s. One of the early purchases, in 1870 for five guineas, was a book of engravings of Adam van Vianen's goldsmith's work, published in Utrecht in 1650 (plate 182). The family of van Vianens, Adam, Paul and Christaen were the most brilliant and inventive goldsmiths in seventeenth-century northern Europe, and this is a tantalising record of what many of Adam's lost works looked like.

There is no space here to cover in detail the complete range of this department: its wallpapers, its cuttings from manuscripts, its portrait engravings, its architectural drawings, its playing cards, jig-saw puzzles and topographical engravings. Practically all aspects of the collections, except oil paintings, are still being added to, but the bulk of the purchase grant now goes on twentieth-century purchases. The gaps in the watercolour collections for the 1920s and 1930s, for example, need to be filled. Among recent acquisitions is a collage and watercolour by the English painter, John Banting, who lived in Paris during that period and was one of the very few English exponents of Surrealism (plate 183). The Circulation department had of course always acquired the work of contemporary artists, such as the John Piper (plate 185) acquired in 1940, and the department has increased the number of acquisi-

185

185.   'The Cottage by the Railway, Great Bedwyn', a water-colour drawing by John Piper. About 1940 (Circ 29-1940).

tions. One of the aims in buying a work is to illustrate all the many and varied media now being used. 'Bull Head 1' (plate 184), for example, is a colour lithograph and line block, and at the time of writing the department is staging an exhibition of the use of photography in printmaking. The curatorial staff who mounted it took advantage of the fact that this was an absolutely contemporary theme, and went to interview print-makers and printers who used this technique, such as Eduardo Paolozzi, Stanley Jones, Chris Prater and Michael Rothenstein. Having the resources of the his-torical collection behind them, they could also pro-duce examples which illustrated the development of photo-mechanical printing through calotype negative, photo-lithography, photogravure and so on.

An exhibition like this brings the conventional prints and drawings side of the department very close to its new subsection which deals with photography. This has recently been incorporated in the title of the department in its second change of name since 1909, when it was called the Department of Engravings, Illustration and Design; in 1960 it became the Depart-ment of Prints and Drawings, and in 1977 the Depart-ment of Prints, Drawings, Paintings and Photo-

graphy. At that point it took over the responsibility for the last of the pictorial material collected by the library, the photographs. This collection had begun with perhaps the earliest photographs to be printed for art historical purposes, the *Minutolische Vorbilder*, portfolios of photographs of exhibits in the Minutoli Institute, a tiny decorative arts museum founded in Liegnitz in Silesia in 1895. The library had constantly added to these, and because the early days of the museum coincided with the pioneering days of photography, sheer age, if nothing else, would have made part of the collection interesting (plate 187). In the 1960s and 1970s photography has become generally recognised as an art form, and the price of certain kinds of photographs has risen hugely, stimulating interest in the whole subject. Thus it was decided to take these old photographs away from the library and put them under a new Assistant Keeper who would also have a budget with which to buy photographs *qua* works of art. (The Science Museum continues to be

187

188

186. The Wyndham Sisters, 1950, a photograph (silverprint) by Sir Cecil Beaton (1904-80). Left to right: Mrs John Wyndham, Lady Cranbourne, Lady Roderick Pratt, photographed in a setting reminiscent of the famous Sargent portrait of their second cousins 'The Wyndham Sisters'. 9¾ ins. by 7⅞ ins. (192-1977).

187. A&P, New York City, Winter 1975-6. C-type colour photograph. From 'Cars', a portfolio of 13 prints by Langdon F. Clay, an American photographer born in 1949. It was published by Caldecott Chubb, New York, in 1977. 9ins. by 13¾ ins. (X 940).

188. Scientist in his Study. A hand-tinted stereoscopic daguerrotype dating from the 1850s, and attributed to John Benjamin Dancer (1812-87). 2¾ ins. by 2¼ ins. (243-1979).

responsible for examples which merely illustrate technical innovation, and the National Portrait Gallery for portraiture.) Four thousand photographs have been collected in the last four years and they fall basically into four categories: masterpieces, such as the widely admired work of Julia Margaret Cameron, which should be available to the public in the original, not in reproductions or later prints made from her negatives; photographs enshrining aesthetic and social values, such as the Cecil Beaton of the three debutante sisters which derives its composition from a famous Sargent portrait of three beautiful sisters (plate 186);

photographs showing changes in taste and critical awareness, and the different 'states' possible with a print, such as a softly tinted Bill Brandt photograph of the 1930s, and an expressionist, highly contrasted print made from the same negative twenty or thirty years later; photographs which serve the departments of the museum, such as fashion or interior design; and lastly photographs by contemporaries. Here, even more than with painters and printmakers, the museum can introduce the general public to a highly specialised and, as yet, rather unknown world, and open its eyes to a huge range of developing possibilities (plate 188).

189. *A page from the book of hours of*
Margaret of Foix. French, 1470-80 (L2285-1910).

10
The Library

The Victoria and Albert Museum Library and the British Museum Library have always had a very different tone. There are numerous anedotes illustrating the exclusivity and elitism of the British Museum during the early decades of its existence, and not surprisingly the same attitudes ruled in its library (now detached and called the British Library). For example, in 1835 Sir Henry Ellis, its principal librarian, produced the following answer when asked whether the reading room might not remain open in the evenings so that working men could use it: 'My own opinion is that the Museum library is rather too much used than too little used.' Late opening would attract 'a class of persons for whom it would be hardly necessary to provide such a library as that of the British Museum; they would be lawyers' clerks, and persons who would read voyages and travels, novels and light literature; a class, I conceive, the Museum library was not intended for'. Forsooth, people might actually enjoy themselves there!

By comparison, the library of the Victoria and Albert Museum has always had a more open and liberal attitude towards readers. Even now any member of the public may enter it with no more formality than signing the visitors' book; he may consult the catalogues, and order almost any of the books down to his desk in the reading room. By contrast at the British Library references are required, photographs taken, identity cards issued. The sharply different attitudes of the two libraries are explained by the quite distinct purposes for which they were founded. The library at the Victoria and Albert Museum is called the National Art Library, and it is a much smaller and more specialised affair, containing mainly books which are relevant to the study of the arts. It was founded in 1837 at exactly the same time as the Schools of Design in Somerset House, with a specifically educational and practical purpose in mind. The Schools were granted money to buy plaster casts, which were the origin of the museum, and books, which were the origin of the library. In 1843 the Schools' third director, Charles Heath Wilson, made it a lending library, which must have been a great help to the students, who were mostly from the upper artisan class. Heath Wilson's idea was not, however, to produce learned men, but to stimulate their understanding and sense of beauty in the most practical way possible. The Annual Report for that

year states sensibly that the 'ornamentist' (as the student was called) was to be educated 'not to write but to work', but that 'the degree of excellence of that which his hand executes is dependent on a correspondent superiority of his suggestive and thinking faculties'. The means were to be provided in 'appropriate and judiciously selected books'. The contrast with the British Museum could not be greater: this was to be a practical library, a supplementary tool for the craftsman, rather than a universal library for learned men.

The beginnings were very small. In March 1845 there were 200 books housed uncomfortably 'in a small ante-room, constantly open as a passage', but 'a convenient ladder with carpeted steps was provided, and the room was efficiently lighted by gas from the ceiling'. By November 1846 it had 850 volumes — 'treatises on the history, theoretic principles and practice of Fine Art in general, elementary manuals on Architecture, Practical Geometry, Optics, Perspective, Anatomy and every obtainable work on the application of art to manufactures and decoration' (this of course was the *raison d'être* of the Schools and the Museum); it also included works 'conducive to mental elevation and refinement such as critical essays on Beauty, Taste and Imagination; the works of some of the great descriptive Poets . . . and, for the excitement of emulation, Biographies of Artists and others, who by genius and perseverance have acquired honourable distinction'.

These confident and improving sentiments were not, however, matched by a corresponding confidence on the part of the teachers, or a willingness to be improved on the part of the students: Heath Wilson was unable to get on with his staff, there were riots in the classrooms, and many of the books were cannibalised, reduced to 'mere fragments, or texts without plates, owing to the . . . usage of cutting up books of plates for the sake of furnishing the classes with examples'.

The first reform of the Schools took place: in 1852 they moved to Marlborough House under the firm directorship of Cole, who appointed the first full time librarian, Ralph Wornum, originally a violent critic of his, but now won round to his team. An important decision was made, still in effect today, to make the library open to the public use; Cole was firmly committed to populist policies, not least because he was an

191. A page from Picolpasso's Li
Tri Libri dell'arte del Vasaio.
Italian (Casteldurante) (1556-9).

empire-builder and they gave him the greatest leverage with the Treasury. The reactions of one rather pious-sounding working man to this benevolent facility have come down to us. 'When I was a journey man in London', remembers Harry Hems, a woodcarver, 'I always spent my evenings and Saturday afternoons there. The majority of my fellow-toilers used to vote one very foolish and wondered why I pored over books when . . . I might "enjoy" myself with them.'

To assist men such as this with their researches Ralph Wornum produced a classified catalogue of books in 1855. This listed them under headings in general categories such as Architecture or Sculpture, and was the ancestor of the subject index. While compiling his work Wornum obviously became aware of the categories in which the library was weak, and he set it on the path towards becoming an academic art historical library, not so much because he expected people like Harry the woodcarver to read art literature, but 'those well able to serve the masses might'.

Art history was still in its infancy so to some extent he had to decide for himself what range the collections should have, but he had a few guidelines and was not working with completely unsifted material. Despite the fact that this was a decorative art museum, it was obvious that books on the fine arts, painting, sculpture and architecture had to provide the core of the collection. The earliest books on these subjects were of course the technical treatises, such as the *Schedula diversarum artium*, written by a Rhenish priest called Theophilus in the twelfth century, or Piccolpasso's *Three Books on the Art of the Potter* (1556-9) (plate 191). This important illustrated manuscript, subsequently often reprinted in facsimile, was one of J. C. Robinson's coups, found in 1859 in Casteldurante, and used by him in his catalogue of maiolica which was never completed.

But students of art history needed to know not only the technical side of the arts, but also the lives of previous great artists, so the early biographies of artists were a necessity: Vasari, Bellori and Baldinucci for Italy; van Mander and Houbraken in the Netherlands; Neudorfer and Sandrart in Germany; Vertue and Walpole in England. Most useful of all were the artists' own reactions to works of art, such as the thoughts and sketches of the painter James Thornhill (1676-1734) decorator of among other things the cupola of St Paul's Cathedral, as he toured the Netherlands in 1711 (plate 190).

The student must also be able to refer to the works of art themselves, and this in the nineteenth century tended to mean portfolios of engravings, such as Raphael's works engraved by Raimondi, or books with engraved illustrations such as *The Supplement to Antiques explained* and represented in *Sculptures* by the learned Father Montfaucon (London 1725), a large work in five volumes whose illustrations were an essential source for eighteenth-century architects and artists, and which in turn is now a vital source for art

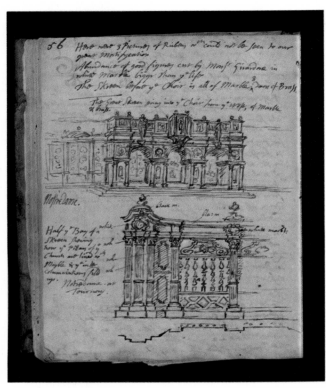

190

190.   James Thornhill's manuscript diary of his journey through the Netherlands in 1711. This page shows a sketch of the choir screen in the church of Notre Dame at Tournay.

historians interpreting the same artists and architects. The library therefore acquired as many works of this kind as possible (plate 192), as well as catalogues of collections, from the one-franc pocket-size catalogues of the Revolutionary Musée Central in Paris to the expensive and now rare catalogue of the Duke of Marlborough's engraved gems.

Art has, at least until the twentieth century, always had to have a subject matter, and to provide all the necessary reference works for tracing the subjects the library had to stray well beyond books on art in the narrow sense. To take one example: throughout the Middle Ages and well into the seventeenth century the most common source for the iconography of religious art was the Bible, and of secular art, Ovid's 'Metamorphoses.' Not only, therefore, does one need copies of both in order to identify inscriptions, personages and events, but the copies must be illustrated, because in the sixteenth and seventeenth centuries the woodcuts and engravings were copied and recopied by craftsmen working in all the arts. Plate 193 shows one of these, the *Metamorphoses* published in Lyons by Jean de Tournes in 1557, which is also an example of fine printing. For similar reasons, works on history, and sixteenth- and seventeenth-century emblem literature, which combined visual images with a concise poetic phrase or 'conceit', are important.

p che glie da sapere che si come
questa Citta e libera
signiora e Regina
di se medesma.

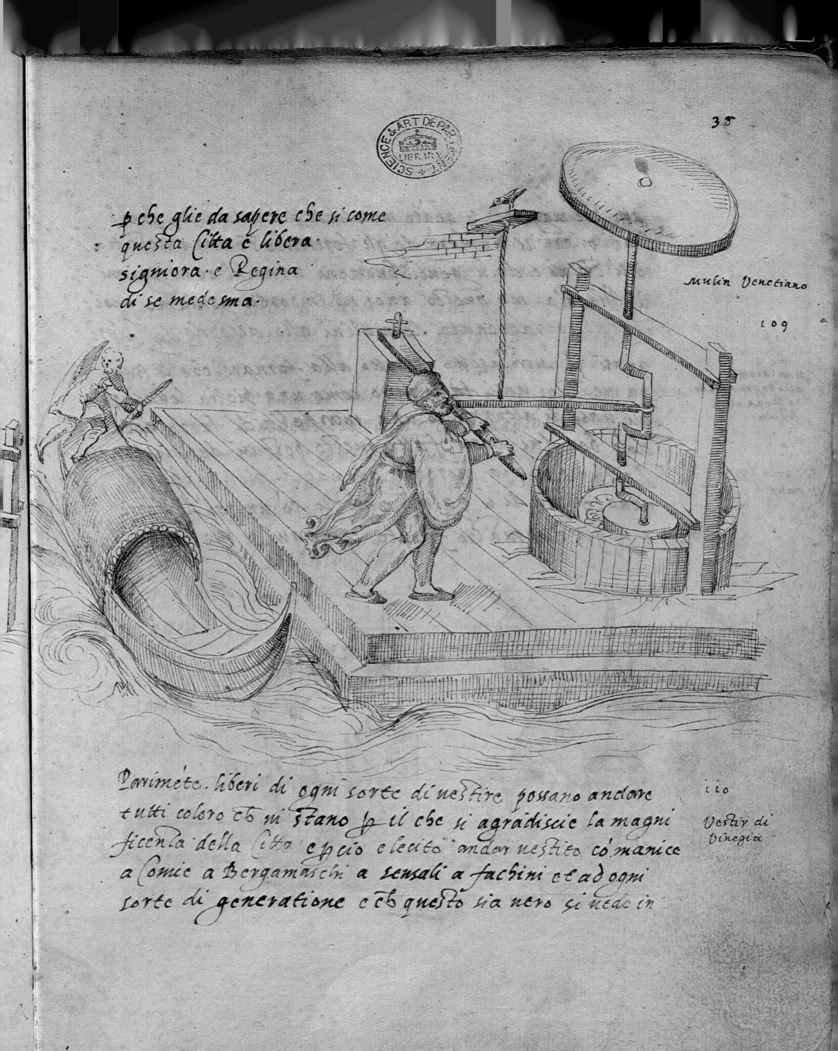

mulin Venetiano

109

Parimeto. liberi di ogni sorte di nestire possano andare
tutti coloro ch ni stano p il che si agradiscie la magni
ficentia della Citta e cio e lecito andar nestito co manice
a Comic a Bergamaschi a sensali a fachini e ad ogni
sorte di generatione e ch questo sia nero si nede in

iio

Vestir di
binegia

192

*192. A page from the sketchbooks of Sir J. A. Crowe and
C. B. Cavalcaselle's* History of Italian Painting, *c.1860-80.*

The study of anatomy and of perspective were vital
to artists and architects from the Renaissance
onwards. It was axiomatic in art schools until recently
that no one could depict a man satisfactorily with his
clothes on until he fully comprehended the
musculature and proportions beneath. So the museum
collected and still collects works on both these
sciences: Vesalius' *De Humani Corporis Fabrica* (the
1543 edition) with the woodcuts by Titian's pupil,
John Stephen of Calcar, and Dürer's and Alberti's
perspective manuals.

Heraldry, the chivalrous visual language of
ownerships, can tell us where a painting or a silver
chalice or a maiolica plate came from, so an important
heraldic reference library was also gradually built up.
Engravings after the old masters have already been

mentioned, but the library also collected books and
sheets of engraved and drawn ornament by masters
such as the sixteenth-century Virgil Solis from
Nürnberg, and the seventeenth-century Adam van
Vianen from Utrecht (see plate 182). It was also in the
vanguard of collecting photographs made for art
historical purposes.

Wornum was not, however, to remain to see the
library filled with all the books in these categories, for
in 1854 he was appointed Keeper of the National
Gallery. In 1857 the museum moved from Marlborough House to South Kensington. The Brompton
boilers provided no satisfactory space for the library,
and so the first accommodation for the 6,000 books,
2,200 prints and 1,000 photographs was temporary.
Eventually they were moved to a makeshift area
partitioned off from the galleries at the north-east
corner of the site. For twenty-five years they remained
there in profound gloom. According to one user of the
library: 'The small portion of the rays of the sun that is
allowed to struggle in is through the deadened glass of
the skylights of the museum itself, and then through a
vertical glass window that separates the reading room
from the Court of the main building.'

J. C. Robinson was nominally in charge in his
capacity as Superintendent of the Art Museum, but in
practice his assistant, R. H. Soden Smith, must have
been responsible for the running of the library as
Robinson was continually away on buying trips.
Robert Henry Soden Smith was a perfect example of a
nineteenth-century English gentleman, singled out for
his 'conspicuous courtesy and unruffled temper,' with
which qualities he made the cramped conditions
tolerable to readers. He was an artistic all-rounder: a
naturalist who specialised in fresh-water shell-fish, an
art-collector; and the author of a slim volume of verse
called *Flowers and Posies.*

During this period Cole hit on a scheme for
drawing official public attention to the library and its
wants, which led to its scope being greatly enlarged.
His partner in this scheme was the architect and minor
Pre-Raphaelite John Hungerford Pollen, to whom
Cole had been introduced by his friend and neighbour,
the famous novelist William Thackeray. Pollen was
employed as General Superintendent of Catalogues —
he himself wrote a catalogue of the gold- and
silversmiths' work in the museum (published in 1878)
— and under his supervision a number of elegant
leather-bound catalogues of aspects of the collections,
with etchings by students of the South Kensington Art
School, appeared during the 1870s.

Cole and he had a better and more ingenious idea
where the library was concerned than merely writing
another catalogue which would be out of date almost
before it was printed. Instead, they would write a
universal catalogue. As Pollen wrote: 'There is but one
way of meeting such a difficulty of cataloguing the
collections. It is by making the catalogue complete,
and gradually bringing the library up to the range of

Het hueuerspel van Mars en Venus.

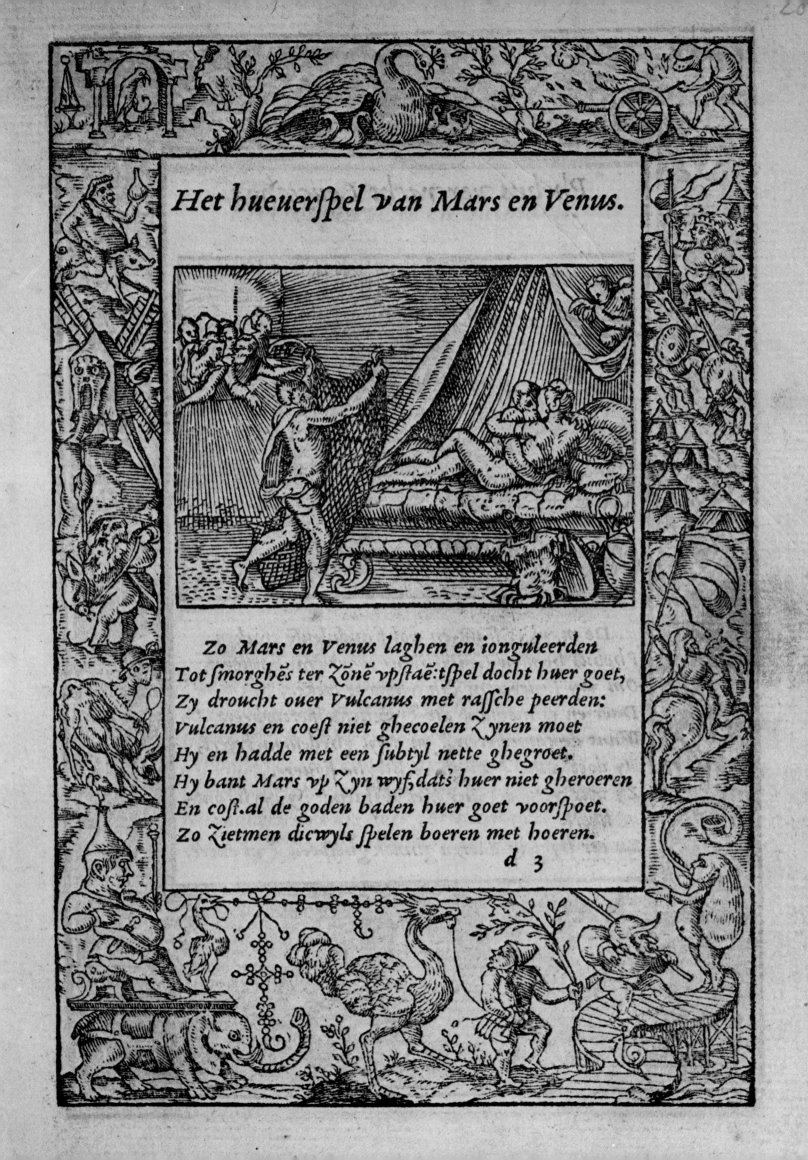

Zo Mars en Venus laghen en ionguleerden
Tot smorghĕs ter Zōnĕ vpstaĕ:tspel docht huer goet,
Zy droucht ouer Vulcanus met rassche peerden:
Vulcanus en coest niet ghecoelen Zynen moet
Hy en hadde met een subtyl nette ghegroet.
Hy bant Mars vp Zyn wyf,dats huer niet gheroeren
En cost.al de goden baden huer goet voorspoet.
Zo Zietmen dicwyls spelen boeren met hoeren.

d 3

194. *One of the present-day reading rooms in the library.*

195

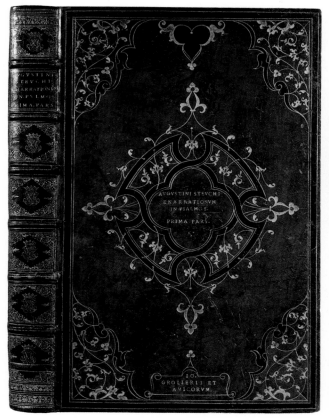

196

195. *The binding of a book belonging to the great collector Jean Grolier, Viscomte d'Aguisy. French, 1550-60 (L3395-1921).*
196. *An Italian book of hours, illuminated for the Serristori family in about 1500 (L1722-1921).*

the catalogue.' This topsy-turvy method of proceeding would have been impossible at that time for a more general library such as the British Museum's, and would be quite unthinkable now even for an art library, because of the quantity of works being published every year. Then it was just about a feasible proposition and it was certainly a brilliant publicity campaign by Cole. Pollen employed a team of hacks who transcribed for tuppence an entry the entries from the printed catalogues of all the libraries in Europe, the British Museum, the Bodleian in Oxford and other libraries elsewhere.

The opinions of eighty English art historians and thirty foreign ones were then solicited. Most sent their best wishes but little in the way of constructive suggestions. Only one, Bernard Quaritch the bookseller, whose business still flourishes, sent detailed criticism suggesting that professional bibliographical standards be observed; but he was ignored.

Eventually the A to B sections were published in the advertising columns of the front page of 'The Times', proof if it were needed that this was something of a publicity stunt. Later portions appeared more obscurely in 'Notes and Queries' or were printed by Her Majesty's Stationery Office. This hefty alphabetical 'Universal Catalogue of Books on Art' appeared in book form in July 1870, increasing the library in importance so far as both the public and the authorities were concerned. In keeping with this new

importance, Cole renamed it the National Art Library, the title which it has maintained to the present day.

Meanwhile there was a shift of power going on inside the museum; J. C. Robinson was toppled in 1867 and Soden Smith was appointed Keeper of the Library in 1868. He remained in charge until his death in 1890, and at the very end of his term the authorities finally heeded his repeated complaints about the inadequate accommodation. In 1884 he and his by now very large collections moved into the three rooms still used by the library (plate 194). The middle one, where the catalogues and card indexes are now kept, contained prints and photographs, while the outer ones were both reading rooms; the western reading room is now used for book stacks and offices, and desks have been fitted into the central room instead.

Soden Smith was an eminent collector of books if not an eminent librarian in the organisational sense, and his twenty-two years in office were marked by many distinguished purchases of prints, drawings and photographs and of specimens of the art of the book — fine illumination, binding, typography and illustration. He was principally interested in fifteenth- and sixteenth-century books of the type such as the Book of Hours for the Serristori family, with its fine calligraphy and illumination (plate 196) (actually a later acquisition), or the illuminated manuscript of Pliny's *Natural History,* painted in Siena around 1460-70, with initials that show craftsmen and farm labourers at work.

197 and 198.   The binding on Luther's translation of the Bible, executed for the Duke of Savoy. German, 1583 (AM4057-1856). Plate 198 shows the decorated fore-edge of this book.

During his keepership the library was bequeathed three remarkable collections. The first and smallest was a group of illustrated books left by the Rev. Chauncy Hare Townsend (died 1868) who is even more prominent in the annals of the present Painting department because he bequeathed them a number of Swiss and German nineteenth-century paintings. The next was the working library of the Rev. Alexander Dyce (1798-1869) a shadowy figure on the outskirts of the English literary scene. His researches were into classical scholarship and playwrights, and Elizabethan and Jacobean poets whose works he edited. Besides numerous printed works the collection includes some manuscript material such as a Shakespeare quarto and a poetical miscellany with verses by John Donne.

In 1876 this was augmented by another literary library, that of John Forster, critic, journalist, historian, and a friend and biographer of Dickens. It includes standard works to be found in a mid-Victorian library as well as the manuscripts of Dickens's novels. It is still extremely useful to be able

199. Two facing pages from P. S. Fournier's
Manuel Typographique *(Paris 1764-66).*
200. A rococo binding on E. Montagu's An Essay
on Shakespeare *(London 1770) (AM 163-1864).*

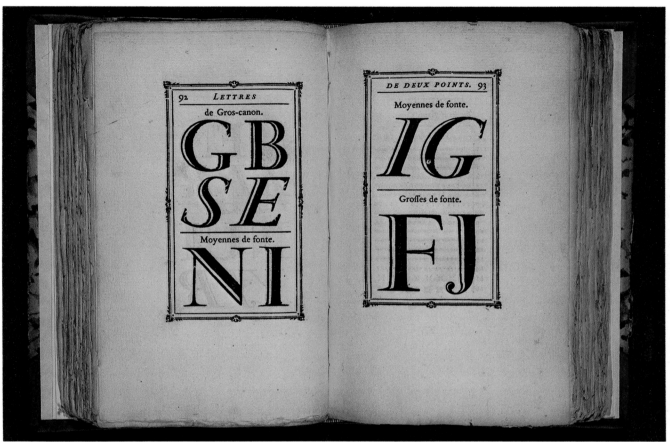

199

200

to use these two nineteenth-century gentlemen's libraries, whose range wanders much wider than the already fairly ample confines of the ordinary collections.

Not surprisingly Soden Smith was anxious to have somewhere to display these sumptuous works — a gallery for the 'Art of the Book' — but he was unsuccessful in getting this, and it was not until the reorganisation of 1909 that a gallery was set aside for this purpose.

After his death in 1890 he was succeeded by a very different sort of man, one who, far from being an urbane diplomat, was described thus in his obituary (1917): 'It may be fully admitted that Mr Weale was not fitted for official life. He was skilled neither in the art of concealing his opinions nor in paying deference to official superiors with whom he disagreed. As a chief, unsparing towards himself, he exacted industry from others . . . indolence joined with incapacity effectively aroused him. His naturally suitable temper could indeed blaze into a furnace of just anger; as when an unwary vendor of obscene prints who had penetrated to his room was pursued by him, shouting with fury, through the reading rooms.'

William Henry James Weale was a lean tall figure with sloping shoulders, clad in a grey coat of unfashionable cut, moving with a shambling gait on out-turned feet; a full grey beard; and short-sighted eyes peering through spectacles from beneath the

201

201. Le Rime *by Cardinal Bembo (Italian c. 1540), which was acquired as a fine example of Renaissance humanist handwriting.*

widest brim imaginable of a black felt hat. He was already a well-known scholar when appointed at the advanced age of fifty-eight, an authority on the Van Eycks, the restoration of historic buildings, monumental brasses, ecclesiastical goldsmiths' work, bookbinding, Flemish and Rhenish pottery, Flemish bells and bell-founders and liturgical studies. This breadth of knowledge combined with a professional approach to librarianship made it especially unfortunate that he fell out with his superiors, in particular the head of the Department of Practical Art, Sir John Donnelly, and was retired the moment he reached the age of sixty-five.

His skills were especially needed where the cataloguing was concerned. Soden Smith had limited himself in a happy-go-lucky way to putting the shelf-mark beside the entry in the *Universal Catalogue* as the books came into the library. Weale considered that this amateurish way of proceeding had gone on long enough, established cataloguing rules based on those in force at the British Museum Library and started the card cataloguing which is now used by all readers. He also set about revising the classified catalogue begun by Wornum, and had thirty-three in preparation at one time; but he laboured under certain difficulties about which he complained frequently. When Soden Smith's old assistant retired, Weale was prevented from filling the post with a man who had been trained up in his department, but instead had inflicted on him a man who worked elsewhere in the museum and knew nothing about books. Promotion was then by an examination, which included a drawing test — a relic of pre-photography days, and of the essentially practical origins of the museum. The offending new man had done particularly well at copying the famous advertisement for Pear's soap showing a woman scrubbing a dirty boy. As a constant irritant Weale also had Donnelly's nephew in the library, compiling a catalogue of engraved portraits, and receiving a larger salary than Weale.

Altogether the museum was at a low ebb and Weale was a ferocious member of the reform party. He

202

*202. An initial from an illuminated missal
written for the use of the Abbey of St Dénis,
Paris, 1350. It was acquired in 1891 under
Weale's librarianship (AM1346-1891).*

203. *The* Victoria Psalter, *designed and illuminated by the artist, designer and theorist Owen Jones, 1861.*

testified bluntly before the Select Committee set up by Parliament to look into its affairs. Indeed, what he had to say was usually so contentious that the room was cleared of spectators when he stood up to testify. No one, however, could stop Donnelly getting rid of him in August 1897 on the pretext that he had reached retirement age, although the Committee said it was 'a grave public scandal'. Donnelly was too formidable to be circumvented and the resolutions of the Select Committee came to nothing until he also reached retirement in 1899. The museum, and the library with it, continued to languish until 1903 when Cecil Harcourt-Smith was appointed to reorganise both. It was after this that the present departments were created and Prints and Drawings were hived off from the library to the new department of Engraving, Illustration and Design, now called the Departments of Prints, Drawings, Photographs and Painting. The logical completion of this process was in 1977 when photographs were also reallocated from the library, and a new assistant Keepership created to look after them.

There was to be one more innovation, under Weale's successor, George Palmer, who abandoned the thirty-three incomplete classified catalogues and began the multi-volume Subject Index to books in the library; this continues to be a most useful tool for students. Under Palmer the library also acquired the bulk of its collection of 129 medieval illuminated manuscripts, largely through the generosity of George Reid, who in 1902 bequeathed 83 of them, for the most part fifteenth-century books of hours. George Salting's vast bequest to the museum also included two illuminated pages and four complete manuscripts, of which plate 202 is one. It is one of the museum's great books of hours, made in France around 1470-80 for Margaret of Foix.

An odd and unexpected collection which arrived in 1910 was that of the celebrated swordsman Captain Alfred Hutton. Stage managers and directors of historical films would do well to consult its many illustrated treatises on the art of fencing and swordplay through the centuries.

The next fifty years were a period of consolidation for the whole museum, the library included. Examples of the art of the book continued to be collected in keeping with changing artistic tastes (plate 203). Under the influence of the Deputy Keeper of the Library, the calligrapher James Wardrop, the museum acquired a manuscript copy of Cardinal Bembo's *Rime* (plate 201), whose fine clear humanist hand typifies the Renaissance and its scholars of antiquity. As the nineteenth century came back into fashion the museum bought the architectural phantasy *St Marie's College* (plate 204) by Augustus Welby Pugin (1834) who was, of course, intimately associated with the early years of the museum.

The library was also in the forefront of collecting that new invention, the *livre d'artiste*. This emerged

204

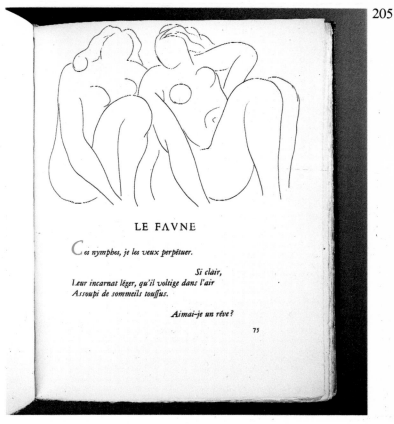

205

LE FAVNE

C es nymphes, je les veux perpétuer.

Si clair,
Leur incarnat léger, qu'il voltige dans l'air
Assoupi de sommeils touffus.

Aimai-je un rêve?

75

204.   *A plate from A. W. Pugin's* St Marie's College, *a sketchbook with ink drawings for an imaginary architectural project (1834) (L5175-1969).*
205.   Poèmes *by S. Mallarmé, illustrated by Henri Matisse (Lausanne, 1932).*

from France, a conscious attempt to produce the book as a work of art, normally with a rather rarefied text, such as some well-chosen verses, or a part or the whole of some well-established classic. The illustrations are

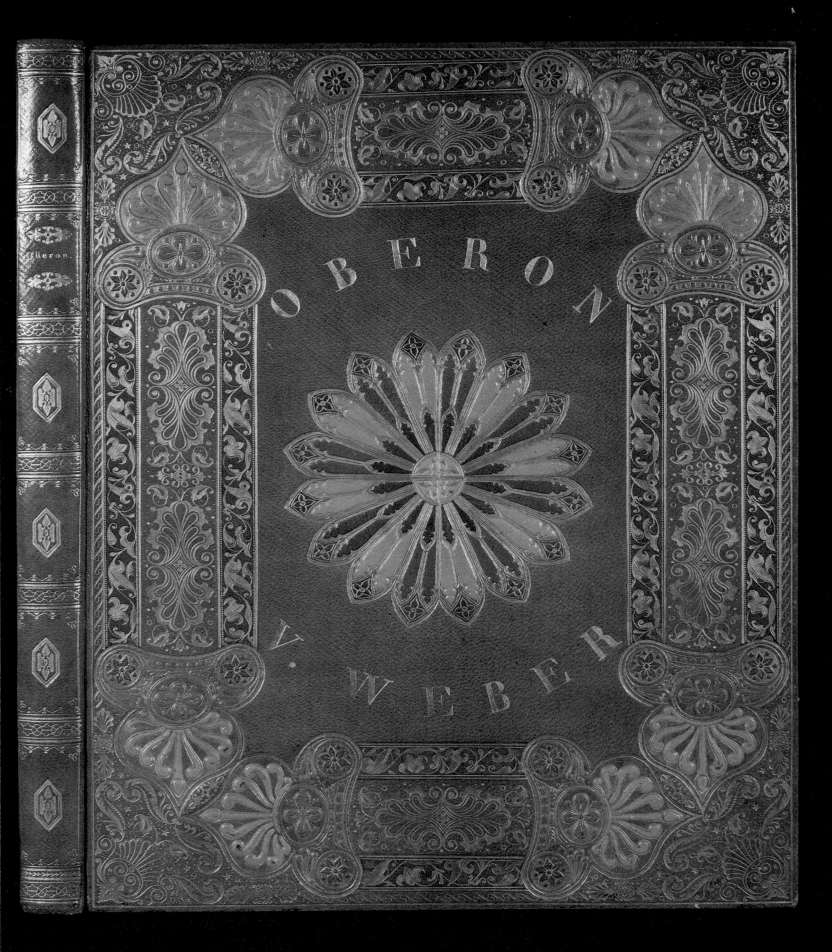

206. *A German binding of c. 1826 by Johann Jacob Selencka of Brunswick: Weber's opera* Oberon *(L5175-1969).*

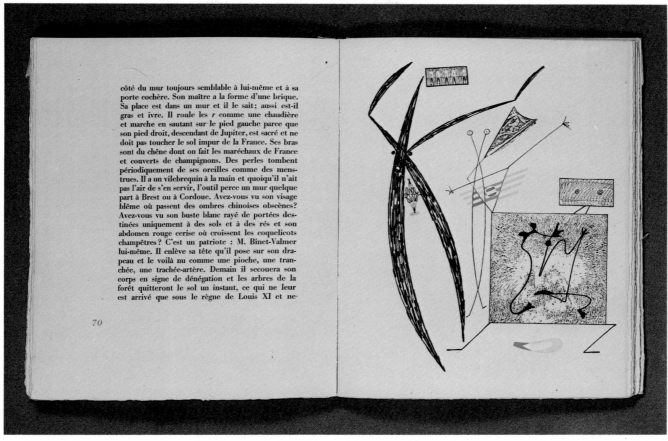

côté du mur toujours semblable à lui-même et à sa porte cochère. Son maître a la forme d'une brique. Sa place est dans un mur et il le sait; aussi est-il gras et ivre. Il roule les r comme une chaudière et marche en sautant sur le pied gauche parce que son pied droit, descendant de Jupiter, est sacré et ne doit pas toucher le sol impur de la France. Ses bras sont du chêne dont on fait les maréchaux de France et couverts de champignons. Des perles tombent périodiquement de ses oreilles comme des menstrues. Il a un vilebrequin à la main et quoiqu'il n'ait pas l'air de s'en servir, l'outil perce un mur quelque part à Brest ou à Cordoue. Avez-vous vu son visage blême où passent des ombres chinoises obscènes? Avez-vous vu son buste blanc rayé de portées destinées uniquement à des sols et à des rés et son abdomen rouge cerise où croissent les coquelicots champêtres? C'est un patriote : M. Binet-Valmer lui-même. Il enlève sa tête qu'il pose sur son drapeau et le voilà nu comme une pioche, une tranchée, une trachée-artère. Demain il secouera son corps en signe de dénégation et les arbres de la forêt quitteront le sol un instant, ce qui ne leur est arrivé que sous le règne de Louis XI et ne-

70

207

208

207. La Brèbis galante *by Benjamin Peret, illustrated by Max Ernst (Paris, Éditions Premières, 1949).*
208. *A binding on the* Apocryphal *commissioned by the museum from Sybil Pye, 1934 (L494-1938).*

specially commissioned from a 'fine artist', great attention is paid to the paper, typography and binding, and normally only a small number are printed, partly because of the high cost of production and sometimes deliberately to increase the works' value as an investment.

The museum owns one of the earliest of these creations, *Parallèlement,* with poetry of a faintly erotic nature by Verlaine and lithographs by Bonnard (plate 209). Among the large subsequent collections are Mallarmé's verses illustrated by Matisse (plate 205) and Peret's *La Brèbis galante* with abstract illustrations by Max Ernst (plate 207). The art of fine binding continues today, but the craft is so limited and so expensive that the library generally commissions examples. One such is plate 208, showing the work of Sybil Pye in 1934.

Children's books have always had a place in the museum as examples of illustration, but in the late 1950s the collection became really representative when Guy Little, a friend of Gabrielle Enthoven, whose collection formed the nucleus of the Theatre Museum, bequeathed his children's books which included large numbers from the late eighteenth and early nineteenth

209.   *Paul Verlaine's* Parallèlement *(Paris,*
(Vollard, 1900) with lithographs by Pierre Bonnard.

209

Ne fronce plus ces sourcils-ci,
Casta, ni cette bouche-ci,
Laisse-moi puiser tous tes baumes,
Piana, sucrés, salés, poivrés,
Et laisse-moi boire, poivrés,
Salés, sucrés, tes sacrés baumes.

33

210   *Drawing from an unpublished work by Beatrix Potter,*
c. *1900.*

centuries. It was partly the existence of this collection of children's books in the museum which prompted the Beatrix Potter enthusiast, Leslie Linder, to give to the museum all his material to do with this famous children's author and illustrator (plate 210). It is an especially suitable resting place for this collection, since Beatrix Potter was a frequent visitor to the museum, and it was here that she sketched the eighteenth-century costumes which later appeared in *The Tailor of Gloucester.*

While these generous gifts came to the library, its stock-in-trade of art historical books continued to be built up until, not surprisingly, in the late 1960s it was again bursting out of its accommodation. Three floors of bookstacks were ingeniously inserted into the very high Medieval Court, Room 43, using the space right up to its barrel-vaulted ceiling. The ground floor is now a modern gallery devoted to early medieval art in a space vaguely evocative of a basilica with its two rows of columns. The original grand nineteenth-century interior, sadly, is completely obscured. Now, in 1980, shelf space is running out again and it looks as though the two vast galleries on either side, Far Eastern and Middle Eastern Art respectively, are threatened with similar schemes.

Nowadays the National Art Library in the Victoria and Albert Museum is just one of many similar institutions: the libraries of the many universities with art history faculties cater for the same needs, and as early as the 1850s the art libraries of the academies of Berlin and Vienna, the Städel Institute in Frankfurt and the Conservatoire des Arts et Métiers in Paris were founded. In Italy there were the Vatican Library and the Biblioteca Marucelliana in Florence. As the European decorative arts museums were founded in imitation of the South Kensington Museum, they also started libraries. The first was in Vienna in 1865, and others followed in Paris, Prague, Zagreb, Budapest, Copenhagen and Hamburg. The only one, however, to outstrip this library was that of the decorative art museum in Berlin founded in 1867. There are also numerous complementary institutions in America; in the last couple of years the famous wedge-shaped extensions of the National Gallery in Washington has been opened, and this has six floors of library and research facilities.

The expansion of one of these libraries, however, is really the expansion of them all, for with computer technology, microphotography and rapid telecommunications, information can be easily transmitted from one to the other, the only obstacle being the occasionally curmudgeonly attitude, worse in some institutions than others, towards the new technology and the circulation of knowledge. It is natural, however, that a library should grow up wherever there is a museum, for as Ralph Wornum once wrote: 'while the museum is necessarily extremely limited in many respects, the library is in a measure infinite. . . . It is the experience of the world pitted against that of an individual'.

References

Altick, R. D., *The Shows of London,* Cambridge, Mass., 1978

Anon, *Catalogue of the International Exhibition of Chinese Art, Royal Academy of Arts,* London 1935-36

Anon, *Catalogue of the Special Loan Exhibition of English Furniture and Silks, Bethnal Green,* 1896

Anon, *Catalogue of Reproductions of Objects of Art,* London 1870

Anon, *Guide to the English Costumes Presented by Messrs Harrods Ltd,* London 1913

Anon, *Fashion, an Anthology compiled by Cecil Beaton,* Catalogue of V & A Exhibition, 1971

Anon, 'A French Critic's Opinion', *Art Journal,* 1897

Anon, *History of the Art Museum of South Kensington especially as regards Premises,* the official government *Art Series,* no 10

Anon, *The National Museum and Galleries, the War Years and After,* III, Report of the Standing Commission on Museums and Galleries, H.M.S.O., 1948

Anon, Obituary of George Eumorfopoulous, *Transactions of the Oriental Ceramic Society,* 1939-40

Anon, *Official Catalogue of the Great Exhibition,* London 1851

Anon, *Précis of the Minutes of the Science and Art Department, arranged in chronological order from 16 February 1852 to 18 July 1863,* London 1864

Anon, 'Re-organisation at South Kensington', I and II, editorials in *Burlington Magazine* XIV, 1908-09

Anon, *Report of Her Majesty's Acting Consul at Hakodate on the Lacquer Industry of Japan,* presented to the Houses of Parliament, 1882

Anon, 'The Symbolism of Chinese Imperial Robes', *Catalogue of the Exhibition of the Vuilleumie Collection, China Institute,* London 1939

Bell, Q., *The Schools of Design,* London 1963

Birdwood, George, *The Industrial Arts of India,* London 1880

Bury, S., 'Pugin's Marriage Jewellery', *V & A Museum Yearbook,* 1969

Burys, and D. Fitzgerald, 'A Design for a Candlestick by George Michael Moser', *V & A Museum Yearbook,* 1969

Charleston, R., and J. Bolingbroke, 'The Sèvres Collection in a New Light', *Apollo,* March 1972

Cole, Major H., *Catalogue of the Objects of Indian Art in the South Kensington Museum,* London 1874

Davis, F., *Victorian Patrons of the Arts,* London 1963

Dilke, Lady, *French Furniture and Decoration in the 18th Century,* London 1901

Dresser, C., 'The Art Manufacturers of Japan from Personal Observation', *Journal of the Society of Arts,* February 1878

Dresser, C., in Cassell's *Technical Educator,* London 1870-72

Edwards, R., Review of A. Coleridge, *Chippendale Furniture,* in *Apollo,* November 1968

Graul, R., 'Zur Neuaufstellung des Victoria und Albert Museum in London', *Kunstchronik,* 19 November 1909-10

Gray, Basil, 'The Development of Taste in Chinese Art in the West, 1872-1972', *Transactions of the Oriental Ceramic Society,* 1923-4

Guest, Montague J., ed., *Journals of Lady Charlotte Schreiber,* London 1911

Hogben, C., ed., *The Art of Bernard Leach,* London 1978

Honey, W. B., *Glass: A Handbook,* London 1946

Irwin, John, 'A Gift from William Morris', *V & A Museum Bulletin,* January 1965

Irwin, John, 'The Sānchī Torso', *V & A Museum Yearbook,* 1972

Kauffmann, C. M., *Catalogue of Foreign Paintings in the Victoria and Albert Museum,* I, London 1973

Kauffmann, C. M., 'The Constantine Alexander Ionides Bequest', V & A Masterpiece Sheet, N.D.

Koechlin, R., 'Le nouveau musée de South Kensington', *La Chronique des Arts,* 6 November 1909

Longhurst, M., *Catalogue of Carvings in Ivory,* London 1929

Mallet, J. V. G., 'C.D.E. Fortnum and Italian Maiolica of the Renaissance', *Apollo,* December 1978

Mitter, Partha, *Much Maligned Monsters,* Oxford 1977

Morris, B., 'William Morris and the South Kensington Museum', *Victorian Poetry,* Fall-Winter 1975

Murdoch-Smith, R., *Handbook of Persian Art,* London 1876

Newton, C., *Photography in Printmaking,* London 1979

Oman, C., 'A Hundred Years of Silver', I and II, *V & A Museum Bulletin,* 1965 and 1966

Palliser, Mrs Bury, *History of Lace,* London 1865

Pollen, J. Hungerford, *Ancient and Modern Furniture and Woodwork,* London 1875

Pope-Hennessy, Sir J., *Catalogue of Italian Sculpture in the Victoria and Albert Museum,* London 1964

Pope-Hennessy, Sir J., *The Raphael Cartoons,* London 1958

Rackham, B., *Catalogue of the Herbert Allen Collection of English Porcelain,* London 1917

Radcliffe, A., and Charles Avery, 'The "Chellini Madonna" by Donatello', *Burlington Magazine,* June 1976

Reitlinger, G., *The Economics of Taste,* II, London 1963

Reynolds, G., *Catalogue of the Constable Collection,* London 1960

Reynolds, G., *Handbook of the Department of Prints, Drawings and Paintings,* London 1964

Robinson, J. C., *Catalogue of the Soulages Collection,* London 1856

Robinson, J. C., ed., *Catalogue of the Special Exhibition of Works of Art on Loan to the South Kensington Museum, June 1862,* London 1863

Robinson, J. C., *Italian Sculpture of the Middle Ages and the Period of the Revival of Art,* London 1862

Scarce, J. 'Travels with Telegraph and Tiles in Persia: from the Private Papers of Major-General Sir Robert Murdoch-Smith', *Art and Archaeology Research Papers,* June 1973

Skelton, R., 'The Indian Collections: 1798-1978', *Burlington Magazine,* May 1978

Spielmann, M. H., 'The Faults of the South Kensington Museum Exposed', *Magazine of Art,* XXII, 1897-98

Strong, R., 'The Victoria and Albert Museum', *Burlington Magazine,* CXX, May 1978

Thornton, P., 'Collector of French Furniture' [John Jones], *Apollo,* March 1972

Walpole, Horace, *The Letters of Horace Walpole, Earl of Oxford,* VI, London 1840

Ward-Jackson, P., *Catalogue of the Italian Drawings in the Victoria and Albert Museum,* I, London 1979

Williamson, G. C., *Murray Marks and his Friends,* London 1919

Index